WTO Antidumping and Subsidy Agreements

A Practitioner's Guide to "Sunset" Reviews in Australia, Canada, the European Union, and the United States

WTO Antidumping and Subsidy Agreements

A Practitioner's Guide to "Sunset" Reviews in Australia, Canada, the European Union, and the United States

by

Terence P. Stewart and Amy S. Dwyer

KLUWER LAW INTERNATIONAL

The Hague • London • Boston

Published by Kluwer Law International,
P.O. Box 85889, 2508 CN The Hague, The Netherlands.

Sold and distributed in the U.S.A. and Canada
by Kluwer Law International,
675 Massachusetts Avenue, Cambridge, MA 02139, U.S.A.

In all other countries, sold and distributed
by Kluwer Law International,
P.O. Box 85889, 2508 CN The Hague, The Netherlands.

Library of Congress Cataloging-in-Publication Data

Stewart, Terence P.
WTO antidumping and subsidy agreements : a practitioner's guide to "Sunset" reviews in Australia, Canada, the European Union, and the United States / by Terence P. Stewart and Amy S. Dwyer.
p. cm.
ISBN 9041106405
1. Antidumping duties--Law and legislation. 2. Subsidies--Law and legislation. 3. Sunset reviews of government programs--Law and legislation. I. Dwyer, Amy. S. II. Title.
K4635.S79 1998
343'.0742--dc21 98-35204
CIP

ISBN 9041106405

Kluwer Law International incorporates the publishing programs of Graham & Trotman Ltd, Kluwer Law and Taxation Publishers, and Martinus Nijhoff Publishers.

ABOUT THE AUTHORS

Terence P. Stewart is the managing partner of Stewart and Stewart, a Washington, D.C. law firm focusing on international trade, customs, international transactions, and administrative law. The firm has a representative office in Moscow and a correspondent office in Charleroi, Belgium. Mr. Stewart received his law degree from Georgetown University (magna cum laude), an M.B.A. from Harvard University and a bachelor of arts from the College of the Holy Cross (magna cum laude). He is a prominent trade law practitioner in the United States having participated in several hundred trade cases before various government agencies. Mr. Stewart's firm has advised clients on trade laws and participated in trade cases in a number of countries. He has advised clients on the Uruguay Round trade negotiations, WTO accession, WTO dispute settlement, various bilateral and regional trade agreements involving the United States, as well as regional agreements in Europe. He is the current president of the Customs and International Trade Bar Association, is an *ex officio* member of the Court of International Trade's Advisory Committee, is a member of the International Trade Law Sections of the American Bar Association and the District of Columbia Bar, the Federal Circuit Court of International Trade and International Trade Commission Appeals Committee, and is a member of other bar associations in the United States. Mr. Stewart is a frequent speaker at bar association, judicial conference and other trade law fora, has written extensively on trade, investment and other laws in the United States, the European Community, Africa, Eastern Europe, various C.I.S. countries and Southeast Asia. Mr. Stewart is admitted to, *inter alia*, the U.S. Supreme Court, four of the U.S. Circuit Courts of Appeals (including the Federal Circuit), the Court of Appeals for the District of Columbia and the U.S. Court of International Trade. Mr. Stewart is on the Board of Directors of the U.S.-Africa Chamber of Commerce and is a member of the Russian American Chamber of Commerce. Mr. Stewart is married to Ellen Guraa Blendheim Stewart and has three daughters, Natalie, Melissa and Hanna.

Amy S. Dwyer is an attorney with the law firm of Stewart and Stewart, where she practices in the areas of international trade regulation, import and export law, antidumping, NAFTA, export regulation, subsidies and countervailing duties, administrative law, and unfair competition law. Ms. Dwyer received her law degree from Boston College, where she was the executive editor/European Economic Community, *Boston College International and Comparative Law Review.* She received her bachelor of arts degree from the College of the Holy Cross. She also studied at the Loyola University of Chicago's Rome Center. Ms. Dwyer is admitted to the bars of Massachusetts, the District of Columbia, the Court of International Trade, and the Court of Appeals for the Federal Circuit. She has written articles on the Inter-American Court of Human Rights, state export restrictions, subsidies, and trade-related aspects of intellectual property rights. She is a member of the American and Massachusetts Bar Associations, and the Customs and International Trade Bar Association. Ms. Dwyer is married to Howard Ravitz and has a son, Evan Michael.

ACKNOWLEDGEMENTS

When we began work on this topic in the summer of 1997, it was with the intention of writing a relatively short article about the U.S. implementation of the WTO Antidumping and Subsidy Agreements' provisions regarding automatic five-year sunset reviews. This change in U.S. law clearly was an important development in the evolution of these trade remedies. Much had already been written and said about how the new sunset provisions should be administered, and some commenters used the pre-WTO experiences of the European Union and Canada, which already had sunset measures in effect, to forecast the proportion of U.S. antidumping and countervailing duty orders which might be revoked as a result of sunset reviews. There was not, however, a comprehensive comparison of the laws, regulations and practices concerning the duration and termination of antidumping and countervailing duty measures in the United States and other countries. We believed such an analysis would be helpful to practitioners, and equally importantly to trade administrators, to better understand the various outcomes of sunset reviews among different countries. As we expanded the scope of our undertaking, it rapidly became apparent that an article was no longer an adequate vehicle, and we therefore decided to write this book. An excerpt of this book that focuses solely on sunset reviews in the United States will appear in a forthcoming issue of the Journal of World Trade.

We thought it appropriate to focus on Australia, Canada, and the EU, along with the United States, since they historically have been the predominant users of antidumping and countervailing duty measures. As other countries liberalize their trade regimes and avail themselves of WTO-consistent trade remedies, we intend over time to supplement this research with examinations of other countries' experiences.

We also believed it important to make this research available to administrators and practitioners at the time that sunset reviews were scheduled to begin in the United States, so that it might inform their work. Thus, we had a self-imposed time constraint to have the book published no later than July 1998. Although our names appear as the authors, we could not have met that deadline without the generous assistance of numerous colleagues. For their help in providing copies of foreign laws and regulations, and for answering many, many questions about the conduct of sunset reviews in their respective systems prior to implementation of the WTO Agreements, we thank Gerhard Hannes Welge of the European Commission, Margaret McLeod and Chris Tuckwell of the Australian Anti-Dumping Authority, and Michel Granger and Josee LeBlanc of the Canadian International Trade Tribunal. We are also grateful to the contributions and assistance provided by attorneys and staff in our firm, including Eric P. Salonen, Patrick J. McDonough, our law librarian Monica L. Luciano, and trade consultant Federico Canuto. Many thanks to our summer law clerks for their assistance in cite-checking, including Victor Chen, Joshua Cohen, Gregory Dundas, Amy Karpel, and Marta Prado. Early contributors who have since moved on to other professional challenges include Todd J. Wagnon and Maryam D. Kamali Miyamoto.

Finally, we want to give special thanks to our Senior Partner Emeritus, Eugene L. Stewart, for his encouragement and support, and his insightful suggestions to improve the work.

Any mistakes or errors in the text are, of course, the responsibility of the authors.

Terence P. Stewart
Amy S. Dwyer
Washington, D.C.
June 1, 1998

PREFACE

During the Uruguay Round of multilateral trade negotiations, member states agreed to establish a time limit for antidumping and countervailing duty measures. The new "sunset" provision required member states to allow a measure to expire after five years from its imposition or last review. In order to maintain a measure, member states would have to find, based on a review, that expiration would be likely to lead to continuation or recurrence of dumping or subsidization and injury. Some member states, such as the European Union (EU), Canada, and Australia, already had comparable sunset requirements in existing legislation and did not have to make substantial changes to their domestic legislation to implement the new sunset requirement. Other member states, such as the United States, were required to modify their domestic legislation to incorporate the new sunset requirements.

As July 1998 marks the commencement of the first round of sunset reviews in the United States, this treatise provides practitioners in antidumping and countervailing duty cases with a timely and useful tool for effective participation in sunset reviews in any member state. In order to provide a context for understanding future post-Uruguay Round sunset decisions, this treatise begins with a brief negotiating history of the provisions.

Because the EU, Canada, Australia, and the United States have historically been the major users of antidumping and countervailing duty measures, this treatise examines their law and practice concerning expiration of measures before and after the Uruguay Round in four separate chapters. Specifically, the treatise reviews the legislative provisions establishing the sunset review mechanism in each country as well as summarizes the factors considered in applying those laws to individual cases. In order to enhance the reader's understanding of how cases are conducted in each member state, the treatise provides the procedural background and deadlines for sunset reviews as well as a summary of a recent case. Finally, the treatise reviews the factors considered by authorities in each of the four countries that typically lead to affirmative determinations. A further supplement will examine the laws, regulations, and practices of other countries.

The text of the treatise is amply supported by citations to the actual laws in each of the four countries as well as individual decisions. Three appendices include side-by-side comparisons of the actual negotiating drafts of the sunset provisions used by the Uruguay Round negotiators as well as the primary sunset review provisions in the domestic legislation of the four countries. The treatise concludes with a comparison of the procedural requirements and substantive considerations in the four sunset review systems.

TABLE OF CONTENTS

I. INTRODUCTION 1

II. THE URUGUAY ROUND NEGOTIATIONS 5
A. Pre-Uruguay Round Sunset Provisions 5
1. Pre-Uruguay Round EU Sunset Provisions 12
2. Pre-Uruguay Round Canadian Sunset Provisions 16
3. Pre-Uruguay Round Australian Sunset Provisions 19
4. Pre-Uruguay Round U.S. Revocation and Termination Provisions 25
a. The Agency Regulations 25
b. The DOC's Practice of Revoking Orders or Terminating Suspended Investigations Under Pre-URAA Law 31
i. Administrative Reviews 31
ii. Changed Circumstances Reviews Under Section 751(b) 35
c. The ITC's Practice in Revoking Orders or Terminating Suspended Investigations Under Pre-URAA Law 37
i. Changed Circumstances Reviews Under Section 751(b) 37
ii. The ITC's Injury Review and Revocation Under Section 104(b) 47
5. The Expiry Rate Under the Four Systems Differed 53
B. The Uruguay Round Negotiating History of the Sunset Provisions 57
1. The Negotiations: A Timeline 57
2. The Negotiations: The Issues 60
3. The Negotiations: The Final Sunset Provisions 65

III. EUROPEAN UNION SUNSET REVIEWS: LEGISLATION AND PRACTICE 71
A. Initiating Expiry Reviews 71
1. Self-Initiation and Requests for Expiry Reviews 71
2. Judging the Adequacy of Responses 73
3. Simultaneous Reviews and Cumulation 73
B. The Expiry Review 75
1. Deadlines 75
2. The Likelihood Tests 76
a. The Commission's Determination of the Likelihood of Continuation or Recurrence of Dumping or Subsidization 76
b. The Commission's Determination of the Likelihood of Continuation or Recurrence of Injury 78
3. Summary of Affirmative Determinations 83
C. Subsequent Sunset Reviews 84
D. Appeals of Expiry Review Determinations 84
E. A Post-Uruguay Round Expiry Review 84
1. The Expiry Review Schedule 84
2. A Seven-Part Decision 85
3. The Decision 86

IV. CANADIAN SUNSET REVIEWS: LEGISLATION AND PRACTICE 89
A. Initiating Expiry Reviews 89
1. Grouping Sunset Reviews and Cumulation 90
2. Self-Initiation and Requests for Expiry Reviews 91
B. The Expiry Review 94
1. Deadlines 94
2. No Early Expiry of Orders or Findings 95
3. The Likelihood Tests 96
a. The CITT's Determination of Likelihood of Continuation or Recurrence of Dumping or Subsidization 97
b. The CITT's Determination of the Likelihood of Continuation or Recurrence of Injury 101
4. Summary of Affirmative Determinations 104

C. Subsequent Expiry Reviews 105
D. Appeals of Expiry Review Determinations 105
E. A Post-Uruguay Round Expiry Review 106
1. The Expiry Review Schedule 106
2. An Eight-Part Decision 107
3. The Decision 108

V. AUSTRALIAN SUNSET REVIEWS: LEGISLATION AND PRACTICE 111
A. Initiating Continuation Inquiries 111
1. Applications for Continuation Inquiries 112
2. Grouping Continuation Inquiries 112
B. The Continuation Inquiry 113
1. Deadlines 113
2. The Likelihood Tests 114
a. The ADA's Determination of Likelihood of Continuation or Recurrence of Dumping or Subsidization 114
b. The ADA's Determination of Likelihood of Continuation or Recurrence of Injury 117
3. Summary of Affirmative Determinations 119
C. Subsequent Continuation Inquiries 120
D. Appeals of Continuation Inquiries 120
E. A Post-Uruguay Round Continuation Inquiry 120
1. The Continuation Inquiry Schedule 120
2. A Nine-Part Decision 121
3. The Decision 123
F. Australia Announces Reforms 124

VI. UNITED STATES SUNSET REVIEWS: LEGISLATION AND PRACTICE 127
A. Procedural Provisions in the Uruguay Round Agreements Act 127
1. Initiating Sunset Reviews 128
a. Grouping Reviews and Cumulation 129
b. Automatic Initiation of Sunset Reviews 134
i. The DOC's Notice of Initiation 135

ii. The ITC's Notice of Institution 142
c. Judging the Adequacy of Substantive Responses for a Full Review 144
i. The DOC's Regulations 145
ii. The ITC's Regulations 147
iii. An Expedited Review Based on "Facts Available" 148
d. Judging the Adequacy of Response Rates for a Full Review 150
i. The DOC's Regulations 152
ii. The ITC's Regulations 153
e. Request for Simultaneous Expedited Review and Injury Investigation for Certain Countervailing Duty Orders 154
f. Waiver of Reviews 155
2. Conducting an Expedited or Full Review: Procedures and Deadlines 157
a. Expedited Reviews 158
b. Full Reviews 158
3. No Early Revocation or Termination of Transition Orders 160
B. The Likelihood Test in the Uruguay Round Agreements Act 162
1. The DOC's Determination of Likelihood of Continuation or Recurrence of Dumping 162
2. The DOC's Determination of Likelihood of Continuation or Recurrence of a Countervailable Subsidy 166
3. The Role of Margins and *De Minimis* Rates 169
4. The ITC's Determination of Likelihood of Continuation or Recurrence of Material Injury 174
a. The URAA's Likelihood Test of Material Injury 174
i. Injury Factors 174
ii. A "Reasonably Foreseeable Time" 176
iii. Other Factors 178
iv. Condition of the Domestic Industry 179
(A) vulnerability of the domestic industry 180
(B) consideration of duty absorption 183
(C) causation 184
b. Comparison of "Likelihood Tests" in Sunset, Section 751(b), and Section 104(b) Reviews 185

i. Section 751(b) 185
ii. Section 104(b) 189
c. Regional Industry Sunset Reviews 190
C. Subsequent Sunset Reviews 191
D. Appeals of Sunset Review Determinations 192

VII. CONCLUSION 195

APPENDIX I 199

APPENDIX II 211

APPENDIX III 217

BIBLIOGRAPHY 253

INDEX 261

CHAPTER I

INTRODUCTION

In 1947, member states negotiated the General Agreement on Tariffs and Trade (GATT) which was amended in seven subsequent negotiating rounds.[1] The eighth so-called "Uruguay Round" commenced in September 1986[2] and was completed in December 1993.[3] In addition to establishing the World Trade Organization (WTO), the Uruguay Round's Final Act modified the international requirements governing antidumping and countervailing duty measures.[4]

During the Uruguay Round, negotiators debated whether or not to include an automatic "sunset" requirement for ending antidumping and

---

[1]Terence P. Stewart, Susan G. Markel & Michael T. Kerwin, *Antidumping*, 2 THE GATT URUGUAY ROUND: A NEGOTIATING HISTORY (1986-1992) 1383-1710 (Terence P. Stewart ed., 1993). For a detailed history of the General Agreement on Tariffs and Trade, see Robert A. Weaver, *Functioning of the GATT System*, 2 THE GATT URUGUAY ROUND: A NEGOTIATING HISTORY (1986-1992) 1891-1996 (Terence P. Stewart ed., 1993); Terence P. Stewart, *Overview of the Uruguay Round of Trade Negotiations*, GATT/WTO Seminar in Conjunction With the Chamber of Commerce and Industry of the Russian Federation (Oct. 16-17, 1995); Terence P. Stewart, *Antidumping, Subsidies and Countervailing Measures: The Negotiations Are Still a Long Way From Completion in* URUGUAY ROUND TRADE NEGOTIATIONS: WHERE DO WE GO FROM HERE? (ABA, March 21-22, 1991).

[2]Stewart, Markel & Kerwin, *supra* note 1, at n.552, *citing Ministerial Declaration of 20 September 1986 (Punta del Este Declaration)*, GATT Doc. No. MIN(86)/6 (Sept. 20, 1986), at 7; *Launching the Uruguay Round*, GATT FOCUS NEWSLETTER (Oct. 1986), at 1.

[3]*See* USITC, THE YEAR IN TRADE 1993: OPERATION OF THE TRADE AGREEMENTS PROGRAM, 45TH REPORT, USITC Pub. 2971, at 1 (June 1991).

[4]Final Act Embodying the Results of the Uruguay Round of Multilateral Trade Negotiations, done at Marrakesh on April 15, 1994, 33 I.L.M. 1143, *reprinted in* H.R. DOC. NO. 103-316, vol. 1, at 1318 (1994) [hereinafter Final Act].

countervailing duty measures. As the four major users of the antidumping and countervailing duty laws, the European Union, Canada, Australia, and the United States participated in the Uruguay Round negotiations and helped shape the sunset review provision. Three of those users, the European Union, Canada, and Australia, maintained a sunset provision which included a deadline for expiration of the measure in the absence of a review to determine its continued need.

The resulting Final Act Embodying the Results of the Uruguay Round of Multilateral Trade Negotiations (Final Act) included an Agreement on Implementation of Article VI of the GATT 1994 (Antidumping Agreement) and an Agreement on Subsidies and Countervailing Measures (Subsidies Agreement), both of which included a five-year expiration or "sunset" requirement.[5] According to the new sunset requirement, member states were required to revoke or terminate an antidumping[6] or countervailing[7] duty measure not later than five years from its imposition or the last review. An antidumping or countervailing duty measure, however, could be main-

---

[5]Agreement on Implementation of Article VI of the General Agreement on Tariffs and Trade 1994, art. 11.3, *in* Final Act, *supra* note 4, at 1453 [hereinafter Antidumping Agreement]; Agreement on Subsidies and Countervailing Measures, art. 21.3, *in* Final Act, *supra* note 4, at 1533 [hereinafter Subsidies Agreement].

[6]Countries collect antidumping duties on imports to remedy the unfair trade practice of foreign exporters who sell their goods at prices that are less than their "normal value" causing or threatening to cause material injury to a domestic industry or material retardation of an industry in the importing country. A product is sold at less than its "normal value" if the export price of the product exported from one country to another is less than the comparable price, in the ordinary course of trade, for the like product when destined for consumption in the exporting country, a third country, or cost of production plus a reasonable amount for administrative, selling, and general costs and for profits. Antidumping Agreement, supra note 5, at arts. 2 & 3 n.49; *see generally* Terence P. Stewart, *The Important Function of Antidumping Laws*, IV.6 INT'L ECON. 46 (Insights, Inst. for Int'l Econ., Nov.-Dec. 1993); Terence P. Stewart, *Administration of the Antidumping Law: A Different Perspective, in* DOWN IN THE DUMPS: ADMINISTRATION OF THE UNFAIR TRADE LAWS 288 (Richard Boltuck & Robert E. Litan eds., 1991).

[7]Countries collect countervailing duties on imports to remedy the unfair trade practice of foreign exporters who sell goods that have benefited from a subsidy causing or threatening to cause injury to the domestic industry or material retardation of the establishment of an industry in the importing country. A subsidy is a financial contribution by a government or any public body within a country and a benefit is conferred. Subsidies Agreement, *supra* note 5, at arts. 1 & 15 n.45.

tained if the government found, based on a review, that revocation, termination, or expiration would be likely to lead to continuation or recurrence of dumping or subsidization and injury.

Although all four countries had some form of sunset review provision prior to the Final Act, only the United States was required to adopt substantial additional review procedures in its implementing legislation. In order to implement changes in the Final Act, U.S. Congress passed the Uruguay Round Agreements Act (URAA) effective January 1, 1995.[8] Based on requirements in the Final Act, the URAA includes a sunset provision that revokes or terminates an antidumping or countervailing duty order or suspended investigation after five years unless a sunset review reveals that dumping or a countervailable subsidy and material injury, whether originally based on a material injury, threat of injury, or material retardation finding, would be likely to continue or recur.[9] Unlike prior law, the sunset requirement applies whether or not the U.S. Department of Commerce (DOC) has conducted administrative reviews in intervening years or the domestic industry continues to be interested in the order or suspension agreement.

The first sunset review under the new U.S. statutory provisions is expected to be initiated in July 1998.[10] In order to provide a useful tool for conducting or participating in sunset reviews in all four countries, this treatise lays the groundwork for analysis with a review of pre-Uruguay Round sunset provisions, a brief negotiating history of the sunset provisions of the Final Act, and a discussion of the implementing legislation and practice in sunset reviews in the European Union, Canada, Australia, and the United States. This treatise concludes with a comparison of similar provisions in the sunset legislation of the four countries.

---

[8]19 U.S.C. §1671 (1980 & 1998 Supp.) (notes). For a discussion of other changes to the antidumping law as a result of the URAA, see Alan F. Holmer, Gary N. Horlick, & Terence P. Stewart, *Enacted and Rejected Amendments to the Antidumping Law: In Implementation or Contravention of the Antidumping Agreement?*, 29 INT'L LAW. 483 (Summer 1995)

[9]19 U.S.C. §1675(d)(2) (1980 & 1998 Supp.).

[10]Transition Orders; Final Schedule and Grouping of Five-Year Reviews, 63 Fed. Reg. 29,372, 29,374 (Dep't Comm. 1998).

CHAPTER II

The Uruguay Round Negotiations

A. *PRE-URUGUAY ROUND SUNSET PROVISIONS*

The Antidumping and Subsidies Agreements (Agreements) represented the first time countries agreed to establish a formal mechanism for conducting sunset reviews of antidumping and countervailing duty orders. Article VI, concerning antidumping duties, and Article XVI, concerning countervailing duties, of the 1947 General Agreement on Tariffs and Trade (GATT) did not include any specific requirement concerning revocation of orders or suspended investigations.[11] Beginning as early as the mid-to-late 1950's, however, the issue of the duration of antidumping and countervailing duty measures was the subject of attention in the GATT.[12] The first so-called "Group of Experts Report" recommended that:

[11]General Agreement on Tariffs and Trade, *opened for signature* Oct. 30, 1947, 61 Stat. 173, T.I.A.S. No. 1700, 55 U.N.T.S. 187, at arts. VI & XVI.

[12]*See, e.g., Anti-dumping and Countervailing Duties*, GATT Sales No. GATT/1958-2 (July 1958) (analysis prepared by the Secretariat of the GATT of the laws and regulations of certain contracting parties that provided for the levying of antidumping and countervailing duties). One of the questions asked of the contracting parties whose laws were reviewed was whether the validity of the proclamation was "limited in time or does it remain in force until repealed?" *Id.* at 32, 51, 56, 69, 81, 95, 113, 121. Australia, Rhodesia, South Africa, Sweden, and the United States responded that the measure remained in force until it was repealed. *Id.* at 32, 81, 95, 113, 121. Belgium responded that "the decision is reviewed at regular intervals in order to take into account any changes in the position. The Royal Order is abrogated as soon as the import price can be regarded as normal." *Id.* at 51. Canada and New Zealand responded that the question, which was the last question in a section concerning selection of items on which AD duties are to be

> [A]nti-dumping duties should remain in force only so long as they were genuinely necessary to counteract dumping which was causing or threatening material injury to a domestic industry.... [A]ny country imposing a duty would naturally be free to review it and ... it might well be desirable for it to do so from time to time in the light of information at its disposal.... [I]t should be open to exporters of the product concerned, if they considered that they had the necessary evidence, to request the importing country to carry out a review of the facts.[13]

In 1964, the International Chamber of Commerce (ICC) sent a report to the GATT recommending, *inter alia*, the drafting of an international code of antidumping procedures.[14] Among the ICC's recommendations for such a code were the provisions that antidumping orders "should be revoked as soon as they are no longer necessary," and that the authorities in the importing country should agree to review the order upon request of exporters in the exporting country or importers in the importing country.[15]

After the Kennedy Round negotiations began in 1963,[16] a Group on Antidumping Policies was established.[17] It was under the auspices of that Group that the United Kingdom prepared a Draft International Code on Antidumping Procedure and Practice in 1965, [18] which included provisions

---

levied, was not applicable since their systems did not have recourse to a "pre-selection of products." *Id.* at 51, 56. Elsewhere, however, Canada noted: "The Government has laid down stringent conditions for the determination that a product is a class or kind made in Canada and the relevant decisions (of which those of general interest are published in the *Canada Gazette*) are continually under review independent from the anti-dumping provisions." *Id.* at 55.

[13] *Anti-dumping and Countervailing Duties, Report adopted on 13 May 1959,* GATT Doc. No. L/978, *reprinted in* GATT BISD (8th Supp.) at 151-152. This was one of two reports that were issued in 1960 and 1961 by a "Group of Experts" that were appointed by the Contracting Parties to study technical antidumping issues. The reports were approved by the Contracting Parties, and were published in March 1961 as a single volume. *Anti-dumping and Countervailing Duties, Report of Group of Experts,* GATT Sales No. GATT/1961-2 (1961). *See generally* Stewart, Markel & Kerwin, *supra* note 1, at 1413-1414.

[14] *Communication from the International Chamber of Commerce,* GATT Doc. No. TN.64/NTB/42 (June 20, 1966) at 1, *cited in* Stewart, Markel & Kerwin, *supra* note 1, at n.178.

[15] *Id.* at 5.

[16] *See* Stewart, Markel & Kerwin, *supra* note 1, at n.177 and accompanying text.

[17] *See id.* at 1418.

[18] *Id.*

concerning the duration of antidumping duties.[19] The Draft Code incorporated the recommendations of the Group of Experts that antidumping duties were to remain in effect only as long as necessary and that authorities were to review the need for the duties if exporters of the merchandise in question so requested.[20] The Draft Code went further, however, and elaborated that antidumping duties should be revoked "as soon as:"

> (i) full relief from duty has been granted . . . over a sufficiently long period to demonstrate that the goods in question will continue to be sold at undumped prices;
>
> (ii) the authorities concerned are satisfied in the light of information at their disposal, or which is submitted to them, that imports of the goods in question . . . can be sold at undumped prices or that the imports, though technically dumped, would no longer cause or threaten material injury to a domestic industry.

As for reviews, the Draft Code provided: "The authorities concerned shall carry out a review of the position if exporters of the goods in question so request and if they submit information substantiating the need for review." The Draft Code did not propose automatic reviews, apparently because it was assumed that "interested parties would draw the attention of the authorities concerned to any change in the position."[21] Indeed, when members of the Group suggested periodic review of antidumping duties, the United Kingdom representative responded that although such a provision could be added, it would likely have little practical effect as "it was in the interest of the parties concerned to ask for a review as soon as they felt that it could be justified."[22]

In 1966, a Draft Revised Antidumping Checklist, which outlined topics that were open for comment among the Group, including duration of antidumping duties, was circulated.[23] Most of the comments of the representatives in the Group concerning both the Draft Code and the Checklist that addressed the duration issue generally endorsed having some rule for the duration of antidumping measures and several supported providing for

---

[19]*Draft Int'l Code on Anti-dumping Procedure and Practice: Note by the United Kingdom Delegation*, GATT Doc. No. Spec(65) 86 (Oct. 7, 1965), at 21-22, *cited in* Stewart, Markel & Kerwin, *supra* note 1, at n.96.

[20]*Id.*

[21]*Id.*

[22]*Notes on Meeting on 20-21 October 1965*, GATT Doc. No. TN.64/NTB/W/2 (Nov. 23, 1965) at 3, *cited in* Stewart, Markel & Kerwin, *supra* note 1, at n. 186.

[23]*See* Stewart, Markel & Kerwin, *supra* note 1, at 1422.

reviews of those measures where there was a request.[24] The Group generally agreed that an antidumping measure should remain in force only as long as necessary to counteract injurious dumping. There did not appear to be support for a rule that specified how long "as long as necessary" might be. Indeed, the United States commented that a provision "limiting dumping duties to some specific period would appear unreasonable."[25] Australia expressed the following concern:

> There would be practical difficulties in formulating conditions for the duration of anti-dumping duties to meet the circumstances of all countries. A 'stop go' procedure would be particularly unsuited to countries with small-scale industries supplying relatively small domestic markets. In such countries the periodic removal of anti-dumping duties could lead to pre-empting or disruption of markets by sporadic dumping.[26]

There was a difference of views as to whether reviews should be conducted automatically, or whether reviews initiated upon request from exporters or importers would be sufficient. There was also the issue of whether evidence of a need for review should be a prerequisite for granting a request. For example, Denmark and Sweden recommended periodic reviews, with Denmark observing "it may be difficult to the exporters and the importers of the dumped products to estimate whether material injury continues to exist."[27] The United States believed that periodical review "with or without an importer request . . . might have merit," although it

---

[24] *See, e.g., Anti-dumping Checklist, Comments by the United Kingdom*, GATT Doc. No. TN.64/NTB/W/10 (April 19, 1966) at 2; *Anti-dumping Checklist, Comments by the European Economic Community*, GATT Doc. No. TN.64/NTB/W/10/Add.1 (April 21, 1966) at 5; *Anti-dumping Checklist, Comments by Japan*, GATT Doc. No. TN.64/NTB/W/10/Add.2 (April 22, 1966) at 2; *Anti-dumping Checklist, Comments by the United States*, GATT Doc. No. TN.64/NTB/W/10/Add.3 (April 28, 1966) at 3; *Anti-dumping Checklist, Comments by Norway*, GATT Doc. No. TN.64/NTB/W/10/Add.4 (April 29, 1966) at 2; *Anti-dumping Checklist, Comments by Denmark*, GATT Doc. No. TN.64/NTB/W/10/Add. 6 (May 5, 1966) at 2; *Anti-dumping Checklist, Comments by Sweden*, GATT Doc. No. TN.64/NTB/W/10/Add. 7 (May 6, 1966) at 3-4; *Anti-dumping Checklist, Comments of Finland*, GATT Doc. No. TN.64/NTB/W/10/Add. 10 (June 30, 1966) at 2; *cited in* Stewart, Markel & Kerwin, *supra* note 1, at n.208.

[25] *Comments by the United States, supra* note 24, at 3.

[26] *Anti-dumping Checklist: Comments by Australia*, GATT Doc. No. TN.64/NTB/W/10/Add. 8 (May 20, 1966), *cited in* Stewart, Markel & Kerwin, *supra* note 1, at n.208

[27] *Comments by Sweden, supra* note 24, at 3-4; *Comments by Denmark, supra* note 24, at 2.

also believed that review requests should be accompanied by evidence that "importation of goods at dumped prices has ceased."[28] Norway thought providing for reviews upon requests from importers accompanied with evidence that substantiated the need for review was sufficient. "With such safeguards there is probably no need for setting a definite time-limit to the duration of anti-dumping measures."[29] Canada took the view that so long as antidumping duties were imposed only on imports that were actually dumped and in an amount no greater than the margin of dumping, "no question of duration of anti-dumping levy should arise."[30] Canada also believed, however, that "the authorities concerned must regularly review the need for the continued imposition of an anti-dumping duty, whether or not a review is requested by any interested party."[31]

As the language of Article 9 indicates, the Group ultimately recommended to the Contracting Parties that reviews either could be conducted by the authorities on their own initiative or upon the request of interested suppliers or importers of the product who submitted information substantiating the need for review. Thus, in the 1967 Kennedy Round Agreement on Implementation of Article VI of the GATT, member states adopted the following requirement for antidumping duty measures:

Article 9
Duration of Anti-Dumping Duties

> (a) An anti-dumping duty shall remain in force only as long as it is necessary in order to counteract dumping which is causing injury.
>
> (b) The authorities concerned shall review the need for the continued imposition of the duty, where warranted, on their own initiative or if interested suppliers or importers of the product so request and submit information substantiating the need for review.[32]

[28]*Comments by the United States*, *supra* note 24, at 3.

[29]*Comments by Norway*, *supra* note 24, at 2.

[30]*Antidumping Checklist: Comments by the Government of Canada*, GATT Doc. No. TN.64/NTB/W/10/Add. 5 (May 5, 1966) at 2, *cited in* Stewart, Markel & Kerwin, *supra* note 1, at n.208.

[31]*Memorandum by the Government of Canada*, GATT Doc. No. TN.64/NTB/W/15 (Feb. 21, 1967) at 5, *cited in* Stewart, Markel & Kerwin, *supra* note 1, at n.200.

[32]Agreement on the Implementation of Article VI of the General Agreement on Tariffs and Trade, art. 9, *reprinted in* GATT BISD (15th Supp.) at 24, 32 (1968).

Like the Kennedy Round Agreement, the 1979 GATT Tokyo Round Agreement did not specifically address sunset reviews. The Tokyo Round Agreement, however, did extend the Article 9 requirements to countervailing duty cases. As shown below, both Article 9.1 of the Tokyo Round Antidumping Code and Article 4.9 of the Tokyo Round Subsidies Code required that duties should remain "in force only as long as, and to the extent necessary to counteract dumping [or subsidization] which is causing injury":[33]

Article 9 *Duration of Anti-Dumping Duties*	*Article 4* *Imposition of Countervailing Duties*
1. An anti-dumping duty shall remain in force only as long as, and to the extent necessary to counteract dumping which is causing injury.	9. A countervailing duty shall remain in force only as long as, and to the extent necessary to counteract the subsidization which is causing injury. The investigating authorities shall review the need for the continued imposition of the duty, where warranted, on their own initiative or if any interested party so requests and submits positive information substantiating the need for review.
2. The investigating authorities shall review the need for the continued imposition of the duty, where warranted, on their own initiative or if any interested party so requests and submits positive information substantiating the need for review.	

[33]Agreement on the Implementation of Article VI of the General Agreement on Tariffs and Trade, art. 9.1, *reprinted in* GATT BISD (26th Supp.) at 181 (1980); Agreement on Interpretation and Application of Articles VI, XVI and XXIII of the General Agreement on Tariffs and Trade, art. 4.9, *reprinted in* GATT BISD (26th Supp.) at 63

Both provisions further required a "review" of the need for continued imposition of the duty.

During the Uruguay Round, the European Union (EU),[34] Canada, Australia, and the United States were major users of antidumping and countervailing duty laws:[35]

Measures In Force By Country

Year	US	EU	Can.	Austl.	Mex.	N.Z.	Braz.
1990AD	201	137	78	24	6	8	0
1990CVD	94	0	31	1	0	0	0
Total	295	137	109	25	6	8	0
1991AD	216	144	69	30	19	13	2
1991CVD	87	1	30	5	0	0	1
Total	303	145	99	35	19	13	3
1992AD	267	159	73	44	23	23	9
1992CVD	93	0	29	12	0	0	13
Total	360	159	102	56	23	23	22
1993AD	304	150	85	76	28	24	23
1993CVD	122	2	29	12	0	1	13
Total	426	152	114	88	28	25	36
1994AD	293	164	95	83	42	22	19
1994CVD	108	3	29	13	0	1	1
Total	401	167	124	96	42	23	20
1995AD	292	173	94	88	96	25	21
1995CVD	73	2	42	13	22	1	6
Total	365	175	136	101	118	26	27
1996 AD	301	172	96	47	95	27	26
1996 CVD	67	2	5	13	11	2	7
Total	368	174	101	60	106	29	33
Average	360	158	112	66	49	21	20

(1980). In *Fresh and Chilled Atlantic Salmon from Norway*, a GATT Panel rejected Norway's argument that continuation of the antidumping duty order was inconsistent with Article 9:1 because imports were no longer causing any present material injury to the domestic industry. Fresh and Chilled Atlantic Salmon from Norway, ADP/87 (April 27, 1994) <http://www.wto.org/wto/dispute/panel.htm>. The panel rejected Norway's arguments noting that if "the mere fact that, following the imposition of anti-dumping duties, the imports in question were no longer causing injury were sufficient to require a Party to terminate the imposition of these duties, the logical result would be that any

Prior to the Uruguay Round, the EU, Canadian, Australian, and U.S. antidumping and countervailing duty laws already included provisions to implement the Kennedy and Tokyo Round Agreements.[36] The manner in which each country implemented the Article 9 requirements, however, differed. The following sections summarize the pre-Uruguay legal provisions that permitted revocation or termination of antidumping and countervailing duty measures in each of the four countries.

1. Pre-Uruguay Round EU Sunset Provisions

In order to implement the Tokyo Round, the EU adopted Council Regulation (EEC) No. 3017/79 on December 20, 1979, covering the antidumping and countervailing duty laws concerning imports from countries not members of the European Economic Community (EU).

---

anti-dumping duty which was effective in removing injury to a domestic industry had to be withdrawn immediately." *Id.*

[34]The term "European Union" is used throughout this article for ease of reference. The authors recognize, however, that the European Union does not have an international legal personality as the European Community. *Compare* Peter L.H. Van den Bossche, *The European Community and the Uruguay Round Agreements, in* IMPLEMENTING THE URUGUAY ROUND 23, 23 n.1 (John H. Jackson & Alan O. Sykes eds., 1997), *with* Frank Montag & Andre Fiebig, *The European Union, in* ANTI-DUMPING UNDER THE WTO: A COMPARATIVE REVIEW 97, 97 n.3 (Keith Steele ed., 1996).

[35]For the "Measures in Force" chart, figures for the years 1990 to 1995 were based on Po-Yee Lee, *Canadian & International Use of Anti-Dumping and Countervailing Measures* 29-38 (Research Branch, CITT May 1997). Figures for the year 1996 were based on WTO notifications. Semi-Annual Reports under Article 16.4 of the Agreement, G/ADP/N/22/NZL; G/ADP/N/22/MEX; G/ADP/N/22/BRA; G/ADP/N/22/CAN; G/ADP/N/22/EEC; G/ADP/N/22/USA; G/ADP/N/22/AUS; Semi-Annual Reports under Article 25.11 of the Agreement, G/SCM/N/23/NZL; G/SCM/N/23/MEX/Corr.1; G/SCM/N/23/MEX; G/SCM/N/23/USA; G/SCM/N/23/AUS; G/SCM/N/23/BRA; G/SCM/N/23/CAN; G/SCM/N/23/EEC. Other major users of antidumping and countervailing duty laws were Mexico, New Zealand, and Brazil.

[36]*See* Stewart, Markel & Kerwin, *supra* note 1, at n.26 (noting that Australia, the United States, the EU, and Canada were responsible for 95 percent of the total new antidumping cases reported to the GATT from 1980 to 1989), *citing* GAO, INTERNATIONAL TRADE: USE OF THE GATT ANTIDUMPING CODE 3, Pub. No. GAO/NSIAD-90-238FS (1990).

According to Regulation 3017/79, an antidumping or countervailing duty investigation could be initiated by any natural or legal person or association acting on behalf of a community industry by filing a complaint with the European Commission[37] alleging injury or threat of injury due to dumped or subsidized imports, or by the submission of evidence to the Commission from any member state in possession of sufficient evidence of dumping, or subsidization and injury.[38]

The Commission then would conduct an investigation issuing questionnaires to EU producers, foreign producers/exporters, and importers, and, if necessary, verify information collected.[39] Verification was conducted in both EU member states as well as foreign countries.[40] The Commission also would conduct a hearing and a meeting upon request by interested parties[41] and issue preliminary and final determinations.[42] In its final determination, "[w]here the facts as finally established show that there is dumping or subsidization and injury caused thereby, and the interests of the community call for community intervention, a definitive anti-dumping or countervailing duty shall be imposed by the Council, acting by qualified majority on a proposal submitted by the Commission after consultation."[43]

---

[37]The European Commission is the executive body of the Community with the predominant role in antidumping and countervailing duty proceedings. The Commission's decisions, however, must be adopted by the European Council, which is the legislative body of the Community. *See* Clive Stanbrook & Philip Bentley, DUMPING AND SUBSIDIES: THE LAW AND PROCEDURES GOVERNING THE IMPOSITION OF ANTI-DUMPING AND COUNTERVAILING DUTIES IN THE EUROPEAN COMMUNITY 11-13 (1996); Montag & Fiebig, *supra* note 34, at 97, 99.

[38]Council Regulation 3017/79, arts. 4-5, 1979 O.J. (L 339) (1979).

[39]*Id.* at art. 7; Terence P. Stewart, *Antidumping Practice of the United States and the European Union*, Vol. 1, Before the Russian Chamber of Commerce and Industry Conference on GATT/WTO at 62 (Oct. 1995).

[40]*See, e.g.*, Plain Paper Photocopiers Originating in Japan, Council Regulation 2380/95, para. 7, 1995 O.J. (L 244) (1995).

[41]Council Regulation 3017/79, *supra* note 38, at art. 7.

[42]*Id.* at arts. 7, 12.

[43]*Id.* at art. 12. The European Council is comprised of ministers from each member state that enact the laws of the Community. *See* Montag & Fiebig, supra note 34, at 98.

Article 14 of Regulation 3017/79 also provided an administrative "interim" review[44] mechanism for outstanding measures if warranted.[45] Based on an interim review, outstanding measures could be amended, repealed or annulled. In 1984, the EU amended Article 14 to require that interested parties requesting interim reviews submit "evidence of changed circumstances sufficient to justify the need for such review."[46] The 1984 Regulation 2176/84 also established a 5-year sunset requirement.[47] According to Article 15 of Regulation 2176/84, interested parties were required to establish that

---

[44]*See* Stanbrook & Bentley, *supra* note 37, at 201-03.

[45]Article 14 of Regulation 3017/79 provides as follows:

> 1. The regulations imposing provisional or definitive anti-dumping or countervailing duties and the decisions to accept undertakings shall be subject to review where warranted. Such review may be held either at the request of a member state or on the initiative of the Commission or if any interested party so requests and submits positive information substantiating the need for review. Such requests shall be addressed either to a member state or to the Commission. A member state receiving any such request shall inform the Commission, which shall notify the other members states. Where the Commission receives the request, it shall inform the member states.
>
> 2. Where, after consultation, it becomes apparent that review is warranted, the proceedings shall be re-opened in accordance with article 7, where the circumstances so require. Such re-opening shall not per se affect the measures in operation.
>
> 3. Where warranted by the review, carried out either with or without re-opening of the proceeding, the measures shall be amended, repealed or annulled by the Community institution competent for their introduction. However, where measures have been taken under the traditional provision of the Act of Accession the Commission shall itself amend, repeal or annul them and shall report this to the Council; the latter may, acting by a qualified majority, decide that different action be taken.

Council Regulation 3017/79, *supra* note 38, at art. 14.

[46]Council Regulation 2176/84, art. 14, 1984 O.J. (L 201) (1984), *reprinted in* GATT, ANTI-DUMPING AND COUNTERVAILING MEASURES LEGISLATION CE-22-23 (June 1987).

[47]Article 15 of Regulation 2176/84 provides as follows:

> 1. Subject to the provisions of paragraph 2, anti-dumping or countervailing duties and undertakings shall lapse after five years from the date on which they entered into force or were last modified or confirmed.
>
> 2. The Commission shall normally, after consultation and within six months prior to the end of the five-year period, publish in the Official Journal of the European Communities a notice of the impending expiry of the measure in question and inform the Community industry known to be concerned. This notice shall state the period within which interested parties may make known their views in writing and may apply to be heard orally by the Commission in accordance with Article 7(5).

the expiry of the measure would lead again to injury or threat of injury before the Commission would conduct a review of the measure. Interested parties, however, did not need to establish changed circumstances to justify initiation of an Article 15 review.[48]

In 1988, the EU added minor additional procedural requirements for sunset reviews.[49] For example, according to Article 15(4) of Regulation 2423/88, "[w]here a review of a measure under Article 14 is in progress at the end of the relevant five year period, the measure shall remain in force pending the outcome of such review."[50] According to post-1988 EU expiry decisions, a review consists of commencing another investigation of dumping in which the Commission would review the annual period prior to the notice of initiation.[51] The Commission would determine whether dumping has continued by calculating margins for the period of review and considers whether injury is still being caused to the domestic industry.[52] Likewise,

---

> Where an interested party shows that the expiry of the measure would lead again to injury or threat of injury, the Commission shall carry out a review of the measure. The measure shall remain in force pending outcome of this review.
>
> Where anti-dumping or countervailing duties and undertakings lapse under this Article the Commission shall publish a notice to that effect in the Official Journal of the European Communities.
>
> 3. Existing anti-dumping or countervailing duties and undertakings shall not lapse under this Article before 1 July 1985.

Id. at art. 15.

48*See* Ivo Van Bael & Jean-Francois Bellis, ANTI-DUMPING AND OTHER TRADE PROTECTION LAWS OF THE EEC 209 (CCH 2nd ed., 1990).

49Council Regulation 2176/84, *supra* note 46, at art. 15.1; *see* Edwin A. Vermulst, ANTIDUMPING LAW AND PRACTICE IN THE UNITED STATES AND THE EUROPEAN COMMUNITIES: A COMPARATIVE ANALYSIS 251 (North-Holland, 1987); Philippe De Smedt, *Survey of the Revised Basic EC Anti-Dumping Regulation*, 17 INT'L BUS. LAW. 13, 18 (1989).

50Council Regulation 2423/88, art. 15(4), 1988 O.J. (L 209) (1988).

51*See, e.g.*, Fibre Building Board (Hardboard) Originating in Czechoslovakia, Poland and the USSR, Council Regulation 1789/89, para. 3, 1989 O.J. (L 176) (1989); Ball Bearings With a Greatest External Diameter Exceeding 30 mm Originating in Japan, Council Regulation 1739/85, para. 7, 1992 O.J. (L 286) (1992); Certain Electronic Weighing Scales Originating in Japan, Council Regulation 993/93, art. 14, 1993 O.J. (L 104) (1993).

52Fibre Building Board (Hardboard) Originating in Czechoslovakia, Poland and the USSR, Council Regulation 1789/89, para. 8, 1989 O.J. (L 176) (1989); Ball Bearings With a Greatest External Diameter Exceeding 30 mm Originating in Japan, Council Regulation 1739/85, paras. 21-23, 1992 O.J. (L 286) (1992).

the Commission would consider whether expiry of the measure would lead to a situation causing or threatening to cause material injury to the domestic industry by evaluating the probable development of volumes and prices of the imported product.[53] Finally, the Commission would assess whether it was in the Community's interest to maintain the measure.[54]

2. Pre-Uruguay Round Canadian Sunset Provisions

In 1984, Canada enacted the Special Import Measures Act (SIMA) to implement the Tokyo Round agreements.[55] According to that law, the Deputy Minister of the National Revenue for Customs and Excise (Revenue Canada) was charged with determining whether imports were being dumped or subsidized.[56] Revenue Canada issued preliminary and final determinations regarding dumping and subsidization. Upon receipt of Revenue Canada's preliminary determination, the Canadian Import Tribunal (CIT)[57] would make an inquiry regarding whether the dumping or the subsidizing of the goods had caused, was causing, or was likely to cause material injury or has caused or is causing retardation.[58] As part of its investigation, the CIT collected questionnaire responses from interested parties, prepared a staff report, and conducted a hearing.[59] Upon an affirmative determination from Revenue Canada, the CIT issued one, final de-

---

[53]Fibre Building Board (Hardboard) Originating in Czechoslovakia, Poland and the USSR, Council Regulation 1789/89, para. 14, 1989 O.J. (L 176) (1989).

[54]Ball Bearings With a Greatest External Diameter Exceeding 30 mm Originating in Japan, Council Regulation 1739/85, para. 40, 1992 O.J. (L 286) (1992).

[55]Special Import Measures Act, ch. 25, 1984 S.C. (Can.), *reprinted in* GATT, ANTI-DUMPING AND COUNTERVAILING MEASURES LEGISLATION CA-1 (June 1987); *see generally* Debra P. Steger, *Canadian Implementation of the Agreement Establishing the World Trade Organization, in* IMPLEMENTING THE URUGUAY ROUND 243, 250 (John H. Jackson & Alan Sykes eds., 1997).

[56]Special Import Measures Act, ch. 25, §§2, 38, 41 & 42, 1984 S.C. (Can.), *reprinted in* GATT, ANTI-DUMPING AND COUNTERVAILING MEASURES LEGISLATION CA-2, -35, -37, -39 (June 1987).

[57]*Id.* §2, *reprinted in* GATT, ANTI-DUMPING AND COUNTERVAILING MEASURES LEGISLATION CA-5 (GATT June 1987). Prior to 1984, the CIT was known as the "Anti-dumping Tribunal." CITT RESEARCH BRANCH, CANADA'S USE OF THE GATT ANTI-DUMPING CODE 23 n.5 (June 1991).

[58]Special Import Measures Act, ch. 25, 1984 S.C., §42(1) (Can.), *reprinted in* GATT, ANTI-DUMPING AND COUNTERVAILING MEASURES LEGISLATION CA-39 (June 1987).

[59]*See* CITT RESEARCH BRANCH, *supra* note 57, at 6.

termination and an order or finding with respect to the imports as necessary.[60] Finally, as with the EU, the SIMA required the Tribunal to consider whether the imposition of a duty or imposition of a duty in the full amount would be in the public interest.[61] Orders or findings could be appealed to the Federal Court of Canada.[62]

The 1984 SIMA established a formal sunset review procedure.[63] Section 16(d) of the Anti-dumping Act and Section 76 of the Special Import Measures Act provided the CIT with the power to review prior findings of material injury still in effect as of December 1, 1984.[64] According to Section 76(5) of the SIMA, an antidumping or countervailing duty order or finding

---

[60]Special Import Measures Act, ch. 25, §43, 1984 (Can.), *reprinted in* GATT, ANTI-DUMPING AND COUNTERVAILING MEASURES LEGISLATION CA-41 (June 1987).

[61]*Id.* §45, *reprinted in* GATT, ANTI-DUMPING AND COUNTERVAILING MEASURES LEGISLATION CA-43 (June 1987).

[62]*Id.* §44, *reprinted in* GATT, ANTI-DUMPING AND COUNTERVAILING MEASURES LEGISLATION CA-42 (June 1987).

[63]CITT, ANNUAL REPORT 1987, at 35; CITT, ANNUAL REPORT FOR FISCAL YEAR ENDING MARCH 31, 1989, at 14.

[64]Special Import Measures Act, ch. 25, §108(8), 1984 *reprinted in* GATT, ANTI-DUMPING AND COUNTERVAILING MEASURES LEGISLATION CA-84 (June 1987).

> Every order or finding made pursuant to section 16 of the former Act that is in force on the day that this Act comes into force or that is made pursuant to that section after the day on which this Act comes into force shall have the same force and effect for the purposes of sections 3 to 5 of this Act, and shall continue in effect according to its terms, as if made under section 43 or 44 of this Act and section 76 of this Act shall apply in respect of the order or finding in all respects as if it had been made under section 43 or 44 of this Act on the later of the day that this Act comes into force and the day on which the order of finding was in fact made pursuant to section 16 of the former Act.

Id. Section 76 of the SIMA provided:

> 76. (1) Subject to this section and paragraph 91(1)(g), every order or finding of the Tribunal is final and conclusive.
>
> (2) At any time after the making of an order or finding described in any of sections 3 to 6, the Tribunal may, on its own initiative or at the request of the Deputy Minister or any other person or of any government, review the order or finding and, in the making of such review, may rehear any matter before deciding it.
>
> (3) The Tribunal shall not initiate any review pursuant to sub-section (2) at the request of any person or government unless such person or government satisfies the Tribunal that initiation of the review is warranted.
>
> (4) Where the Tribunal reviews an order or finding pursuant to sub-section (2),

would be revoked as of the expiration of five years without the initiation of a review. Although Section 76 of the SIMA was amended in 1988 and again in 1993, those changes did not affect Section 76(5) requiring expiry reviews.[65] The 1988 amendments did, however, establish the Canadian International Trade Tribunal (CITT) which replaced the Canadian Import Tribunal.[66]

Unlike the EU Commission, the CITT's review does not entail the calculation of dumping margins for a specific period of investigation. Instead, the CITT will consider Revenue Canada's calculated margins during the five year period of review. Upon completion of an expiry review, the CITT will either continue or rescind a finding.[67] If the finding is rescinded, duties are no longer collected on imports. The CITT may also continue a finding

---

the Tribunal shall, on completion of the review, make an order rescinding the order or finding or continuing it with or without amendment, as the circumstances require.

(5) Where the Tribunal has not initiated a review pursuant to sub-section (2) with respect to an order or finding before the expiration of five years after

(a) if no order continuing the order or finding has been made pursuant to sub-section (4), the day on which the order or finding was made, or

(b) if one or more orders continuing the order or finding have been made pursuant to sub-section (4), the day on which the last such order was made,

the order or finding shall be deemed to have been rescinded as of the expiration of five years.

Special Import Measures Act, ch. 25, §76, 1984 S.C. (Can.), *reprinted in* GATT, ANTI-DUMPING AND COUNTERVAILING MEASURES LEGISLATION CA-58-59 (June 1987).

[65]An Act to Implement the Free Trade Agreement Between Canada and the United States of America, ch. 65, §§23-45, 1988 S.C. (Can.), *reprinted in* WTO Committee on Anti-Dumping Practices & Committee on Subsidies and Countervailing Measures, *Notification of Laws and Regulations Under Articles 18.5 and 32.6 of the Agreements: Canada*, G/ADP/N/1/CAN/1, G/SCM/N/1/CAN/1, at 2009-38 (March 24, 1995); An Act to Implement the North American Free Trade Agreement, ch. 44, §§201-03, 1993 S.C. (Can.), *reprinted in* WTO Committee on Anti-Dumping Practices & Committee on Subsidies and Countervailing Measures, *Notification of Laws and Regulations Under Articles 18.5 and 32.6 of the Agreements: Canada*, G/ADP/N/1/CAN/1, G/SCM/N/1/CAN/1, at 2066-68 (March 24, 1995).

[66]Canadian International Trade Tribunal Act, ch. 56, 1988; *see* Ronald C. Cheng, *Canada*, ANTI-DUMPING UNDER THE WTO: A COMPARATIVE REVIEW 73, 75, 95 (Keith Steele ed., 1996).

[67]*See* Waterproof Rubber Footwear Originating in or Exported From Czechoslovakia, Poland, the Republic of Korea, Taiwan, Hong Kong, Malaysia, Yugoslavia and the People's Republic of China, Review No.: RR-92-001, at 8 (Oct. 21, 1992); Certain Waterproof Rubber Footwear Originating in or Exported From Czechoslovakia, Poland, the

or amend it to exclude a product, a country or sometimes a specific exporter.[68]

Unlike Section 76 of the SIMA which governs orders or findings, Section 53 governs the review of undertakings. Specifically, in the 1984 SIMA, the Deputy Minister was charged with conducting a review of an undertaking "before the expiration of three years from the date on which he accepted it and before the expiration of the subsequent period, if any."[69] The Deputy Minister would then renew it for another three years. An undertaking that was not renewed would expire which would terminate all proceedings "respecting the dumping or subsidizing of the goods to which the undertaking relates, unless, in any case where the Deputy Minister has accepted two or more undertakings, the Deputy Minister, for good reasons, otherwise directs." The first review under Section 76 was decided on October 4, 1989.[70]

3. Pre-Uruguay Round Australian Sunset Provisions

Prior to 1988, the antidumping law was administered by the Australian Customs Service.[71] In the Anti-Dumping Authority Act of 1988, Australia established the Anti-Dumping Authority.[72] According to the 1988 Act, the Comptroller-General of Customs accepted complaints of injurious dumping or subsidization and made a "prima facie" decision whether to accept an application for investigation of injurious dumping, conducted the preliminary antidumping or countervailing duty investigations, and issued a preliminary determination on whether dumping was causing material injury or threat thereof to the Australian industry producing like goods.[73] If the Comptroller-General reached a positive finding, it prepared a report on

---

Republic of Korea, Taiwan, Hong Kong, Malaysia, Yugoslavia and the People's Republic of China, Review No.: RR-97-001, at 9 (Oct. 20, 1997).

[68]CITT, *Information on Dumping and Subsidizing Inquiries and Reviews* at 4.

[69]Special Import Measures Act, ch. 25, §53, 1984 S.C. (Can.), *reprinted in* GATT, ANTI-DUMPING AND COUNTERVAILING MEASURES LEGISLATION CA-48 (June 1987).

[70]12 Gauge Shotshells (Ammunition) Originating in or Exported from the Union of the Soviet Socialist Republics, Poland, Czechoslovakia and Hungary, Review No.: RR-89-001 (Oct. 4, 1989).

[71]AUSTRALIAN ANTI-DUMPING AUTHORITY, ANNUAL REPORT 1988-89 at 15.

[72]GATT, 1 TRADE POLICY REVIEW: AUSTRALIA 54 (1994).

[73]*Id.*; AUSTRALIAN ANTI-DUMPING AUTHORITY, ANNUAL REPORT 1988-89 at 17, 20-21.

the reasons for its finding, and the matter was referred to the Anti-Dumping Authority.[74]

The Anti-Dumping Authority (ADA) worked within the Industry, Technology and Commerce "portfolio" and reported to the Minister for Industry, Technology and Commerce and the Minister for Science, Customs and Small Business.[75] The ADA was charged with making a recommendation to the Minister whether or not to take antidumping or countervailing duty action in respect of particular goods, to revoke antidumping or countervailing duty action already taken, to review on request Customs' negative "prima facie" decision or preliminary finding, and to prepare reports to the Minister on anti-dumping matters.[76] Upon receipt of a preliminary finding, the Authority requested information from all parties and reviewed Customs' report.[77] The Authority would also visit producers, exporters, and importers.[78] The Authority then arranged a public "meeting of parties" to discuss the issues in the case and made its report and recommendation to the Minister. The ADA would issue exporter-specific antidumping or countervailing duty measures unless there were several suppliers from the same country and it was impractical to do so, in which case country-specific measures were published.[79]

In 1986, the Customs Tariff (Anti-Dumping) Act of 1975, as amended, included Section 20 permitting revocation of orders.[80] In January 1986, the

---

[74] AUSTRALIAN ANTI-DUMPING AUTHORITY, ANNUAL REPORT 1988-89 at 17, 21.

[75] *Id.* at 18.

[76] *Id.* at 17-18.

[77] *Id.* at 21.

[78] *Id.*

[79] *Id.* at 22; Lawrie Willet AO, *Review of Australia's Anti-Dumping and Countervailing Administration* 17, 118-19 (Sept. 1996); Customs Act 1901, as amended, §269TP, *reprinted in* AUSTRALIAN CUSTOMS LAW AND PRACTICE (CCH) ¶74,751.

[80] Section 20 of the Customs Tariff (Anti-Dumping) Act of 1975, as amended, provided:

> 20. (1) The Minister may, by notice published in the Gazette, revoke a notice published in pursuance of this Act and shall do so if he is satisfied that, if the notice were not in force, he would not be authorized by this Act to cause the notice to be published.
>
> (2) A notice of revocation under sub-section (1) has the effect from a date specified in the notice, which, except in the case of the revocation of a notice that directed the manner of ascertaining the amount of a special duty of Customs imposed by this Act, may be a date earlier than the date of publication of the notice of revocation in the Gazette.

Australian Administrative Guidelines indicated that, in order to implement Article 9 of the Tokyo Round Agreement, the Department would regularly review normal values and the continuing need for dumping duties or undertakings.[81] According to those Guidelines, a dumping "gazettal" would be reviewed after two years "as to the continued need for dumping gazettals to remain in force. If justified, enquiries are made with the Australian industry concerned to determine whether there is a foreseeable threat of the injury recurring if the measures are removed."[82] The Guidelines also provided the following procedures for revoking dumping duties:

> A7/3/1 Customs Tariff (Anti-Dumping) Act, Section 20 provides that the Minister may revoke a notice imposing dumping or countervailing duty if he considers that anti-dumping or countervailing action is no longer warranted. Revocation must be by notice published in the Gazette — sample at Appendix A7:1.
>
> A7/3/2 The effective date of revocation will be specified in the notice published in the Gazette (sub-section 20(2)), and dumping or countervailing duty ceases to be payable on goods entered for home consumption on or after that date (sub-section 20(3)). Except where the Minister has directed that an amount of dumping or countervailing duty applies under section 8(5) or 10(5)), the effective date of revocation may be earlier than the date of publication of the revocation of notice (sub-section 20(2)).
>
> A7/3/3 Revocation will follow departmental review of dumping, subsidy and injury whereby it is established that the continuance of dumping or countervailing duty is not warranted. The review may be undertaken upon request, or as part of the Department's continuing review programme. (See A7/1/1).

> (3) Upon the revocation of notice that declared that a section of this Act applies to goods, the special duty on the goods ceases to be payable, and shall not be charged or collected on goods entered for home consumption on or after the date of effect of the notice of revocation.

Australian Customs Tariff (Anti-Dumping) Act of 1975, as amended, §20, *reprinted in* GATT, ANTI-DUMPING AND COUNTERVAILING MEASURES LEGISLATION, *supra* note 56, at AU-52.

[81]*Australian Dumping and Countervailing Administrative Guidelines (Division A5, Section 6), reprinted in Inventory of Review and Sunset Clause Provisions in the Legislation and Administrative Procedures of Parties to the Code*, GATT Doc. No. ADP/W/106 (Jan. 16, 1986) [hereinafter *Inventory*], *cited in* Stewart, Markel & Kerwin, *supra* note 1, at n.1183.

[82]*Id.*

A7/3/4 Prior to revocation of dumping or countervailing duty a meeting of parties may be convened to ensure that all interested parties have the opportunity to put their case and rebut opposing arguments.

A7/3/5 In addition to a publication of the Minister's notice of revocation in the Gazette, the Department will notify revocation by Australian Customs Notice (ACN) and advise known interested parties including the government of the exporting country. State Collectors will also be advised by Dumping Commodities Register (DCR) and Confidential Instructions (CI's), to enable collection of dumping or countervailing duty to cease as directed.[83]

In response to industry dissatisfaction with the Customs Tariff (Anti-Dumping) Act of 1975, the Australian government asked Professor Gruen to review the law and to suggest changes.[84] In March 1986, Professor Gruen recommended an amendment to ensure that an antidumping action could not stay in place for more than a set period of time without a review by the Industries Assistance Commission of the industry concerned.[85] The Minister for Industry, Technology and Commerce, Senator John Button, issued the Australian government's response to the Gruen Report on October 30, 1986.[86] The Australian government stated that it intended to introduce a provision under which antidumping duties measures would cease after three years' continuous application.[87]

As a result of the Gruen Report, Australia established a three-year sunset period in 1988 which was extended to five years in 1992.[88] In 1988, Aus-

---

[83]*Id.*

[84]AUSTRALIAN ANTI-DUMPING AUTHORITY, ANNUAL REPORT 1988-89 at 15.

[85]*Id.*

[86]*Id.* at 16.

[87]*Id.*

[88]Customs Act 1901, as amended, §269TM(1), *reprinted in* AUSTRALIAN CUSTOMS LAW AND PRACTICE (CCH) ¶74,701; *see* AUSTRALIAN ANTI-DUMPING AUTHORITY, ANNUAL REPORT 1988-89 at 16-17; AUSTRALIAN ANTI-DUMPING AUTHORITY, ANNUAL REPORT 1990-91, at 35-36; AUSTRALIAN ANTI-DUMPING AUTHORITY, ANNUAL REPORT 1991-92, at 12, 14; Gerd Hollander & Fred Gruen, *Australia's Antidumping Policies and Practices* 7 (Oct. 3, 1997), presented at the Brookings Trade Policy Forum on "Private Practices and Trade Policy: The Future of International Rules on Antidumping and Competition" (Nov. 13-14 1997).

tralia amended the Customs Tariff (Anti-Dumping) Act of 1975 to restrict the duration of notices and undertakings to a maximum of three years.[89] Australia then extended the sunset period to five years in Section 269TM of the Customs Act of 1901, as amended, which required dumping or countervailing duty notices and undertakings which were in force as of July 10, 1992, or which commenced after that date to expire automatically five years

---

[89]Customs Tariff (Anti-Dumping) Amendment Act 1988, §13.

Period during which certain notices and undertakings to remain in force

12B. (1) Where a notice is published after the commencement of this section under a relevant notification provision in respect of goods of a particular kind, that notice shall, unless sooner revoked:

(a) if, at the time of publication of the first-mentioned notice, no previous notice relating to like goods in force under a relevant notification provision and no previous undertaking relating to like goods is in force under a relevant undertaking provision — expire 3 years after the date on which the first-mentioned notice is published; and

(b) if, at the time of publication of the first-mentioned notice, a previous notice relating to like goods is in force under the relevant notification provision or a previous undertaking relating to like goods is in force under a relevant undertaking provision — expire 3 years after the date on which that notice or undertaking, or, if there is more than one previous notice or undertaking, the first such notice or undertaking, was published or entered into, as the case requires.

(2) Where an undertaking is entered into after the commencement of this section under a relevant undertaking provision in respect of goods of a particular kind, that undertaking shall, unless provision is made for its earlier expiration:

(a) if, at the time when the first-mentioned undertaking was entered into, no previous undertaking relating to like goods is in force under a relevant undertaking provision and no previous notice relating to like goods is in force under a relevant notification provision — expire 3 years after the date that first-mentioned undertaking was entered into; and

(b) if, at the time when the first-mentioned undertaking is entered into, a previous undertaking relating to like goods is in force under a relevant undertaking provision or a previous notice relating to like goods is in force under a relevant notification provision — expire 3 years after the date on which that previous undertaking or notice, or, if there is more than one such undertaking or notice, the first such undertaking or notice was entered into or published, as the case requires.

(3) In subsections (1) and (2):

(a) a reference to a previous notice in relation to particular goods shall be taken to include a reference to a notice published before commencement of this section; and

(b) a reference to a previous undertaking shall be taken to include a reference to an undertaking entered into before the commencement of this section.

after the date on which they were published unless revoked before that time.[90] In the Customs Legislation (Tariff Concessions and Anti-Dumping) Amendment Act of 1992, Australia further allowed interested parties to apply for continuation of the measure.[91] The 1992 Act amended the Anti-Dumping Authority Act of 1988 to include Section 8A governing continuation inquiries:

> **Authority may make recommendations of continuation of dumping duty notices etc.**
>
> 8A. (1) Not later than eight months before an anti-dumping measure expires, the Authority must publish in the Gazette and in a newspaper circulating in each State, in the Australian Capital Territory and in the Northern Territory, a notice:
>
> (a) informing that the dumping duty notice, countervailing duty notice or undertaking is due to expire on a specified day (the 'specified expiry day'); and
>
> (b) inviting interested parties to apply to the Authority in accordance with this section, within 60 days, for the continuation of the anti-dumping measure.[92]

The first sunset review decision or "continuation inquiry" under Section 8A was issued in December 1994.[93]

Id. According to the accompanying notes on these provisions:

> The proposed new subsections 12(B)(1), (2), and (3) provide that a notice imposing duties, or any "undertakings" . . . made pursuant to the provisions of the Principal Act after the commencement of this Bill will only remain in force for a maximum period of three years, (if no notice has been previously issued for like goods) or, if a previous notice has been issued with regards to like goods, all notices will expire three years after the date the first notice was published.

The Parliament of the Commonwealth of Australia, House of Representatives, Customs Tariff (Anti-Dumping) Amendment Bill 1988, Explanatory Memorandum at Notes (Clause 13) (1988).

[90]Customs Act 1901, as amended, §269TM, *reprinted in* AUSTRALIAN CUSTOMS LAW AND PRACTICE (CCH) ¶70,000, 74,701; *see* High Density Polyethylene from the Republic of Korea, Saudi Arabia and Singapore, Anti-Dumping Authority Report No. 172, at 5 (June 1997).

[91]Customs Legislation (Tariff Concessions and Anti-Dumping) Amendment Act 1992, §7.

[92]*Id.*

[93]Bulk Brandy from France, Anti-Dumping Authority Report No. 141, at 6 (Dec. 1994).

The Australian Anti-Dumping Authority conducted a continuation inquiry concerning the expiration of both antidumping and countervailing duty orders and suspension agreements (or "undertakings").[94] According to Australia's sunset provisions, the Minister would revoke an antidumping or countervailing duty action if he was satisfied that, were the action not in place, he would not be empowered to put it in place.[95] Like the EU Commission, the ADA determined whether the domestic industry was currently experiencing injury and recalculated the margin during the course of a continuation review.[96]

4. Pre-Uruguay Round U.S. Revocation and Termination Provisions

a. *The Agency Regulations*

Prior to 1980, the Customs Service of the U.S. Treasury Department was charged with determining whether imports were being dumped or subsidized according to the antidumping and countervailing duty laws. The International Trade Commission (ITC) was charged with determining whether an industry in the United States was injured, likely to be injured, or was prevented from being established by reason of dumped imports[97] or subsidized duty-free imports.[98]

Although the pre-1979 statute did not specifically provide for revocation of orders or termination of suspended investigations,[99] Customs did

---

[94]Customs Legislation (Tariff Concessions and Anti-Dumping) Amendment Act 1992, §7.

[95]AUSTRALIAN ANTI-DUMPING AUTHORITY, ANNUAL REPORT 1991-92, at 9.

[96]Bulk Brandy from France, Anti-Dumping Authority Report No. 141, at 16, 22 (Dec. 1994).

[97]*Sec* Pub. L. No. 67-10, May 27, 1921, tit. II, §201(a), 42 Stat. 9; 19 U.S.C. §160(a) (1970).

[98]Prior to the Trade Act of 1974, U.S. countervailing duty law did not provide an "injury test" for any imports found to have benefited from countervailable subsidies. In 1974, Congress amended the law to provide an injury test only for subsidized imports that entered the United States free of duty. *See* Pub. L. No. 93-618, January 3, 1975, tit. III, §331(a), 88 Stat. 2049; 19 U.S.C. §1303(a) (1975).

[99]According to the DOC:

> "Revocation" is a term of art that refers to the end of an antidumping or countervailing proceeding in which an order has been issued. "Termination" is the companion

have a practice and a regulation governing the revocation of orders.[100] Prior to the June 1976 amendments to Customs' regulations, Customs permitted modification or revocation of dumping findings: (1) based on an application detailing any change in circumstances existing for a "substantial" period of time, (2) based on any other reasons showing that the basis for the dumping finding no longer existed, or (3) on Customs' own initiative. The countervailing duty regulations, however, did not contain a similar provision.[101]

In June 1976, Customs amended its regulations governing revocation. The new regulations permitted revocation of an antidumping finding (1) based on an application with detailed information that "any sales at less than fair value have been terminated for a substantial period of time" and that there would be no future sales at less than fair value, (2) sales at less than fair value "ha[d] not existed" for at least two years from the date of the dumping finding, or (3) on Customs' own initiative if the finding had been in effect for four years and there was no likelihood of resumption of sales at less than fair value. Finally, the regulations required that the agency review the period up to the date of tentative revocation for findings based on no sales at less than fair value for at least two years subsequent to the date of publication of the dumping finding.[102] No comparable amendments were made to the countervailing duty regulations.[103]

Likewise, the ITC could review an injury finding on its own motion, at the request of an interested party, or upon advice from Customs that there were "changed circumstances." Absent "good cause," the ITC would not review an injury determination within two years of a final determination.[104]

> term for the end of a proceeding in which the investigation was suspended due to the acceptance of a suspension agreement. Generally, a revocation or termination may occur only after the Department or Commission have conducted one or more reviews under section 751 of the Act.

19 C.F.R. §351.222(a) (1997). As explained *infra*, Section 751 of the Tariff Act of 1930, as amended (19 U.S.C. §1675), provides for administrative reviews, changed circumstances reviews, and sunset reviews.

[100] 19 C.F.R. §153.41 (1975); Leonard M. Shambon, *Revocation Under the Antidumping and Countervailing Duty Laws?: You Should Live So Long!*, 2 THE COMMERCE DEPARTMENT SPEAKS 241, 247-48 (PLI, 1987).

[101] 19 C.F.R. §153.41(a) (1975); *see* Shambon, *supra* note 100, at 247-48.

[102] 19 C.F.R. §153.44(a) (1979); *see* Shambon, *supra* note 100, at 248-51.

[103] 19 C.F.R. §159.47 (1979); *see* Shambon, *supra* note 100, at 251-52.

[104] *See* Trade Agreements Act of 1979, S. REP. NO. 249, 96th Cong., 1st Sess. 79, *reprinted in* U.S.C.C.A.N. 381, 465 (1979); 19 C.F.R. §§207.5, 207.9 (1979).

In order to implement the results of the Tokyo Round, the United States enacted the Trade Agreements Act of 1979. At around the same time, the authority over administering the antidumping and countervailing duty laws was transferred from the Customs Service to the U.S. Department of Commerce (DOC).[105] In the 1979 Act, Congress adopted Section 751 of the Tariff Act of 1930, as amended (19 U.S.C. §1675). Section 751(a) included an administrative review provision which required the DOC to conduct an administrative review of an antidumping or countervailing duty order or suspended investigation at least once during each 12-month period.[106] The purpose of the administrative review is to determine the amount of any antidumping duty or countervailing duty on imports entered during the previous year and to review the current status of and compliance with any suspension agreement. The DOC published the results of an administrative review together with notice of any duty to be assessed on past entries, estimated duty to be deposited on future entries, or investigation to be resumed.

Section 751(b) included the changed circumstances review provisions. Section 751(b) required the DOC or the ITC to conduct a review of an order or suspension agreement based on receipt of information or a request for review which showed "changed circumstances sufficient to warrant a review."[107] In the absence of good cause shown, however, the DOC or the ITC could not review a final determination or suspension less than 24 months after the date of publication of notice of that determination or suspension.[108]

---

[105]Reorg. Plan No. 3 of 1979, §5(a)(1)(C), 44 Fed. Reg. 69,275, 93 Stat. 1381, eff. Jan. 2, 1980, as provided by Section 1-107(a) of Ex. Ord. No. 12188, Jan. 2, 1980, 45 Fed. Reg. 993, set out as notes under 19 U.S.C. §2171.

[106]The 1979 Act required automatic annual administrative reviews. When that became too burdensome, Congress amended Section 751(a) to require administrative reviews "upon request." Trade and Tariff Act of 1984, Pub. L. No. 98-573, §611(a)(2)(A).

[107]19 U.S.C. §1675(b) (1979). In addition, Section 751(b) required the ITC to consider whether, in light of changed circumstances, a suspension agreement to eliminate the injurious effect of exports of the subject merchandise continued to eliminate completely the injurious effects of imports of the merchandise. If the decision of the ITC was negative with respect to the suspension agreement, Section 751(e) stated that the agreement would be treated as not accepted, and the ITC and DOC would proceed as if the agreement had been violated on that date. 19 U.S.C. §1675(e) (1979).

[108]19 U.S.C. §1675(b)(2) (1979).

Finally, Section 751(c) authorized the DOC to revoke an order or terminate a suspended investigation based on the results of a review under Section 751:[109]

> (c) **Revocation of countervailing duty order or antidumping duty order** — The administering authority may revoke, in whole or in part, a countervailing duty order or an antidumping duty order, or terminate a suspended investigation, after review under this section. Any such revocation or termination shall apply with respect to unliquidated entries of merchandise entered, or withdrawn from warehouse, for consumption on and after a date determined by the administering authority.[110]

The DOC then revised its regulations in 1980 to incorporate these changes.[111] The regulations permitted revocations (1) based on a finding that sales at less than fair value or subsidies have ceased for at least two years, there is no likelihood of resumption of sales at less than fair value or subsidies, and a written statement agreeing to reinstatement for future dumping or subsidies, or (2) based on the DOC's own initiative after three years if there is no likelihood of resumption of imports, the less than fair value sales or subsidies have been eliminated, or other changed circumstances warrant revocation.[112]

Congress amended Section 751(c) in the Trade and Tariff Act of 1984 to prohibit revocation of countervailing duty orders or suspended investigations based on a foreign government's export tax, duty, or other charge

---

[109] *See* Bernard Carreau, *Revocation of Antidumping and Countervailing Duty Orders: New Procedures and Recent Trends in Commerce Practice*, 669 THE COMMERCE DEPARTMENT SPEAKS 43 (PLI, 1990).

[110] 19 U.S.C. §1675(c) (1979).

[111] 19 C.F.R. §§353.54 & 355.42 (1980); *see* Shambon, *supra* note 100, at 258.

[112] 19 C.F.R. §§353.54 & 355.42 (1980); *see* Shambon, *supra* note 100, at 271-76. Once again, the DOC required a review up to the tentative determination to revoke if the date for determining the two year period was the date of the order. 19 C.F.R. §§353.54 & 355.42 (1980). After the new 1980 regulations, however, the DOC adopted two practices of revoking orders (1) based on the cessation of shipments for four years, and (2) based on a finding of one year of sales at not less than fair value and two years of no shipments. Shambon, *supra* note 100, at 271. The DOC would issue a tentative determination to revoke with its preliminary review determination, but would issue its final determination to revoke in the subsequent administrative review. *Id.* at 273-74.

intended to offset the subsidy received.[113] In addition, Congress required the DOC to conduct verification of foreign respondents' questionnaire responses prior to revocation or termination.[114]

The United States again amended the revocation/termination provisions of its countervailing duty regulations in 1988 and its antidumping duty regulations in 1989.[115] Pursuant to those regulations, the United States would revoke an order or terminate a suspended investigation if: (1) the DOC found that producers have not sold the subject merchandise at dumped prices for a period of at least three consecutive years and are not likely to in the future;[116] (2) the DOC found that producers have not applied for or received net subsidies for a period of at least five years and are not likely to in the future;[117] (3) the DOC found that the government of the affected country has eliminated all subsidies on the merchandise by abolishing all programs found countervailable for a period of at least three consecutive years and is not likely to reinstate them or substitute new programs in the future;[118] (4) the DOC found changed circumstances, including a finding that the order is no longer of interest to domestic interested parties based on an affirmative statement from the petitioner or based on five con-

---

[113] Section 1675(c) provided as follows:

> **(c) Revocation of countervailing duty order or antidumping duty order**
> The administering authority may revoke, in whole or in part, a countervailing duty order or an antidumping duty order, or terminate a suspended investigation, after review under this section. The administering authority shall not revoke, in whole or in part, a countervailing duty order or terminate a suspended investigation on the basis of any export taxes, duties, or other charges levied on the export of merchandise to the United States specifically intended to offset the subsidy received. Any such revocation or termination shall apply with respect to unliquidated entries of merchandise entered, or withdrawn from warehouse, for consumption on and after a date determined by the administering authority

19 U.S.C. §1675(c) (1984).

[114] 19 U.S.C. §1677e(b)(2) (1984).

[115] Countervailing Duties: Final Rule, 53 Fed. Reg. 52,306 (Dep't Comm. 1988) (Final Rule); Antidumping Duties: Final Rule, 54 Fed. Reg. 12,742 (Dep't Comm. 1989) (Final Rule).

[116] 19 U.S.C. §1675(c) (1988); 19 C.F.R. §353.25(a)(1) (1989).

[117] 19 U.S.C. §1675(c) (1988); 19 C.F.R. §355.25(a)(2) (1989).

[118] 19 U.S.C. §1675(c) (1988); 19 C.F.R. §355.25(a)(1) (1989).

secutive years without a request for review;[119] or (5) the ITC found lack of injury due to changed circumstances.[120]

The new regulations significantly changed eligibility for revocation or termination. First, the language requiring the DOC to assess future imports was modified from requiring a finding of "no likelihood of resumption" of dumped or subsidized imports to a finding that it is "not likely" that companies will dump or apply for or receive net subsidies or that the foreign government will reinstate the same or other programs.[121] Second, the new language eliminated revocations based on no shipments.[122] Third, the number of years required was extended from two years to three years for antidumping cases and government elimination of subsidies and five years for company non-use of countervailable subsidies.[123] Fourth, the regulations gave the DOC explicit authority to revoke countervailing duty orders in part on a company-specific basis as done for antidumping duty orders.[124] Fifth, the regulations attempted to eliminate the "gap period" problem of requiring current information up to the tentative determination to revoke which could be long after the two year base period. Instead, the regulations made it clear that revocation would be effective the day after the end of the base period thereby eliminating the gap period.[125] Sixth, the new regula-

---

[119] 19 U.S.C. §1675(b) (1988); 19 C.F.R. §§353.25(d); 355.25(d) (1989).

[120] 19 U.S.C. §1675(b) (1988); 19 C.F.R. §207.45 (1989).

[121] *See* Carreau, *supra* note 109, at 63-65, *comparing* 19 C.F.R. §§353.55(c) & 355.42(c) *with* 19 C.F.R. §§353.25(a)(1), 355.25(a)(1) & (2). According to one commentator, the "no likelihood" standard implied a high degree of certainty whereas the "not likely" standard implied probability. *Id.* at 65.

[122] *See id.* at 64, 86 (noting that from 1980 to 1987, the second most common basis for revoking antidumping orders was revocations based on a changed circumstances finding of no shipments).

[123] *See id.* at 48, 53.

[124] *See id.* at 54.

[125] Sections 353.25(c)(3) and 355.25(c)(3) of the agency regulations provided as follows:

> If the Secretary revokes an order or revokes an order in part, the Secretary will order the suspension of liquidation ended for the merchandise covered by the revocation on the first day after the period under review, and will instruct the Customs Service to release any cash deposit or bond.

19 C.F.R. §§353.25(c)(3) & 355.25(c)(3) (1989); *see* Carreau, *supra* note 109, at 49-50; *cf.* Timken Co. v. United States, Slip Op. 97-164, at 29 (CIT Dec. 3, 1997).

tions required applicants to certify the number of clean years and submit a reinstatement certification.[126] Finally, the new regulations established an automatic "sunset" requirement that an order or suspended investigation would be revoked or terminated if after five years an interested party did not request an administrative review or object to revocation.[127]

b. *The DOC's Practice of Revoking Orders or Terminating Suspended Investigations Under Pre-URAA Law*

i. Administrative Reviews

Prior to the URAA, Section 751(c) of the Tariff Act of 1930, as amended (19 U.S.C. §1675(c)), permitted the DOC to revoke, in whole or in part, an antidumping or countervailing duty order or suspended investigation in the context of an administrative review based, *inter alia*, on a finding of compliance with the law.[128] For example, in response to a request for a partial revocation of an antidumping duty order in administrative review, the DOC would first consider whether or not the respondent had established lack of dumping for three consecutive years.[129] Only if the respondent had established lack of dumping did the DOC consider whether there was no likelihood of resumption of dumping.[130] Under this standard, evidence of three consecutive years of zero or *de minimis* margins would not

---

[126]19 C.F.R. §§353.25(b) & 355.25(b) (1989); *see* Carreau, *supra* note 109, at 55-62. According to the DOC's comments on the new regulations, reinstatement in an order would only be possible for partial company revocation given the DOC's position that it could not reinstate a revoked order absent a new investigation. *Id.* at 60, *citing* Preamble, 53 Fed. Reg. at 52,332.

[127]19 C.F.R. §§353.25(d)(4) & 355.25(d)(4) (1989); *see* Carreau, *supra* note 109, at 104.

[128]19 U.S.C. §1675(c) (1994). Pre-Uruguay Round Section 1675(c) is now, for the most part, 19 U.S.C. §1675(d)(1) after the URAA amendments. 19 U.S.C. §1675(d)(1) (1997).

[129]*See* 19 C.F.R. §353.25(a)(2) (1994).

[130]Lack of dumping could not be established on the basis of no shipments. *See, e.g.*, Color Television Receivers from the Republic of Korea, 61 Fed. Reg. 59,402, 59,405 (Dep't Comm. 1996) (Final Results Admin. Rev.).

automatically entitle a respondent to revocation or termination. Rather, the respondent bore the burden of proving that there was no likelihood of resumption of dumping.[131]

To make its likelihood determination, the DOC first considered company-specific pricing data and margins in preceding periods. If that data was insufficient for evaluating the likelihood of future dumped sales, however, the DOC would consider general pricing and market conditions to determine whether respondents could make sales competitively in the United States without selling at dumped prices, including conditions and trends in the domestic and home market industries, currency movements, and the ability of the foreign entity to compete in the U.S. marketplace in the absence of an order or suspension agreement.[132] Evidence that a respondent "may have dumped" in the period following the third administrative review period was relevant to a likelihood determination.[133] Evidence of an economic incentive to dump was also relevant to the DOC's analysis.[134]

---

[131] *See* Sanyo Electric Co., Ltd. v. United States, 15 CIT 609, 614 (1991) (respondent must establish to the satisfaction of the Secretary that there is no likelihood of the resumption of LTFV sales), *citing* Manufacturas Industriales De Nogales, S.A. v. United States, 666 F. Supp. 1562, 1566 (CIT 1987); *see* Brass Sheet and Strip from Germany, 61 Fed. Reg. 49,727, 49,731 (Dep't Comm. 1996) (Final Results Admin. Rev.) ("The principle remains unchanged that the Department must be satisfied that there is no likelihood of resumption of dumping, and this determination is still not solely dependent on three years of no margins."); *but see* Tatung Co. v. United States, 18 CIT 1144 (1994) (ordinarily past behavior constitutes substantial evidence of expected future behavior); Steel Wire Rope from the Republic of Korea, 62 Fed. Reg. 17,171, 17,173 (Dep't Comm. 1997) (Final Results Admin. Rev.); Dynamic Random Access Memory Semiconductors of One Megabyte or Above from the Republic of Korea, 62 Fed. Reg. 39,809, 39,811 (Dep't Comm. 1998) (Final Results Admin. Rev.).

[132] Toshiba Corp. v. United States, 15 CIT 597, 601(1991); *Sanyo Electric Co., Ltd.*, 15 CIT at 611 (Court approves of consideration of market factors that are indicative of present and future competitive pricing pressures in the United States that bear on the issue of whether subject merchandise would be sold at LTFV prices in the future); Brass Sheet and Strip from Germany, 61 Fed. Reg. 49,727, 49,730 (Dep't Comm. 1996) (Final Results Admin. Rev.); Certain Forged Steel Crankshafts from the United Kingdom, 62 Fed. Reg. 16,768, 16,771 (Dep't Comm. 1997) (Final Results Admin. Rev.) (ITA finds change in ownership alone does not establish likelihood of resumption of dumping).

[133] Dynamic Random Access Memory Semiconductors of One Megabyte or Above from the Republic of Korea, 62 Fed. Reg. 39,809, 39,813 (Dep't Comm. 1997) (Final Results Admin. Rev.).

[134] *Id.* at 39,818.

For example, the Court of International Trade in *Toshiba Corp. v. United States* affirmed the DOC's finding that there was insufficient evidence to determine whether there was no likelihood of resumption of dumping. In *Toshiba*, respondent argued that the DOC erred in disregarding evidence that it had no incentive to ship subject merchandise to the United States in making its likelihood determination. The DOC, however, found that the company-specific data available for Toshiba was insufficient to evaluate the likelihood of future LTFV sales when (1) the data used for calculating zero margins was seven years old, (2) evidence that respondent's market share increased while selling at fair value based on merchandise manufactured in the United States, and (3) no company-specific data submitted for home market prices. The DOC found that general market factors, such as the existence of substantial dumping margins of other respondents from the same and other countries, the high costs of production, and the high value of the foreign currency, raised concerns with respect to the likelihood of resumption issue.[135]

The Court affirmed the DOC's finding in *Toshiba Corp.* noting:

> While it cannot be disputed that if there are no shipments there will be no sales at LTFV, the regulation does not require Commerce to consider evidence that sales will not occur. A revocation proceeding is inherently predictive, and rarely, if ever will Commerce be able to predict with certainty what will occur upon revocation.[136]

The Court found that the DOC was correct in disregarding such "ambiguous" evidence of lack of incentive to resume shipments absent evidence that Toshiba could not export or had forsworn exports to the United States. Finally, the Court in *Toshiba* rejected the suggestion that the test under 19 U.S.C. §1675(c) should be whether the resumption of sales at LTFV prices is "imminent or can reasonably be expected" because "[t]he Secretary need not affirmatively find that LTFV sales are likely to be unsatisfied that there is no likelihood of LTFV sales."[137]

---

[135]*Toshiba Corp.*, 15 CIT at 603 (ITA also noted evidence that respondent and other Japanese companies were conducting a large amount of research and development to produce subject merchandise which could be exported to the United States).

[136]*Id.* at 599, *citing* Matsushita Elec. Indus. Co., Ltd. v. United States, 750 F.2d 927, 933 (Fed. Cir. 1984); *see* Sanyo Electric Co., Ltd., 15 CIT at 611.

[137]*Toshiba Corp.*, 15 CIT at 600; *cf.* Kerr-McGee Chemical Corp. v. United States, 765 F. Supp. 1576 (CIT 1991).

Among the general conditions the DOC would consider in deciding whether there was no likelihood of resumption of dumping was whether, despite zero or *de minimis* margins, there had been a decline in import volumes of the subject merchandise.[138] For example, in *Brass Sheet and Strip from Germany*, the DOC refused to find no likelihood of resumption of dumping when, *inter alia*, respondent's declining sales volumes suggested that it would have difficulty in selling subject merchandise above fair value.[139] While the DOC has noted that strong, profitable markets tend not to precipitate dumping, a market downturn could preclude revocation.[140]

The DOC would reject requests for revocation based on lack of shipments for any one of the three years.[141] According to the DOC, "the absence of shipments is no indication of the absence of price discrimination, which is the basis for revocation" under non-sunset revocation/termination provisions.[142] The DOC would also consider exchange-rate relationships in determining whether dumping sales are likely.[143] For example, the DOC would consider whether the relative strengthening of the home market currency could increase home market prices relative to U.S. prices and thereby increase the likelihood of future dumped sales.[144] The mere fact that the home market currency was appreciating, however, was not as compelling if respondents were able to secure zero or *de minimis* margins during the period of appreciation and further appreciation was unlikely.[145]

The DOC also entertained requests for revocation or termination of countervailing duty orders or suspended investigations. The DOC would

---

[138]Brass Sheet and Strip from Germany, 61 Fed. Reg. at 49,730.

[139]*Id.* at 49,730-31.

[140]Brass Sheet and Strip from Canada, 63 Fed. Reg. 6519, 6523 (Dep't Comm. 1998) (Prelim. Results Admin. Rev.); Dynamic Random Access Memory Semiconductors of One Megabyte or Above from the Republic of Korea, 62 Fed. Reg. at 39,816-17.

[141]*See, e.g.*, Color Television Receivers from the Republic of Korea, 62 Fed. Reg. at 59,405.

[142]Antidumping Duties; Final Rule, 54 Fed. Reg. 12,742, 12,758 (Dep't Comm. 1989) (Final Rule).

[143]Brass Sheet and Strip from Germany, 61 Fed. Reg. at 49,731; Tatung Company v. United States, 18 CIT 1137 (1994).

[144]Brass Sheet and Strip from Germany, 61 Fed. Reg. at 49,731; Steel Wire Rope from the Republic of Korea, 62 Fed. Reg. at 17,174 (ITA will ignore appreciation of foreign currency, however, where respondents have shown that past instances of currency appreciation did not change pricing practices.).

[145]Steel Wire Rope from the Republic of Korea, 62 Fed. Reg. at 17,174.

first consider whether or not the government of country or the exporters satisfied the conditions for revocation or termination. If a country was requesting revocation or termination because they abolished a program for three consecutive years, the DOC would determine whether or not the government made an actual change in the law prior to revocation or termination.[146] If exporters requested revocation or termination based on their non-use of a program, the DOC would consider whether each of those exporters established non-use for a period of five consecutive years by participating in administrative reviews.[147] Because the DOC's regulations did not permit partial termination of a suspended investigation for certain exporters, the DOC explained its policy for suspension agreements in the following manner:

> [W]e have determined that section 355.25(a)(2) permits termination of a suspended investigation whenever the Department determines that the exporters or producers that originally signed the suspension agreement have consistently accounted for at least 85 percent of the imports of the subject merchandise for a period of at least five consecutive years, during which time they did not apply for or receive any net subsidy on the subject merchandise. In addition, any new signatories must be found to have complied with the terms of the agreement during the time they are covered.[148]

ii. Changed Circumstances Reviews Under Section 751(b)

The DOC was also permitted to revoke an order or terminate a suspended investigation based on a changed circumstances review pursuant to

[146]*See* Asociacion Colombiana de Exportadores de Flores v. United States, Slip Op. 95-59, at 12 (April 6, 1995) (Court affirms DOC's determination that an actual change in the law was required to "abolish" a program and that a retroactive abolition is insufficient.).

[147]*See* Ceramic Tile from Mexico, 60 Fed. Reg. 39,937 (Dep't Comm. 1995) (Final Results Admin. Rev.), 60 Fed. Reg. 26,717 (Dep't Comm. 1995) (Prelim. Results Admin. Rev.) (ITA denies revocation for 14 companies because the "companies did not participate in five consecutive administrative reviews in which they were found not have received any net subsidy, including the review in which they are requesting revocation, and with no intervening period in which a review of the company was not conducted.").

[148]Fresh Cut Flowers from Costa Rica, 59 Fed. Reg. 24,687, 24,688 (Dep't Comm. 1994) (Final Results Admin. Rev.); *see* Roses and Other Cut Flowers from Colombia; Miniature Carnations from Colombia, 61 Fed. Reg. 45,941, 45,943 (Dep't Comm. 1996) (Final Results Admin. Rev.).

Section 751(b).[149] Usually, the DOC would revoke or terminate under Section 751(b) based on the domestic industry's expression of a lack of continued interest in an order.[150] Upon request, however, the DOC would conduct changed circumstances reviews to determine whether or not a company, product, or country should be covered by an order or agreement based on changed circumstances.

For example, in *Sugar and Syrups from Canada*, the DOC considered whether a company was a successor-in-interest to a company subject to the antidumping duty order in a changed circumstances review.[151] The only changes to the company subject to the order was that it had changed its legal name and the Executive Vice President had become the President and CEO of the new company. The DOC concluded that the new company was indeed a successor-in-interest and should receive the same treatment under the antidumping duty order. The DOC would also initiate a changed circumstances review based on evidence that a company excluded from an order has recommenced dumping and reinstate the order based on an affirmative determination.[152]

In *Sugar from France*, the DOC partially revoked the order with respect to homeopathic sugar pellets when the petitioners informed the agency that it had no interest in maintaining the finding on that product.[153]

Finally, in *Solid Urea from the German Democratic Republic*, the DOC examined the effect of the reunification of Germany (by combination of

---

[149]*See generally* Carreau, supra note 109, at 89-97.

[150]*See, e.g.*, Portable Electric Typewriters from Japan, 59 Fed. Reg. 22,584 (Dep't Comm. 1994) (Final Results).

[151]Sugar and Syrups from Canada, 61 Fed. Reg. 51,275 (Dep't Comm. 1996) (Final Results), 61 Fed. Reg. 48,885 (Dep't Comm. 1996) (Prelim. Results Admin. Rev.); *see* Industrial Phosphoric Acid from Israel, 59 Fed. Reg. 6944 (Dep't Comm. 1994) (Final Results).

[152]*See* Certain Welded Stainless Steel Pipes from Taiwan, 59 Fed. Reg. 6619, 6620 (Dep't Comm. 1994) (Amended Final LTFV Deter. and Order); Frozen Concentrated Orange Juice from Brazil, 59 Fed. Reg. 53,136, 53,138 (Dep't Comm. 1994) (Final Results Admin. Rev.); Sweaters Wholly or in Chief Weight of Man-Made Fiber from Taiwan, 57 Fed. Reg. 43,785 (Dep't Comm. 1992) (Initiation); Jia Farn Manufacturing Co., Ltd. v. United States, Slip Op. 93-42 (CIT 1993).

[153]Sugar from France, 61 Fed. Reg. 40,609 (Dep't Comm. 1996) (Final Results Admin. Rev.), 61 Fed. Reg. 20,236 (Dep't Comm. 1996) (Prelim. Results Admin. Rev.).

the former German Democratic Republic and the Federal Republic of Germany) on the antidumping duty order covering solid urea from the former German Democratic Republic. The DOC concluded that it would maintain the antidumping duty order only on the five states originally from the German Democratic Republic and would allow entry of shipments from the pre-unification territory of the FRG without regard to antidumping duties.[154]

c. *The ITC's Practice in Revoking Orders or Terminating Suspended Investigations Under Pre-URAA Law*

i. Changed Circumstances Reviews Under Section 751(b)

As explained above, Pre-Uruguay Round Section 751(b)(1) of the Tariff Act of 1930, as amended (19 U.S.C. §1675(b)(1)), permitted the DOC or the ITC to conduct an administrative review of an affirmative final determination or suspension agreement based on a request or information showing changed circumstances.[155] Foreign interested parties used Section 751(b) to request modification or revocation of an antidumping or countervailing duty order or termination of a suspended investigation by alleging that revocation or modification would not cause injury to the domestic industry.[156]

---

[154]Solid Urea from the Former German Democratic Republic, 63 Fed. Reg. 7122 (Dep't Comm. 1998) (Final Results Admin. Rev.), 60 Fed. Reg. 21,067 (Dep't Comm. 1995) (Prelim. Results Admin. Rev.).

[155]19 U.S.C. §1675(b)(1) (1980 & 1994 Supp.).

[156]For example, the ITC could consider whether or not exclusion of a product from the scope of the order would cause injury. *See, e.g.*, Liquid Crystal Display Television Receivers from Japan, Inv. No. 751-TA-14, USITC Pub. 2042, at 1 (Dec. 1987); Synthetic L-Methionine from Japan, Inv. No. 751-TA-4, USITC Pub. 1167, at 7 (July 1981); Salmon Gill Fish Netting of Manmade Fibers from Japan, Inv. No. 751-TA-11, USITC Pub. 1921, at 1 (Dec. 1986). The ITC explained that modification of an order might be appropriate under the following circumstances:

> One possible rationale for modifying the order could be a determination that through technological development a particular imported product no longer has a competing

A changed circumstance review could be initiated by the ITC on its own motion or based on a request demonstrating sufficient evidence of changed circumstances.[157] Upon receipt of a request for a changed circumstances review, the ITC would engage in a two-part analysis.[158] First, the ITC would determine whether or not the request was sufficient to warrant a review. The ITC would publish a notice in the *Federal Register* requesting comments on whether changed circumstances were sufficient to warrant institution of a review investigation.[159] Interested parties would then have thirty days to comment on whether the ITC should institute a changed circumstances review.[160] Within thirty days of the public comment period, the ITC would issue its determination as to whether the request showed changed circumstances sufficient to warrant a review and, if so, the ITC would institute a review which would be completed within 120 days.[161]

A request has been sufficient to warrant a review when the available information persuaded the ITC that:

> counterpart in the domestic market. In this case, it could make sense to drop that product from the finding, assuming complete revocation was not justified, upon a showing that there was indeed no competition between the import and any segment of the domestic industry protected from material injury by the order.

Television Receiving Sets from Japan, Inv. No. 751-TA-2, USITC Pub. 1153, at 19 (June 1981). With respect to the ITC's changed circumstance review, the DOC regulations provided:

> If the Commission determines in an administrative review under section 751(b) of the Act that an industry in the United States would not be materially injured, or would not be threatened with material injury, or the establishment of an industry in the United States would not be materially retarded, by reason of imports of the merchandise covered by an antidumping duty order [or countervailing duty order] or suspension agreement, the Secretary will revoke, in whole or in part, the order or terminate the suspended investigation, and will publish in the Federal Register notice of "Revocation of Order (in Part)" or, if appropriate, "Termination of Suspended Investigation."

19 C.F.R. §§353.25(e) & 355.25(e).

[157] 19 U.S.C. §1675(b)(1) (1980 and 1994 Supp.).

[158] *See* A. Hirsch, Inc. v. United States, 737 F. Supp. 1186 (CIT 1990).

[159] 19 C.F.R. §207.45(a) (1994); *see also* Stainless Steel Plate from Sweden, 56 Fed. Reg. 35,044, 35,045 (USITC 1993).

[160] 19 C.F.R. §207.45(b) (1980 & 1994 Supp.).

[161] 19 C.F.R. §207.45(c) (1980 & 1994 Supp.).

(1) there have been significant changed circumstances from those in existence at the time of the original investigation;

(2) those changed circumstances are not the natural and direct result of the imposition of the antidumping or countervailing duty order, and

(3) the changed circumstances indicate that the domestic industry would be materially injured should the order be revoked, thereby warranting a full investigation.[162]

The burden of establishing "changed circumstances" was fairly heavy.[163] In making its decision, the ITC recognized that Congress had not intended prior injury determinations to be disturbed lightly.[164]

In actual cases, the ITC has found sufficient changed circumstances to warrant review based on evidence that domestic producers have ceased production;[165] evidence that the domestically-produced products no longer

---

[162] *See* Certain Cold-Rolled Carbon Steel Flat Products from Germany and the Netherlands, 61 Fed. Reg. 17,319, 17,320 (USITC 1996); *see also* A. Hirsh, Inc. v. United States, 737 F. Supp. 1186, 1188 (CIT 1990); Avesta AB v. United States, 724 F. Supp. 974 (CIT 1989), *aff'd* 914 F.2d 232 (Fed. Cir. 1990), *cert. denied*, 111 S. Ct. 1308 (1991).

[163] *See* Avesta AB v. United States, 689 F. Supp. 1173, 1181 (CIT 1988), *citing* Matsushita Elec. Indus. Co., Ltd. v. United States, 750 F.2d 927, 932 (Fed. Cir. 1984). According to the Court of International Trade, the evidence submitted in support of a request for review may or may not be persuasive on the issue of revocation.

[164] *See* Certain Cold-Rolled Carbon Steel Flat Products from Germany and the Netherlands, 61 Fed. Reg. 17,319, 17,320 (USITC 1996); Royal Business Machines, Inc. v. United States, 507 F. Supp. 1007, 1014 n.18 (CIT 1980), *aff'd*, 659 F.2d 659 F.2d 692 (CCPA 1982); Avesta AB, 689 F. Supp. at 1180.

[165] *See* Salmon Gill Fish Netting of Manmade Fibers from Japan, Inv. No. 751-TA-11, USITC Pub. 1921, at 4 n.5 (Dec. 1986); *see also* Salmon Gill Fish Netting of Manmade Fibers from Japan, Inv. No. 751-TA-7, USITC Pub. 1387, at 2 (June 1983). The ITC has refused to initiate a review based on evidence of changed circumstances that are the direct and anticipated result of the imposition of import relief. *See* Avesta AB v. United States, 914 F.2d 233, 237 (Fed. Cir. 1990), *cert. denied*, 111 S. Ct. 1308 (1991). The ITC will consider evidence of import patterns and market conditions to determine whether or not to initiate a review. With respect to import patterns, the ITC has denied requests for reviews based on evidence that (1) imports to the United States had increased on a value basis, (2) there had been no decrease of imports through a purchase of local manufacturing facilities, (3) the decrease in the volume of production was attributable to the order, or (4) petitioner's assertion of a change in technology was based on a continuation of a trend which was discussed in the original investigation. A. Hirsh, Inc. v. United States, 729 F. Supp. 1360, 1363 (CIT 1990). In considering market conditions, the ITC

compete with the imported product due to the latter's technological advances;[166] evidence of increased demand for imported juice over domestic juice due, in part, to a Florida freeze;[167] evidence of declining imports, increasing demand, increasing import prices, U.S. product changes, and one exporter becoming a U.S. producer;[168] evidence of declining imports, increasing prices, increasing import share from third countries, and contractions in the domestic industry;[169] and evidence that the domestic industry does not compete with a particular product covered by an order.[170]

The second part of the analysis consisted of a review which focused on the potential effect of revocation on the domestic industry. Upon institution of a review, interested parties would have 21 days in which to file an entry of appearance. On the basis of questionnaire responses and other information collected during the review, the ITC staff would prepare a prehearing staff report and interested parties would be permitted to file prehearing and posthearing briefs. The ITC would also conduct a hearing and receive testimony from interested parties.[171] The ITC would issue one final determination.

As part of the review, the ITC would reconsider its like product and domestic industry definitions. The ITC would then consider whether an industry in the United States would be materially injured, or would be threatened with material injury or the establishment of an industry in the United States would be materially retarded by reason of the merchandise covered by the antidumping or countervailing duty order or suspension agreement

---

has denied requests based on evidence that (1) an established domestic United States industry benefited from the market conditions created by the order, or (2) a restructuring of the United States market and importer's domestic market was attributable to the order imposed and not other factors. *Id.*

[166]Liquid Crystal Display Television Receivers from Japan, Inv. No. 751-TA-14, USITC Pub. 2042, at 8-9 (Dec. 1987).

[167]Frozen Concentrated Orange Juice from Brazil, Inv. No. 751-TA-10, USITC Pub. 1623, at 2 (Dec. 1984).

[168]Drycleaning Machinery from the Federal Republic of Germany, Inv. No. 751-TA-9, USITC Pub. 1617, at A-1 n.7 (Dec. 1984).

[169]Birch Three-Ply Door Skins from Japan, Inv. No. 751-TA-6, USITC Pub. 1271, at 5, A-1 (July 1982).

[170]*See* Synthetic L-Methionine from Japan, Inv. No. 751-TA-4, USITC Pub. 1167, at 4 (July 1981).

[171]*See* Stainless Steel Plate from Sweden, 56 Fed. Reg. at 35,046.

were it to be modified or revoked.[172] Thus, unlike the original investigation, the inquiry is "entirely prospective and predictive."[173]

The ITC adopted a two-part inquiry for determining injury.[174] First, the ITC forecast the likely behavior of the foreign producers, exporters, and the importers in the event that the order was revoked or modified. In the first part of the test, the ITC would consider factors such as capacity utilization or supplies of the raw product; marketing networks and strategies; conditions in the United States market; past behavior; the imports' share of the United States market; corporate planning; ability of the foreign producers to respond rapidly to shifts in United States demand; the stated intent of the foreign producer, exporter, or the importer or both; performance in other export markets; and all relevant economic factors. The ITC would not, however, consider "the presence or absence of a dumping margin, or its magnitude within a limited range" because margins were not considered

[172]Liquid Crystal Display Television Receivers from Japan, Inv. No. 751-TA-14, USITC Pub. 2042, at 3-4 (Dec. 1987), citing 19 C.F.R. §207.45 (1987); *see* American Permac v. United States, 831 F.2d 269 (Fed. Cir. 1987); Salmon Gill Fish Netting and Manmade Fibers from Japan, Inv. No. 751-TA-11, USITC Pub. 1921, at 5 n.9 (Dec. 1986); Frozen Concentrated Orange Juice from Brazil, Inv. No. 751-TA-10, USITC Pub. 1623, at 1 (Dec. 1984); Electric Golf Cars from Poland, Inv. No. AA1921-147A (Review), USITC Pub. 1069, at 25-26, 35-36 (June 1980) (Commissioner Stern applies a threat analysis); Potassium Chloride from Canada, Inv. No. 751-TA-3, USITC Pub. 1137, at 10 (April 1981) (Commissioners consider material injury factors of volume, price, and impact). Due to the lack of a standard of review in the statute, the ITC developed 19 C.F.R. §207.45 which modeled its standard of review on section 104 of the Trade Agreements Act of 1979, 19 U.S.C. §1671 note, which provides for review of certain countervailing duty orders. Television Receiving Sets from Japan, Inv. No. 751-TA-2, USITC Pub. 1153, at 6-7 (June 1981); *see infra* Chapter II, Section A.4.c(ii). According to the Statement of Administrative Action, post-Uruguay Round Section 751(b) incorporates a new standard of review which is identical to that used in post-Uruguay Round sunset reviews and which conforms with prior agency practice in Section 751(b) reviews. Statement of Administrative Action, *reprinted in* H.R. Doc. No. 103-316, vol. 1, at 878 (1994).

[173]Frozen Concentrated Orange Juice from Brazil, Inv. No. 751-TA-10, USITC Pub. 1623, at 7 (Dec. 1984).

[174]*See, e.g.*, Frozen Concentrated Orange Juice from Brazil, Inv. No. 751-TA-10, USITC Pub. 1623, at 10, 15 (Dec. 1984); Salmon Gill Fish Netting and Manmade Fibers from Japan, Inv. No. 751-TA-11, USITC Pub. 1921, at 5 (Dec. 1986); Drycleaning Machinery from the Federal Republic of Germany, Inv. No. 751-TA-9, USITC Pub. 1617, at 5 (Dec. 1984).

useful in predicting how a company would set prices when no longer constrained by an order.[175] As part of the test, the ITC would assume that dumped or subsidized sales would "continue or resume" if the order or suspension agreement were modified or revoked.[176]

Second, the ITC considered the potential impact of imports, as affected by the revocation, on the U.S. industry's current condition to determine whether they would cause material injury, threat thereof, or material retardation.[177] The ITC would only consider the effect of imports from producers that have not otherwise been excluded from an order.[178]

With respect to statements of intentions, the Court of Appeals for the Federal Circuit in *Matsushita* noted that, in the absence of direct evidence, the ITC appropriately relied on circumstantial evidence of importers' intent such as production capacity, domestic and foreign demand, and incentives or motivations to increase imports. The Court noted that "[s]uch

---

[175]Television Receiving Sets from Japan, Inv. No. 751-TA-2, USITC Pub. 1153, at 8 (June 1981).

[176]Drycleaning Machinery from the Federal Republic of Germany, Inv. No. 751-TA-9, USITC Pub. 1617, at 10 (Dec. 1984); Salmon Gill Fish Netting of Manmade Fibers from Japan, Inv. No. 751-TA-5, USITC Pub. 1234, at 8 (March 1982); Television Receiving Sets from Japan, Inv. No. 751-TA-2, USITC Pub. 1153, at 8 (June 1981). The ITC would presume that dumped or subsidized imports would resume or continue after revocation or termination in a Section 751(b) review because otherwise a petitioner would have requested a DOC review under Section 751(a) based on cessation of dumping or subsidies.

[177]American Permac, Inc., 831 F.2d at 272; see Frozen Concentrated Orange Juice from Brazil, Inv. No. 751-TA-10, USITC Pub. 1623, at 10, 15 (Dec. 1984); Television Receiving Sets from Japan, Inv. No. 751-TA-2, USITC Pub. 1153, at 7 (June 1981). The ITC in *Television Receiving Sets from Japan* concluded that a Section 751(b) inquiry required (1) consideration of the relevant facts as they currently existed, (2) assessment of the intentions of the exporters and importers as to the prospective revocation or modification of the order, and (3) projection of those factors into the future. *See also* Salmon Gill Fish Netting of Manmade Fibers from Japan, Inv. No. 751-TA-7, USITC Pub. 1387, at 8-9 (June 1983); Frozen Concentrated Orange Juice from Brazil, Inv. No. 751-TA-10, USITC Pub. 1623, at 7 (Dec. 1984); Salmon Gill Fish Netting of Manmade Fibers from Japan, Inv. No. 751-TA-11, USITC Pub. 1921, at 5 (Dec. 1986).

[178]Potassium Chloride from Canada, Inv. No. 751-TA-3, USITC Pub. 1137, at 6, 12 (April 1981); Television Receiving Sets from Japan, Inv. No. 751-TA-2, USITC Pub. 1153, at 4 n.3 (June 1981).

factors are always relevant and, indeed may be more reliable that self-serving declarations."[179] In the context of Section 751(b) reviews, the ITC also acknowledged that it must "assess the validity of statements on intentions, which could easily be self-serving."[180] Therefore, "[s]tatements on intentions should be examined in light of other objective information on the record."[181]

With respect to the export orientation of the foreign producers or exporters, the ITC will consider the degree of government involvement and control, including export price controls, export quotas, and minimum prices, used to ensure the long-term growth of the exporting industry.[182] At least one Commissioner has considered the effect of exchange rates as they affect exports to the United States.[183] With respect to foreign producers/exporters' performance in export markets, the ITC would consider whether uncertainty in export markets would create a possibility for trade diversions to the U.S. market in the future.[184]

With respect to the likely impact of revocation on the domestic industry, the ITC would assess the domestic industry's vulnerability to imports.[185] The fact that the domestic industry's vulnerability was not due to

---

[179]Matsushita Elec. Indus., Co., Ltd., 750 F.2d at 934.

[180]Birch Three-Ply Door Skins, Inv. No. 751-TA-6, USITC Pub. 1271, at 9 n.28 (July 1982).

[181]*Id.* at 11 n.35 (views of Commissioner Frank) (evidence of export proclivities includes court cases relating to exporter's efforts to circumvent trade rules); *see* Drycleaning Machinery from the Federal Republic of Germany, Inv. No. 751-TA-9, USITC Pub. 1617, at 9 (Dec. 1984) (evidence of an intention to increase exports to the U.S. market includes petitioners' increased numerical export goal to the United States and a product designed for the U.S. market).

[182]Frozen Concentrated Orange Juice from Brazil, Inv. No. 751-TA-10, USITC Pub. 1623, at 17-18 (Dec. 1984).

[183]Birch Three-Ply Door Skins from Japan, Inv. No. 751-TA-6, USITC Pub. 1271, at 11 n.35 (July 1982) (views of Commissioner Frank).

[184]Television Receiving Sets from Japan, Inv. No. 751-TA-2, USITC Pub. 1153, at 4 (June 1981).

[185]Frozen Concentrated Orange Juice from Brazil, Inv. No. 751-TA-10, USITC Pub. 1623, at 5 (Dec. 1984); Drycleaning Machinery from the Federal Republic of Germany, Inv. No. 751-TA-9, USITC Pub. 1617, at 3 (Dec. 1984); Birch Three-Ply Door Skins from Japan, Inv. No. 751-TA-6, USITC Pub. 1271, at 7 (July 1982) (views of Commissioner Frank) (At least one Commissioner found that the time span applicable to a

dumped or subsidized imports, however, was not relevant.[186] Rather, the ITC would assess whether the current condition of the industry would be able to withstand the likely effect of changes from revocation. The ITC would predict the impact of imports, as affected by revocation, on the domestic industry's productive capacity, capacity utilization, shipments, inventories, employment, exports, and profitability.[187] The ITC has noted that "if imports act to hinder or prevent the industry's recovery, we conclude that this would be injury to the industry" because as the opportunity for recovery slips by, the industry is unable to recover fully.[188]

The ITC presumed that the existence of an outstanding antidumping order would change the pricing behavior of importers and exporters of merchandise subject to the order.[189] The ITC would consider whether the imports were currently underselling the domestic product,[190] and whether a reduction in the price offered for the imported product as result of revocation would significantly affect domestic producers.[191]

Section 751 review where material injury would be likely to occur included time spans in which exporters are able to make rapid movements to increase the number of production shifts, to bring back equipment and plants that are well maintained but on idled-or standby-status, or to divert products shipped or produced.).

[186]Birch Three-Ply Door Skins from Japan, Inv. No. 751-TA-6, USITC Pub. 1271, at 3, 7 (July 1982) (ITC finds that an industry would be materially injured by reason of imports if the order were revoked despite the fact that the drop in housing starts seriously affected the domestic industry.).

[187]Frozen Concentrated Orange Juice from Brazil, Inv. No. 751-TA-10, USITC Pub. 1623, at 22 (Dec. 1984).

[188]*Id.* at 23.

[189]Salmon Gill Fish Netting of Manmade Fibers from Japan, Inv. No. 751-TA-7, USITC Pub. 1387, at 10 (June 1983); Salmon Gill Fish Netting of Manmade Fibers from Japan, Inv. No. 751-TA-5, USITC Pub. 1234, at 7 (March 1982).

[190]Frozen Concentrated Orange Juice from Brazil, Inv. No. 751-TA-10, USITC Pub. 1623, at 23 (Dec. 1984).

[191]Birch Three-Ply Door Skins from Japan, Inv. No. 751-TA-6, USITC Pub. 1271, at 10 (July 1982). For example, in *Salmon Gill Fish Netting*, the ITC concluded that revocation would not materially injure the domestic industry when the larger portion of the domestic industry's production was devoted to a product that was not a close substitute for the imported product. Salmon Gill Fish Netting and Manmade Fibers from Japan, Inv. No. 751-TA-11, USITC Pub. 1921, at 17 (Dec. 1986); Salmon Gill Fish Netting of Manmade Fibers from Japan, Inv. No. 751-TA-7, USITC Pub. 1387, at 11-13

Section 751(b) specifically provided that, for ITC reviews, "the party seeking revocation of an antidumping or countervailing duty order shall have *the burden of persuasion* with respect to whether there are changed circumstances sufficient to warrant revocation of the antidumping or countervailing duty order."[192] Congress adopted the "burden of persuasion" standard in the Trade and Tariff Act of 1984 in response to the Court of International Trade's decision in *Matsushita Elec. Indus. Co., Ltd. v. United States*, 569 F. Supp. 853 (CIT 1983).[193]

In July 1983, the Court of International Trade in *Matsushita* reversed an ITC determination that import levels would threaten the domestic industry with injury absent the antidumping duty order. The Court of International Trade found that the ITC's changed circumstance review must establish the "continuing need" for the injury determination or lead to revocation.[194] By October 1984, Congress had decided to amend Section 751(b) to assign the "burden of persuasion" to the party seeking revocation.[195] The Conference Report disagreed with the *Matsushita* decision:

> The Managers believe that the *Matsushita* decision incorrectly places the burden of persuasion on the domestic industry in section 751 review investigations. The effect of the *Matsushita* decision is that the ITC's investigation must establish through substantial evidence the *continued need for the antidumping duty order*. This standard creates a difficult task for the domestic industry, since the existence of an antidumping duty order is a discipline on the pricing practices of foreign manufacturers. Because the order offsets the effects of any dumping, the order makes its difficult for the industry to show present material injury resulting from the effects of dumping or to point to present demonstrable adverse trends which establish a threat of material injury.

(June 1983); *see* Frozen Concentrated Orange Juice from Brazil, Inv. No. 751-TA-10, USITC Pub. 1623, at 19 (Dec. 1984).

[192] 19 U.S.C. §1675(b)(1) (1994) (emphasis added). Originally, the Trade and Tariff Act of 1984 adopted the new burden test for antidumping duty orders only. *See* Frozen Concentrated Orange Juice from Brazil, Inv. No. 751-TA-10, USITC Pub. 1623, at 9 n.11 (Dec. 1984).

[193] The Court of Appeals for the Federal Circuit reversed *Matsushita Elec. Indus. Co., Ltd. v. United States*, 569 F. Supp. 853 (CIT 1983) in *Matsushita*, 750 F.2d at 927.

[194] Matsushita, 569 F. Supp. at 859.

[195] *Conference Report to Accompany H.R. 3398*, H.R. REP. NO. 98-1156, §611 (1984).

> The purpose of section 751 review investigations is to determine whether there are changed circumstances sufficient to warrant revocation of an antidumping order. The ITC must evaluate the changed circumstances alleged to determine whether revocation is appropriate in light of current factor and conditions of trade.
>
> . . .
>
> The absence of any burden of proof does not mean, however, that a section 751 review is without a burden of persuasion. A foreign manufacturer, after all, is subject to an antidumping order because it was previously found to have engaged in injurious dumping. For that reason, a section 751 review does not begin from an entirely neutral starting point. *The party seeking revocation of the order has a burden of persuasion, in the sense that at the end of the investigation, the ITC must be convinced that revocation of the order is appropriate.* In short, the ITC must determine that, in light of the "changed circumstances," the revocation of the order will not result in material injury or threat of material injury to the U.S. industry.[196]

Congress made it clear that no party carried the burden of proof in *any* ITC review. At the same time, however, the Section 751 review did not begin from a "clean slate."[197] Therefore, the party previously found to contravene the law had the burden to persuade the agency that revocation or termination was appropriate.

Finally, the ITC indicated that it would not give retroactive effect to its changed circumstances determinations. In *Salmon Gill Fish Netting*, petitioners requested that the ITC recommend that the DOC revoke the antidumping duty order as of the date when all significant domestic production had ended despite the fact that the order continued for another ten years after that date.[198] Although the ITC did not reach the issue in that case, the ITC noted that all of its rules and all of its Section 751 reviews were conducted "with the idea that review investigations are prospective in nature."[199]

---

[196] *Id.* at 182-83 (emphasis added).

[197] *Id.* at 182; Matsushita, 750 F.2d at 932; American Permac, Inc. v. United States, 831 F.2d at 273-74.

[198] Salmon Gill Fish Netting and Manmade Fibers from Japan, Inv. No. 751-TA-11, USITC Pub. 1921, at 18-19 (Dec. 1986).

[199] *Id.* at 19.

ii. The ITC's Injury Review and Revocation Under Section 104(b)

Prior to the Uruguay Round, the ITC could also conduct a review under Section 104(b) to determine whether or not certain countervailing duty orders should be revoked. Section 303 of the Tariff Act of 1930, as amended (19 U.S.C. §1303) originally established a countervailing duty law which applied only to dutiable merchandise and did not provide an injury test.[200] In 1947, Article VI, paragraph 6(a) of the General Agreement on Tariffs and Trade required member states to provide an injury test before imposing countervailing duties.[201] The United States, however, was not required to provide an injury test because Section 303 was "grandfathered" by the GATT Protocol of Provisional Application which required parties to apply Article VI "to the fullest extent not inconsistent with existing legislation."[202] In 1974, the United States amended Section 303 to expand its countervailing duty law to cover duty-free merchandise and provided an injury test for duty-free merchandise only if required by international obligations.[203] Thus, prior to the Tokyo Round Agreement in 1979, the United States could issue countervailing duty orders or suspension agreements without conducting an injury test for dutiable merchandise pursuant to Section 303 of the Tariff Act of 1930, as amended (19 U.S.C. §1303).

As a result of the Tokyo Round, signatories to the Subsidies Code, in-

---

[200]*See* Ceramica Regiomontana, S.A. v. United States, 853 F. Supp. 431, 433 (CIT 1994), *citing* 19 U.S.C. §1303; Cementos Guadalajara, S.A. v. United States, 686 F. Supp. 335, 337 (CIT 1988).

[201]General Agreement on Tariffs and Trade, Oct. 30, 1947, 61 Stat. All, T.I.A.S. No. 1700, 55 U.N.T.S. 184, at art. VI, para. 6(a) [hereinafter GATT]. Paragraph 6(a) provides as follows:

> 6. (a) No contracting party shall levy any anti-dumping or countervailing duty on the importation of any product of the territory of another contracting party unless it determines that the effect of the dumping or subsidization, as the case may be, is such as to cause or threaten material injury to an established domestic industry, or is such as to retard materially the establishment of a domestic industry.

Id.

[202]GATT Protocol of Provisional Application, Oct. 30, 1947, 61 Stat. Part 6, T.I.A.S. No. 1700, 55 U.N.T.S. 308, at A2051, para. 1(b).

[203]Trade Act of 1974, Pub. L. 93-618, 88 Stat. 2050.

cluding the United States, were specifically required to conduct an injury test prior to imposing countervailing duties.[204] In order to implement its obligations under the Subsidies Code, the United States enacted the Trade Agreements Act of 1979.[205] The 1979 Act retained the existing Section 303 which would apply to countries that did not sign the Subsidies Code or an equivalent agreement. In addition, the 1979 Act incorporated the injury test requirement for countervailing duty orders covering dutiable and duty-free merchandise for countries that did sign the Subsidies Code or an equivalent agreement in a new Section 701 of the Tariff Act of 1930, as amended (19 U.S.C. §1671).

In Section 104(b), Congress enacted transitional rules to provide an injury test for outstanding countervailing duty orders upon request within three years.[206] According to Section 104(b), the Commission would determine:

> **(b) Other countervailing duty orders.** —
>
> . . .
>
> **(2) Determination by the Commission.** — In a case described in paragraph (1) with respect to which it has received a request for review, the Commission shall commence an investigation to determine whether —
>
> (A) an industry in the United States —
>
> (i) would be materially injured, or
>
> (ii) would be threatened with material injury, or

[204]GATT, *supra* note 201, at art. VI, para. 6(a); Agreement on Interpretation and Application of Articles VI, XVI, and XXIII of the General Agreement on Tariffs and Trade, arts. 1, 6 (1979), *reprinted in* GATT BISD (26th Supp.) (March 1980).

[205]Trade Agreements Act of 1979, Pub. L. No. 96-39, 93 Stat. 144.

[206]19 U.S.C. §1671 (note).

> **(1) Review by Commission upon request.** — In the case of a countervailing duty order issued under section 303 of the Tariff Act of 1930 (19 U.S.C. 1303) —
>
> (A) which is not a countervailing duty order to which subsection (a) applies,
>
> (B) which applies to merchandise which is a product of a country under the Agreement, and
>
> (C) which is in effect on January 1, 1980, or which is issued pursuant to court order in an action brought under section 516(d) of that Act before that date,
>
> the Commission, upon request of the government of such a country or of exporters accounting for a significant proportion of exports to the United States of merchandise which is covered by the order, submitted within 3 years after the effective date of title VII of the Tariff Act of 1930 shall make a determination under paragraph (2) of this subsection.

19 U.S.C. §1671 (note at Section 104(b)(1)).

(B) the establishment of an industry in the United States would be materially retarded,

by reason of imports of the merchandise covered by the countervailing duty order if the order were to be revoked.[207]

A negative determination by the ITC would result in revocation of the countervailing duty order.[208]

Upon receipt of a request from a government or from exporters accounting for a significant proportion of exports to the United States of merchandise covered by the order, the ITC would institute an investigation. Interested parties would have 21 days in which to file an entry of appearance. On the basis of questionnaire responses and other information collected during the review, the ITC staff would prepare a prehearing staff report and interested parties would be permitted to file prehearing and posthearing briefs. The ITC would also conduct a hearing and receive testimony from interested parties.[209] The ITC would issue one final determination.[210]

In order to determine whether injury would result from revocation of the countervailing duty order, the ITC would evaluate the current health of the domestic industry and the likely effects of removing the duty on imports and prices.[211] In addition, the ITC would consider recent changes in the product mix of exports and other changes in the foreign exporting industries and the conditions of competition in the relevant markets.[212]

To determine the current health of the domestic industry, the ITC

[207] 19 U.S.C. §1671 (note at Section 104(b)(2)).

[208] 19 U.S.C. §1671 (note at Section 104(b)(4)(B)).

[209] Sugar Content of Certain Articles from Australia, 50 Fed. Reg. 23,086 (USITC 1985).

[210] In *Non-Rubber Footwear from Brazil*, Brazil requested an injury review on October 1981, after the Subsidies Code entered into force on January 1, 1980. According to a GATT Panel, the United States was not required to revoke the order as of January 4, 1980, the date of suspension of liquidation, rather than the date of the request for review. Non-Rubber Footwear from Brazil, SCM/94 <http://www.wto.org/wto/dispute/panel.htm>.

[211] *See* Optic Liquid-Level Sensing Systems from Canada, Inv. No. 104-TAA-2, USITC Pub. 1164, at 7, 9-11 (July 1981); Unprocessed Float Glass from Belgium and Italy, Inv. Nos. 104-TAA-11 and 12, USITC Pub. 1344, at 8 (Feb. 1983).

[212] Unprocessed Float Glass from Belgium and Italy, Inv. No. 104-TAA-11, USITC Pub. 1344, at 3 (Feb. 1983); Rayon Staple Fiber from Sweden, Inv. No. 104-TAA-13,

would consider evidence of profits and losses, capacity, capacity utilization, inventories, employment,[213] consumption, sales prices,[214] domestic production,[215] domestic shipments, imports,[216] and investment.[217] A review of Section 104(b) decisions reveals a tendency to make a determination against revocation where the industry was currently experiencing difficulties.[218]

In its "effects" analysis, the ITC considered the magnitude of current margins and their effect on current sales,[219] the level of participation of the domestic industry in the investigation,[220] the price-sensitivity of sales, the likelihood of an increase or surge of imports and weighed that information against the current state of the domestic industry.[221]

With respect to net subsidy information, the ITC considered the following factors:

USITC Pub. 1360, at 3 (March 1983); Certain Scissors and Shears from Brazil, Inv. No. 104-TAA-19, USITC Pub. 1456, at 3 (Dec. 1983).

[213]Rayon Staple Fiber from Sweden, Inv. No. 104-TAA-13, USITC Pub. 1360, at 5 (March 1983).

[214]Certain Castor Oil Products from Brazil, Inv. No. 104-TAA-20, USITC Pub. 1483, at 6 (Jan. 1994).

[215]Barley from France, Inv. No. 104-TAA-6, USITC Pub. 1227, at 4 (March 1982).

[216]*See* Galvanized Fabricated Structural Steel Units for the Erection of Electrical Transmission Towers from Italy, Inv. No. 104-TAA-4, USITC Pub. 1204, at 5-6 (Dec. 1981) (Commission considers expansion plans of domestic industry).

[217]Sugar Content of Certain Articles from Australia, Inv. No. 104-TAA-26, USITC Pub. 1748, at 12 (Sept. 1985).

[218]*See* Rayon Staple Fiber from Sweden, Inv. No. 104-TAA-13, USITC Pub. 1360, at 5-6 (March 1983); Cotton Yarn from Brazil, Inv. No. 104-TAA-21, USITC Pub. 1530, at 7 (May 1984); Certain Castor Oil Products from Brazil, Inv. No. 104-TAA-20, USITC Pub. 1483, at 5 (Jan. 1984).

[219]*See, e.g.*, Certain Nonrubber Footwear from Brazil, India, and Spain, Inv. Nos. 104-TAA-16, 17, and 18, USITC Pub. 1388, at 8 (May 1983) (views of Chairman Eckes); Certain Scissors and Shears from Brazil, Inv. No. 104-TAA-19, USITC Pub. 1456, at 11 (Dec. 1983).

[220]Certain Spirits from Ireland, Inv. No. 104-TAA-3, USITC Pub. 1165, at 7 (July 1981); Barley from France, Inv. No. 104-TAA-6, USITC Pub. 1227, at 5 (March 1982); Molasses from France, Inv. No. 104-TAA-8, USITC Pub. 1248, at 6 (May 1982).

[221]Optic Liquid-Level Sensing Systems from Canada, Inv. No. 104-TAA-2, USITC Pub. 1164, at 9-11 (July 1981); Barley from France, Inv. No. 104-TAA-6, USITC Pub. 1227, at 6-7 (March 1982).

(a) whether the underlying subsidy has increased or decreased;
(b) how stable the net subsidy is;
(c) trends in import volumes and price, including
  (i) rates of increase or decrease;
  (ii) capacity to generate exports to the United States; and
  (iii) availability of other export markets.[222]

For example, in *Certain Spirits from Ireland*, the ITC concluded that the domestic industry's failure to participate in the investigation, the minuscule level of duty, and insignificant import market share did not indicate that injury was likely upon revocation.[223] According to the ITC, the lower the margin, the less effect revocation would have on prices, and the less price-sensitive buyers were, the less effect a price reduction caused by revocation would have on sales.[224] In addition to the magnitude of the margin, the ITC would also consider what effect changes in the duty deposit rate had on imports.[225] The fact that a subsidy was scheduled to expire on a certain date would weigh in favor of revoking the order.[226]

In determining the likely effect of revocation, the ITC has declined to consider the effects of an antidumping duty order covering some of the same imports. For example, in *Sugar from the European Community*, the ITC found that the domestic industry would be threatened with material injury upon revocation of the countervailing duty order.[227] The ITC re-

---

[222]Sugar Content of Certain Articles from Australia, Inv. No. 104-TAA-26, USITC Pub. 1748, at 9 (Sept. 1985); *see* Bottled Green Olives from Spain, Inv. No. 104-TAA-22, USITC Pub. 1531, at A-6 (May 1984).

[223]Certain Spirits from Ireland, Inv. No. 104-TAA-3, USITC Pub. 1165, at 7-8 (July 1981); *see* Galvanized Fabricated Structural Steel Units for the Erection of Electrical Transmission Towers from Italy, Inv. No. 104-TAA-4, USITC Pub. 1204, at 7 (Dec. 1981).

[224]*See* Galvanized Fabricated Structural Steel Units for the Erection of Electrical Transmission Towers from Italy, Inv. No. 104-TAA-4, USITC Pub. 1204, at 7-8 (Dec. 1981).

[225]*See* Cotton Yarn from Brazil, Inv. No. 104-TAA-21, USITC Pub. 1530, at 9 (May 1984); Certain Tomato Products from Greece, Inv. No. 104-TAA-23, USITC Pub. 1594, at 11 (Oct. 1984).

[226]Bicycles Tires and Tubes from the Republic of Korea and Taiwan, Inv. Nos. 104-TAA-14 and 15, USITC Pub. 1382, at 11-12 (views of Commissioners Stern) (May 1983).

[227]Sugar from the European Community, Inv. No. 104-TAA-7, USITC Pub. 1247, at 9-10 (May 1982).

fused, however, to find that the industry was otherwise adequately protected by the antidumping duty order on sugar from Belgium, France, and West Germany.[228] Specifically, the ITC pointed out that the antidumping duty order's protection did not cover seven of the ten EC member states at that time and that:

> The countervailing duty order and the antidumping duty order address separate and distinct unfair trade practices. It is apparent from the statutory provisions concerning each practice that Congress intended separate consideration. The fact that the statutory scheme provides for an offset for countervailing duties in assessing antidumping duties further indicates that Congress envisioned situations where both types of duties would be required.[229]

Likewise, the existence of a quota on the product is not dispositive.[230] The ITC would also consider whether revocation would result in any increased burden on government income or price support programs.[231]

Like the Section 751(b) reviews, statements of intent of potential exporters and importers would also be relevant in a Section 104(b) investigation.[232] The fact that potential exporters claimed that they did not intend to increase exports to the United States after revocation, however, was insufficient evidence for a negative determination. Rather, the ITC will also consider the exporters' business interests, the exporting countries' capacity and export orientation, as well as U.S. market conditions to determine the likely effect of revocation.[233]

---

[228]*Id.* at 7.

[229]*Id.* at 10.

[230]Cotton Yarn from Brazil, Inv. No. 104-TAA-21, USITC Pub. 1530, at 11 (May 1984).

[231]Barley from France, Inv. No. 104-TAA-6, USITC Pub. 1227, at 7 (March 1982).

[232]*See* Bicycles Tires and Tubes from the Republic of Korea and Taiwan, Inv. Nos. 104-TAA-14 and 15, USITC Pub. 1382, at 9 (Commission also assumed that any subsidy-related injury had been remedied) (views of Commissioners Stern), at 15 (views of Commissioner Haggert) (May 1983).

[233]Rayon Staple Fiber from Sweden, Inv. No. 104-TAA-13, USITC Pub. 1360, at 6-8 (March 1983); Certain Castor Oil Products from Brazil, Inv. No. 104-TAA-20, USITC Pub. 1483, at 10 (Jan. 1984).

5. The Expiry Rate Under the Four Systems Differed

As explained above, all four countries maintained some form of automatic sunset procedure prior to the GATT Final Act. Those sunset procedures, however, were applied in the context of different underlying legal systems. For example, U.S. law provided for revocation or termination after review based on compliance with the law (*i.e.*, a sufficient number of clean years) or based on changed circumstances showing an explicit lack of interest or lack of injury.[234] U.S. law also provided for an automatic revocation or termination without a review based on an implicit lack of interest after a number of years of no reviews and no objection to revocation.[235]

In contrast, the EU, Canadian, and Australian laws provided for expiry unless a review was requested and re-established a continued need for the order. The different expiry provisions in EU, Canadian, and Australian laws reflected, in part, their different underlying systems of collecting duties and the different standards applied in such reviews. Unlike the United States which assessed duties on a retrospective basis, the EU, Canada, and Australia assessed duties on a prospective basis.[236] Under the U.S. system, antidumping duty margins, for example, are estimated during the original investigation and established on the basis of actual sales data during the course of an administrative review.[237] In the U.S. retrospective system, the fact that there was an order outstanding on a product did not become an impediment to trade if, through administrative reviews, dumping is eliminated.

In contrast, Canada established a "normal value" price below which the importer's sales are dumped. The margin of dumping, if any, however, was set by reference to prices or costs which could have been outdated.[238] Like Canada, Australia also established a benchmark price, and dumping

---

[234]*See* 19 C.F.R. §§353.25, 355.25 (1994).

[235]*Id.* at §§353.25(d)(4), 355.25(d)(4) (1994).

[236]*See* Stewart, Markel & Kerwin, *supra* note 1, at 1607; Terence P. Stewart, *Antidumping Practice of the United States and the European Union*, Vol. 1, Before the Russian Chamber of Commerce and Industry Conference on GATT/WTO at 70 (Oct. 1995); Peter A. Magnus, *The Canadian Antidumping System, in* ANTIUMPING LAW AND PRACTICE: A COMPARATIVE STUDY 167, 191, 202 (John H. Jackson & Edwin A. Vermulst eds., 1989).

[237]19 U.S.C. §§1675(a) (1994).

[238]Edwin A. Vermulst, *The Anti-Dumping Systems of Australia, Canada, the EEC and the United States of America: Have Anti-Dumping Laws Become a Problem in International Trade?,* 10 MICH. J. INT'L L 765, 779 (Summer 1989).

duties were paid on transactions with lower purchase prices.[239] In the EU's prospective system, importers were required to apply for a refund for overpayment of antidumping duties.[240] The refund procedure, however, would not adjust the duty rate. Only in an interim review of dumping could the duty rate be updated.[241] As a result, duties could conceivably be overcollected (or undercollected) before the end of a five-year sunset period. Therefore, one could perceive that the need for a sunset procedure is greater when duties are collected on outstanding measures without an administrative review procedure to correct outdated margins.

Because the United States did not maintain a comparable sunset procedure, it is difficult to compare the rate of total U.S. revocations of antidumping and countervailing duty orders to revocations in the EU, Canada, and Australia. Of the 13 Section 751(b) changed circumstances reviews conducted by the ITC, 46 percent of the reviews resulted in revocation or termination.[242] Unlike changed circumstance reviews, U.S. authorities will self-initiate sunset reviews in the United States.

Of the 69 findings to be reviewed from 1989 to 1997, the CITT rescinded 22 findings or 32 percent of the total number of findings or 46 percent of completed reviews.[243] Of the 56 measures reviewed by the Australian Anti-Dumping Authority from 1994 to 1997, the Anti-Dumping Authority recommended expiration for 32 measures or 57 percent.[244] Finally, no com-

---

[239]*See id.* at 780; Australian Anti-Dumping Authority, Annual Report 1988-89, at 6.

[240]Stanbrook & Bentley, *supra* note 37, at 194; *see* Greyson Bryan & Dominique Guy Boursereau, *Antidumping Law in the European Communities and the United States: A Comparative Analysis*, 18 Geo. Wash. J. Int'l L. & Econ. 631, 698-99 (1985).

[241]Stanbrook & Bentley, *supra* note 37, at 193.

[242]Of the 22 Section 104(b) reviews conducted by the ITC, 81 percent of the reviews resulted in revocation. Section 104(b) reviews, however, differ from sunset reviews because they are not based on a pre-existing injury determination. The total number of reviews conducted by the ITC includes only those reviews that resulted in a final determination and, therefore, excludes reviews initiated, dismissed, suspended, or terminated.

[243]Government of Canada Rebuttal Comments to the ITC at 4 (1/21/98) (noting that the CITT continued 25 findings, 16 orders expired without reviews, and the reviews of 6 findings were still pending). According to the CITT, "actions" are measured on a country-specific basis while "findings" include a number of actions concerning the same product. *See* CITT, Annual Report 1995-96 at 55 n.1.

[244]The results of the reviews conducted by the Australian Anti-Dumping Authority were calculated on a country-specific basis.

parable statistics were available for the results of EU expiry reviews. The EU expiry law has eliminated a significant number of measures. For example, from 1985 to 1996, the EU allowed a total of 270 measures to expire automatically without review.[245] From 1985 to 1990, the EU law resulted in expiration of 75 percent of the measures to which the expiry law was applied.[246] Yet, even without a formal sunset review provision, the United States revoked a total of 43 percent of its antidumping and countervailing duty orders issued from January 1, 1980, to July 16, 1997.[247]

Based on these statistics, it can be expected that member states will retain a significant percentage of the measures where the domestic industry perceives the need for relief and actively participates. As subsequent chapters will show, the CITT's expiry review system is comparable to the one proposed by the United States. For example, the United States and the Canada provide similar rights to interested parties in allowing them to participate actively in investigations and reviews. In contrast, the administration of measures in Australia and the European Union has not historically been as transparent or provided the same level of participation to domestic producers.[248] Therefore, it can be anticipated that U.S. revocation rates could be more comparable to Canadian rates.

The mere existence of a sunset review procedure can also serve the purpose of eliminating measures that are no longer necessary. For example, with Canada's application of a sunset law in 1989, the number of expired or rescinded actions increased in 1988, 1989, and 1990, and then tapered off by 1991:[249]

---

[245] Bael & Bellis, *supra* note 48, at 210; *Fourteenth Annual Report from the Commission to the European Parliament on the Community's Anti-Dumping and Anti-Subsidy Activities: 1995*, COM(96) 428 final, at 37 (Brussels, Sept. 16, 1997).

[246] *See Ninth Annual Report of the Commission on the Community's Anti-Dumping and Anti-Subsidy Activities: 1990*, SEC(91) 974 final, at 21 (Brussels, May 31, 1991).

[247] Statistical Summary from the International Trade Administration, U.S. Department of Commerce <http://www.ita.doc.gov/import_admin/records/stats/>.

[248] *See, e.g.*, Willet, *supra* note 79, at 9, 12-13; H. Keith C. Steele, *The Australian Antidumping System*, *in* ANTIDUMPING LAW AND PRACTICE: A COMPARATIVE STUDY, *supra* note 236, at 223, 240-44; Jean-Francois Bellis, *The EEC Antidumping System*, *in* ANTIDUMPING LAW AND PRACTICE: A COMPARATIVE STUDY, *supra* note 236, at 41, 50-52, 96.

[249] Lee, *supra* note 35, at 2, Table 1; *see* CITT Research Branch, *Canada's Use of the GATT Anti-Dumping Code* 7 (June 1991).

Year	Added	Actions Expired/Rescinded	In Place (Dec. 31)
1988	3	22	140
1989	2	14	128
1990	10	60	78
1991	12	17	73
1992	4	7	70
1993	16	0	86
1994	19	9	96
1995	6	5	97

Similarly, a large number of actions were terminated under the Australian system between the time of the Gruen Report in 1986 suggesting a sunset provision and adoption of a sunset provision in 1988:[250]

Year ended 6/30	No. of actions terminated	Average duration (years)	Longest duration (years)
1986	50	4.3	9.6
1987	60	3.6	8.3
1988	66	5.3	8.8
1989	43	5.2	9.7
1990	8	4.0	6.0
1991	7	1.9	3.0

In the United States, the total number of orders prior to the first sunset review in 1998 dropped from 401 in 1994 to 325 by March 1998, or by 19 percent.[251] The number of antidumping and countervailing duty orders revoked increased markedly in 1994 and 1995, perhaps in anticipation of sunset reviews:[252]

[250]Hollander & Gruen, *supra* note 88, at table 3, *citing* Australian Customs Service. The duration information for 1990 is based on only two actions. *Id.*

[251]*Compare* Lee, *supra* note 35, at 2, Table 1, *with Procedures for Conducting Five-Year ("Sunset") Reviews of Antidumping and Countervailing Duty Orders*, 63 Fed. Reg. 13,516, 13,517 (Dep't Comm. 1998).

[252]Statistical Summary from the International Trade Administration, U.S. Department of Commerce <http://www.ita.doc.gov/import_admin/records/stats/revoke1.htm>.

Number of U.S. Antidumping and Countervailing Duty Orders Revoked																	
Date:	80	81	82	83	84	85	86	87	88	89	90	91	92	93	94	95	96
AD	2	8	1	2	8	16	8	9	0	5	10	7	1	3	28	12	6
CVD	5	15	7	9	7	25	4	2	1	5	4	6	0	1	5	35	1
Total	7	23	8	11	15	41	12	11	1	10	14	13	1	4	33	47	7

B. *THE URUGUAY ROUND NEGOTIATING HISTORY OF THE SUNSET PROVISIONS*

1. The Negotiations: A Timeline

In 1985, prior to the Uruguay Round, the Committee on Anti-Dumping Practices asked the Secretariat to compile an inventory of pertinent sections of the legislation and administrative procedures of the Parties to the Code to consider the utility of a sunset clause.[253] With this inventory, Uruguay Round trade negotiators from various countries were prepared to address the issue of the duration of antidumping and countervailing duty measures early in the negotiations. By 1987, various countries were debating the merits of requiring a firm sunset provision in domestic laws.[254] In response to various proposals from Australia, Japan, Korea, Singapore, the Nordic Countries, and Canada[255] and over the objections of the United

[253]Specifically, the United Kingdom, on behalf of Hong Kong and with the support of Singapore and the EU, requested a review of GATT signatories' sunset requirements contained in their national legislation. *See* Stewart, Markel & Kerwin, *supra* note 1, at n.1183 and accompanying text, *citing Minutes of the Meeting Held on 21 and 24 October 1985*, GATT Doc. No. ADP/M/16 (Jan. 9, 1986), at 6; *Inventory*, *supra* note 81.

[254]*See* Stewart, Markel & Kerwin, *supra* note 1, at nn.588, 1196, *citing* Note by the Secretariat, GATT Doc. No. MTN.GNG/NG8/5, at 2 (Dec. 15, 1987); *Submission from the Nordic Countries*, GATT Doc. No. MTN.GNG/NG8/W/15 (Nov. 16, 1987), at 3; Patrick J. McDonough, *Subsidies and Countervailing Measures, in* 1 THE GATT URUGUAY ROUND: A NEGOTIATING HISTORY (1986-1992) at n.234 (Terence P. Stewart ed., 1993), *citing Meeting of October 29, 1987, Note by the Secretariat,* GATT Doc. No. MTN.GNG/NG10/4 (Nov. 10, 1987), at 1-2.

[255]*See* Stewart, Markel & Kerwin, *supra* note 1, at nn.1192-98 and accompany text, *citing Submission by Australia*, GATT Doc. No. MTN.GNG/NG8/W/66 (Dec. 22, 1989), at 3; *Communication from Japan*, GATT Doc. No. MTN.GNG/NG8/W/30 (June 20,

States,[256] Uruguay Round negotiators developed draft texts to memorialize the state of the negotiations. The sunset review provisions in the Antidumping Agreement primarily evolved out of the Tokyo Round's article 9 in the Carlisle, New Zealand, and Dunkel draft texts while the sunset provisions in the Subsidies Agreement evolved out of the Tokyo Round's article 4.9 in the Cartland and Dunkel draft texts. A copy of the draft texts is contained in Appendix I to this treatise.

Briefly, the phrasing of the language in the sunset provision was primarily addressed in negotiations on the Antidumping Agreement. On August 14, 1990, the Carlisle I draft text was superseded by "Carlisle II."[257] Carlisle II, however, failed to resolve contentious issues by presenting the various proposed texts in brackets. In the end, the negotiating parties accepted the Carlisle II draft as a "working tool" to be used in conjunction with the first draft, Carlisle I, in further negotiations.[258] The goal of then Deputy Director General Carlisle was to divide the antidumping negotiations into three parts by focusing on less controversial issues, moderately

---

1988), at 12-13; *Explanations by the Republic of Korea on the Occasion of Submitting Concrete Negotiating Text on the Anti-dumping Code*, GATT Doc. No. MTN.GNG/NG8/W/40/Add.1 (Nov. 23, 1989), at 5; *Submission from the Nordic Countries*, GATT Doc. No. MTN.GNG/NG8/W/15 (Nov. 16, 1987), at 3; *Proposed Elements for a Framework for Negotiations: Principles and Objectives for Anti-dumping Rules, Communication from the Delegation of Singapore*, GATT Doc. No. MTN.GNG/NG8/W/55 (Oct. 13, 1989), at 7; *Communication from the Republic of Korea*, GATT Doc. No. MTN.GNG/NG8/W/40 (Nov. 22, 1988), at 11; *Drafting Proposals of the Nordic Countries Regarding Amendments of the Anti-dumping Code*, GATT Doc. No. MTN.GNG/NG8/W/76 (April 11, 1990), at 5; McDonough, *supra* note 254, at nn.291-94, 757-59, *citing Framework for Negotiations, Communication from Canada*, GATT Doc. No. MTN.GNG/NG10/W/25 (June 28, 1989), at 7-8; *Elements on the Framework for Negotiations, Submission by Japan*, GATT Doc. No. MTN/GNG/NG10/W/27 (Oct. 6, 1989), at 3; *Elements of the Framework for Negotiations, Submission by India*, GATT Doc. No. MTN.GNG/NG10/W/33 (Nov. 30, 1989), at 5; *Elements of the Framework for Negotiations, Submission by the Nordic Countries*, GATT Doc. No. MTN.GNG/NG10/W/30 (Nov. 27, 1989), at 9.

[256]McDonough, *supra* note 254, at n.759 and accompanying text, *citing Meeting of October 19-20, 1989, Note by the Secretariat*, GATT Doc. No. MTN.GNG/NG10/14 (Nov. 15, 1989), at 3; *Meeting of 30 April–1 May 1990, Note by Secretariat*, GATT Doc. No. MTN/GNG/NG10/18 (May 28, 1990), at 6-7.

[257]Stewart, Markel & Kerwin, *supra* note 1, at n.824.

[258]*Id.* at nn.827-29 and accompanying text.

controversial, and more controversial issues (including sunset) during a series of talks scheduled for September and October 1990.[259]

Negotiations on the antidumping provisions, however, broke down in October 1990.[260] One of the unresolved issues at the time of the breakdown was the sunset provision.[261] In order to restart negotiations on October 30, 1990, then Director-General Arthur Dunkel assigned the New Zealand delegate the responsibility of developing an acceptable compromise text for future negotiations.[262] On November 6, 1990, the New Zealand draft (New Zealand I) superseded the Carlisle drafts.[263]

The New Zealand I draft was sharply criticized by the United States and the EU and was revised in a second draft on November 15, 1990.[264] The United States and EU, however, rejected the New Zealand II draft which was revised on November 23, 1990.[265] Although the EU accepted the draft, the United States, Japan, and other Asian exporters rejected the third draft as a basis for future negotiations.[266] The antidumping negotiations failed to progress during 1991. In November 1991, the then-head of the informal working group on antidumping, Rudolph Ramsauer, attempted to stimulate negotiations by issuing a new draft text. In that text, Mr. Ramsauer identified the sunset provision as one of the "major open issues" that required "urgent political decisions."[267]

Like the other drafts, the Ramsauer draft was criticized by the United States and EU. That draft, however, was quickly superseded by Mr. Dunkel's draft text (Dunkel Draft) on December 20, 1991.[268] During the final negotiations, the Subsidies Agreement language was revised to reflect the sunset language of the Antidumping Agreement.[269] Negotiations were concluded in 1993 and countries signed the GATT Final Act Embodying the Results of the Uruguay Round of Multilateral Trade Negotiations on April 15, 1994.

---

[259] *Id.* at nn.830-31 and accompanying text.

[260] *Id.* at nn.835-37 and accompanying text.

[261] *Id.*

[262] *Id.* at n.838 and accompanying text.

[263] *Id.* at n.844 and accompanying text.

[264] *Id.* at nn.848-50 and accompanying text.

[265] *Id.* at nn.851-54 and accompanying text.

[266] *Id.* at n.856 and accompanying text.

[267] *See id.* at nn.868-98 and accompanying text.

[268] *Id.* at nn.902-05 and accompanying text.

[269] *See* Appendix I.

2. The Negotiations: The Issues

Negotiations on sunset provisions during the Uruguay Round addressed a number of issues: initiation of a review, burden of proof, duration of the measures, and treatment of existing measures. Consistent with existing law in some member states, the Cartland I and Carlisle I drafts made continuation of a measure contingent on the findings of a "review."[270] It was in the New Zealand I draft that negotiators entertained the idea of requiring the domestic industry to have the burden of submitting a "duly substantiated request" for initiation of a review. By New Zealand III, however, negotiators inserted the provision allowing governments to have the option of self-initiating sunset reviews. According to the final Agreements, sunset reviews could be initiated by the authorities or upon a duly substantiated request made by or on behalf of the domestic industry.

During the negotiations, much of the difficulty in reaching an agreement centered on whether to place the burden of proving or disproving the continued need for an order on injured domestic parties or on the foreign exporters.[271] Generally, countries supporting a more definite sunset provision believed that, absent "good cause," the order should end. According to those countries, the domestic industry should bear the burden of maintaining an order rather than the companies found to have been dumping.[272] In contrast, countries supporting a more flexible sunset provision were concerned with adding to the domestic industry's difficulties the burden of having to defend their right to an order after having already proven

[270] *Id.*

[271] *See* Stewart, Markel, & Kerwin, *supra* note 1, at n.1201 and accompanying text.

[272] *See id.* at 229-30. Some of the concerns of the countries seeking more definite "sunset" provisions were:

- the perceived ability of "user" countries to keep orders in place for extended periods with no administrative tools to have the orders' continued viability or need tested;
- the difficulty or inability of foreign producers to demonstrate likely consequences of revocation;
- a belief that Article VI should be construed narrowly and circumscribed strictly; and
- difficulty in getting dumping duties to reflect existing pricing practices.

Id. at 1613.

their claim and after receiving no compensation for their injury in the interim.[273]

In the initial Cartland I and Carlisle I drafts, authorities were directed to find "good cause for the continuation" of the measure. Carlisle II, however, eliminated the "good cause" language and instead included language that a review should determine whether "continued imposition of the duty is necessary to offset dumping and prevent injury from recurring." In New Zealand III, the injury language was amended to incorporate a "continuation or recurrence" standard.[274] As a result, the draft required authorities to recognize that injury could continue despite an outstanding measure. The antidumping provisions of the Dunkel Draft required the administering authority to determine whether continuation of the duties was "*necessary to prevent* the continuation or recurrence of injury by dumped imports."[275]

The United States, however, objected to the Dunkel Draft language on sunset reviews. [276] Just before the conclusion of the Uruguay Round, there-

---

[273]*Id.* at 1611. Some of the concerns of countries seeking flexibility in the termination of orders were:

- lack of compensation to injured parties properly puts the burden for terminating orders on those dumping and found to have caused harm — indeed, efforts by some delegations to make threat of material injury and material injury more difficult standards compound the difficulty of accepting short termination periods, as companies are not permitted to "catch up."
- in retrospective systems, producers and exporters are not penalized by maintenance of an order when corrective price action is taken;
- an inability of domestic producers to identify likely courses of conduct of foreign competition if orders are revoked while dumping continues;
- a belief that Article VI is not an exception, but an integral part of the GATT, which clearly condemns injurious dumping.

Id. at 1613.

[274]*See* Appendix I.

[275]*See id.* at Dunkel Draft, art. 11.3 (emphasis added). The language of the draft focusing on whether an order or suspended investigation was "necessary" to prevent the continuation or recurrence of injury would have imposed a standard of review that was similar or identical to the standard rejected for "changed circumstances" reviews under Section 751(b) in the Trade and Tariff Act of 1984. *See infra* note 155 and accompanying text.

[276]*See U.S. Tables Proposal For 11 Changes To GATT Antidumping Text: Special Report*, INSIDE U.S. TRADE (12/3/93).

fore, U.S. negotiators tabled a proposal on November 26, 1993, to modify the sunset provisions of the antidumping and subsidies agreements. Specifically, the United States proposed to clarify that there was no burden on either party. In the following excerpt, the U.S. proposed additions are bolded and proposed deletions are italicized:

> 1. Revise paragraph 3 of Article 11 of the AD text as follows:*
>
> 11.3 Notwithstanding the provisions of paragraphs 1 and 2, any definitive anti-dumping duty shall be terminated on a date not later than five years from its imposition (or from the date of the most recent review under paragraph 2 if that review has covered both dumping and injury, or under this paragraph), unless the authorities determine, in a review initiated before that date on their own initiative or upon a duly substantiated request made by or on behalf of the domestic industry within a reasonable period of time [prior] to that date, that **there is good cause 1/** for the continued imposition of the duty *is necessary to prevent the continuation or recurrence of injury by the dumped imports.1/* 2/The duty may remain in force pending the outcome of this review.
>
> ---
>
> **1/ "Good cause" exists when the authorities determine that official injury within the meaning of Article 3 is likely to continue or recur if the definitive duty is terminated. In the context of such review, no interested party shall be expected to carry this burden of proving that injury is or is not likely to continue or recur.**
>
> 2/ When the amount of the anti-dumping duty is assessed on [a]retrospective basis, a finding in the most recent assessment proceedings under subparagraph 3.1 of Article 9 that no duty is to be yielded shall not by itself require the authorities to determine under this paragraph that **there is no good cause** to continue imposition of the anti-dumping duty *is not necessary.*
>
> * We are seeking parallel changes in the SCM text.[277]

The Dunkel Draft language requiring a showing that the "continued imposition of the duty is necessary to prevent the continuation or recurrence of injury by dumped imports" was revised in the final Agreements to read that the "expiry of the duty would be likely to lead to continuation or recurrence of dumping and injury."[278]

---

[277] *U.S. Antidumping Proposals: Special Report*, INSIDE U.S. TRADE (Dec. 3, 1993).

[278] Antidumping Agreement, *supra* note 5, at art. 11.3; Subsidies Agreement, *supra* note 5, at art. 21.3.

Another issue Uruguay Round negotiations addressed was how long an order should last before being revoked. Based on a 1986 review of national antidumping laws, the Committee on Antidumping Practices found that signatories with sunset provisions had sunset deadlines varying from one to five years.[279] During the negotiations in 1989 and 1990, Australia, Korea, and the Nordic countries argued that a three-year duration would be reasonable while the EU and India proposed a five-year duration.[280] Canada and Japan both argued that an antidumping and countervailing duty order should be extended for a three-year period after the first sunset review.[281]

The concept of ending an order or suspension agreement after a five-year period was established in the initial subsidies draft, Cartland I, and the initial antidumping draft, Carlisle I.[282] Carlisle II bracketed the duration of an antidumping order as being either three or five years. The New Zealand drafts, however, incorporated the idea of permitting sunset reviews every five years as long as the antidumping order remained outstanding. The final sunset review provision retained the five-year deadline and permitted continuation of a measure indefinitely as long as the results of five-year reviews so justified.

---

[279]Stewart, Markel & Kerwin, *supra* note 1, at nn.1185-90 and accompanying text.

[280]*Id.* at n.1198-99 and accompanying text, *citing Submission by Australia*, GATT Doc. No. MTN.GNG/NG8/W/66 (Dec. 22, 1989), at 3; *Communication from the Republic of Korea*, GATT Doc. No. MTN.GNG/NG8/W/40 (Nov. 22, 1988), at 11; *Drafting Proposals of the Nordic Countries Regarding Amendments of the Anti-dumping Code*, GATT Doc. No. MTN.GNG/NG8/W/76 (April 11, 1990), at 5; *Communication from the European Communities to the GATT Uruguay Round — Anti-dumping*, GATT Doc. No. MTN.GNG/NG8/W/74 (March 21, 1990), at 5; McDonough, supra note 254, at n.346 and accompanying text, *citing Elements of the Framework for Negotiations, Submission by India*, GATT Doc. No. MTN.GNG/NG10/W/33 (Nov. 30, 1989), at 4-6.

[281]Stewart, Markel & Kerwin, *supra* note 1, at n.1200 and accompanying text, *citing Submission of Japan on the Amendments to the Anti-Dumping Code*, GATT Doc. No. MTN.GNG/NG8/W/48 (Aug. 3, 1989), at 7; *Submission by Canada*, GATT Doc. No. MTN.GNG/NG8/W/65 (Dec. 22, 1989), at 5; McDonough, *supra* note 254, at n.758 and accompanying text, *citing Framework for Negotiations, Communication from Canada*, GATT Doc. No. MTN.GNG/NG10/W/25 (June 28, 1989), at 7; *Elements on the Framework for Negotiations, Submission by Japan*, GATT Doc. No. MTN.GNG/NG10/W/27 (Oct. 6, 1989), at 3.

[282]*See* Appendix I.

Finally, the negotiators focused on the treatment of existing orders in sunset reviews. During the negotiations, some countries argued for the immediate revocation of orders or termination of suspended investigations older than five years as of the date of entry of the WTO Agreement.[283] The United States, however, argued against immediate application of the Agreement. The result is Article 18.3 of the Antidumping Agreement and Article 32.4 of the Subsidies Agreement which provide in pertinent part:

> 18.3 Subject to subparagraphs 3.1 and 3.2, the provisions of this Agreement shall apply to investigations, and reviews of existing measures, initiated pursuant to applications which have been made on or after the date of entry into force for a Member of the WTO Agreement.
>
> . . .
>
> 18.3.2 For purposes of paragraph 3 of Article 11, existing anti-dumping measures shall be deemed to be imposed on a date not later than the date of entry into force for a Member of the WTO Agreement, except in cases in which the domestic legislation of a Member in force on that date already included a clause of the type provided for in that paragraph. . . .
>
> . . .
>
> 32.4 For purposes of paragraph 3 of Article 21, existing countervailing measures shall be deemed to be imposed on a date not later than the date of entry into force for a Member of the WTO Agreement, except in cases in which the domestic legislation of a Member in force at that date already included a clause of the type provided for in that paragraph. [284]

Therefore, member states that did not already have a comparable sunset review procedure in their domestic legislation were allowed to consider all outstanding orders or suspension agreements as "issued" on the effective date of the WTO Agreement for that country. For those countries, such as the United States, the first sunset reviews would be conducted within five years of the effective date of the WTO Agreement.

---

[283] Statement of Administrative Action, *reprinted in* H.R. DOC. NO. 103-316, vol. 1, at 817 (1994).

[284] Antidumping Agreement, *supra* note 5, at art. 18.3; *see* Subsidies Agreement, *supra* note 5, at art. 32.4.

3. The Negotiations: The Final Sunset Provisions

The final sunset provisions of the Antidumping and Subsidies Agreements are reproduced on the following page. In sum, the final provisions require member states to terminate measures not later than five years from imposition (or the most recent review) unless the authorities (1) initiate a review before that date on their own initiative or upon request, and (2) determine that expiry of the measure would be likely to lead to continuation or recurrence of dumping or subsidization and injury. The burden of conducting a review and making a substantiated determination resides with the authorities.

In addition to the specific provisions governing the conduct of sunset reviews, other substantive provisions in the Agreements also apply to sunset reviews. For example, the Agreements generally define the term "domestic industry" as "domestic producers as a whole of the like products or . . . those of them whose collective output of the products constitutes a major proportion of the total domestic production of those products. . . ."[285] The definition of domestic industry can exclude producers related to exporters or importers and can include regional industries. The Agreements define dumping and subsidization.[286] The Agreements also define the term "injury" as "material injury to a domestic industry, threat of material injury to a domestic industry or material retardation of the establishment of such an industry. . . ."[287]

The Agreements require that an injury determination be based on positive evidence and involve objective examination of (1) the volume of the dumped imports, (2) the effect of the dumped imports on prices (including significant price undercutting or depression or suppression) in the domestic market for like products, and (3) the consequent impact of these imports on domestic producers of such products, including an evaluation of all relevant economic factors affecting the industry. In making an injury determination, the Agreements permit authorities to cumulatively assess imports.[288]

---

[285]Antidumping Agreement, *supra* note 5, at art. 4; Subsidies Agreement, *supra* note 5, at art. 16.

[286]Antidumping Agreement, *supra* note 5, at art. 2; Subsidies Agreement, *supra* note 5, at arts. 1-3, 8.

[287]Antidumping Agreement, *supra* note 5, at art. 3 n.9; Subsidies Agreement, *supra* note 5, at art. 15 n.45.

[288]Antidumping Agreement, *supra* note 5, at art. 3; Subsidies Agreement, *supra* note 5, at art. 15.

Antidumping Agreement	*Subsidies Agreement*
11.3 Notwithstanding the provisions of paragraphs 1 and 2, any definitive anti-dumping duty shall be terminated on a date not later than five years from its imposition (or from the date of the most recent review under paragraph 2 if that review has covered both dumping and injury, or under this paragraph), unless the authorities determine, in a review initiated before that date on their own initiative or upon a duly substantiated request made by or on behalf of the domestic industry within a reasonable period of time prior to that date, that the expiry of the duty would be likely to lead to continuation or recurrence of dumping and injury.* The duty may remain in force pending the outcome of such a review. ——— *When the amount of the anti-dumping duty is assessed on a retrospective basis, a finding in the most recent assessment proceeding under subparagraph 3.1 of Article 9 that no duty is to be levied shall not by itself require the authorities to terminate the definitive duty.	21.3 Notwithstanding the provisions of paragraphs 1 and 2, any definitive countervailing duty shall be terminated on a date not later than five years from its imposition (or from the date of the most recent review under paragraph 2 if that review has covered both subsidization and injury, or under this paragraph), unless the authorities determine, in a review initiated before that date on their own initiative or upon a duty substantiated request made by or on behalf of the domestic industry within a reasonable period of time prior to that date, that the expiry of the duty would be likely to lead to continuation or recurrence of subsidization and injury.* The duty may remain in force pending the outcome of such a review. ——— *When the amount of the countervailing duty is assessed on a retrospective basis, a finding in the most recent assessment proceeding that no duty is to be levied shall not by itself require the authorities to terminate the definitive duty.

The Agreements also impose several procedural and evidentiary requirements on the conduct of sunset reviews. For example, the Agreements require authorities in the member states to notify interested parties and the public regarding the initiation of a review as well as any final determinations. [289] Each notice must set forth, or otherwise make available through a separate report, all relevant information on the matters of fact and law and reasons for the final decision as well as the reasons for the acceptance or rejection of relevant arguments or claims made by the exporters or importers.[290]

The Agreements also require authorities to provide all interested parties notice of the information required and ample opportunity to present in writing all evidence which they consider relevant.[291] Specifically, exporters or foreign producers must be given 30 days to respond to questionnaires with due consideration given to any request for an extension. Subject to the requirements to protect confidential information, evidence shall be made available promptly to other interested parties. Interested parties shall have a full opportunity to defend their interests through opportunities to meet parties with adverse interests to exchange opposing views as well as the right, on justification, to present other information orally. The authorities shall also provide an opportunity for submission of relevant information by industrial users of the product and representative consumer organizations in cases where the product is commonly sold at the retail level.

In addition to the right of participation, the Agreements require the authorities to disclose to interested parties all information that is relevant to the presentation of their cases and relied on by the authorities and to impose requirements protecting the confidentiality of certain information. The Agreements also require authorities to confirm the accuracy of submitted data as well as permit on-site verifications in the territories of other

---

[289]Antidumping Agreement, *supra* note 5, at arts. 6, 11.4, 12.3; Subsidies Agreement, *supra* note 5, at arts. 12, 21.4, 22.7. Articles 11.4 and 12.3 of the Antidumping Agreement, and Articles 21.4 and 22.7 of the Subsidies Agreement expressly require sunset reviews to comply with the evidentiary and procedural requirements of articles 6 and 12, and articles 12 and 22 of the Agreements, respectively.

[290]Antidumping Agreement, *supra* note 5, at arts. 12.1, 12.2.2; Subsidies Agreement, *supra* note 5, at art. 22.5.

[291]Antidumping Agreement, *supra* note 5, at art. 6; Subsidies Agreement, *supra* note 5, at art. 12.

member states. The results of any verification must be disclosed subject to any confidentiality requirements. The Agreements permit the authorities to rely on facts available in their preliminary or final determinations in cases where interested parties refuse access to, or otherwise do not provide, necessary information within a reasonable period or significantly impede the investigation. The authorities, however, must take into account any difficulties experienced by interested parties, in particular small companies, in supplying information requested, and shall provide any assistance practicable.

Finally, the Agreements deem existing measures to be imposed on a date not later than the date of entry into force for a Member of the WTO Agreement unless domestic legislation already included a sunset provision.[292] For countries, such as the United States, that do not already have a comparable sunset review procedure in their domestic legislation, the first sunset reviews would be initiated within five years of the effective date of the WTO Agreement. The Agreements specifically state that the procedural requirements are not intended to prevent the authorities from proceeding expeditiously in reaching determinations. The Agreements further require sunset reviews to be carried out "expeditiously" and normally concluded within 12 months of initiation.[293]

The following chart summarizes significant requirements in the Agreements which affect the conduct of sunset reviews in member states:

[292]Antidumping Agreement, *supra* note 5, at art. 18.3; *see* Subsidies Agreement, *supra* note 5, at art. 32.4.

[293]Antidumping Agreement, *supra* note 5, at arts. 6 & 11.4; Subsidies Agreement, *supra* note 5, at arts. 12 & 21.4.

Requirements	*Agreements*
expiration	not later than five years from imposition or review
initiation	by authorities or upon a duly substantiated request made by or on behalf of the domestic industry
initiation deadline	before the five year deadline
notice of initiation	to all interested parties and public notice
questionnaire	notice of required information; 30 days to respond
facts available	permits resort to facts available when necessary information not provided or parties impede investigation; consideration of difficulties to supply information; provide assistance practicable
opportunity to comment	ample opportunity to present in writing all evidence; evidence shall be made available promptly to other interested parties; opportunity to meet those parties with adverse interests to exchange views and right, on justification, to present other information orally; opportunity for industrial users and consumers organizations to comment
confidential information	protection of confidential information
verification	confirm accuracy of data; permit on-site verification
likelihood test	likely to lead to continuation or recurrence of dumping or subsidization and injury
retrospective analysis	a finding in the most recent assessment proceeding that no duty is to be levied shall not by itself require the authorities to terminate the definitive duty
injury test	examine (1) volume, (2) prices, including significant undercutting, depression, or suppression, and (3) impact on domestic producers, including relevant economic factors affecting industry
disclosure	disclose all information relied on by authorities and results of verification
final determination	notice with reasons; normally issued within 12 months

CHAPTER III

European Union Sunset Reviews: Legislation and Practice

A. *INITIATING EXPIRY REVIEWS*

1. Self-Initiation and Requests for Expiry Reviews

In order to implement the Antidumping and Subsidies Agreements, the EU Council adopted Regulations 3283/94 on antidumping and 3284/94 on subsidies, as amended.[294] Article 11(2) of Regulation 3283/94 and Article 13(2) of Regulation 3284/94, as amended, provide the sunset or "expiry" review procedures for antidumping and countervailing duty measures, respectively. According to those regulations, an antidumping or countervailing duty measure will expire five years from its imposition or five years from the conclusion of the most recent review which has covered both dumping and injury.

In contrast to pre-Uruguay Round law which required "interested parties" to substantiate a request for an expiry review, EU implementing law permits the Commission to conduct the review by self-initiating a review or upon receipt of a request made by or on behalf of "Community producers."[295]

---

[294]Council Regulation 3283/94, 1994 O.J. (L. 349) (1994), *as amended* Council Regulation 355/95, 1995 O.J. (L 41) 2 (1995); Council Regulation 1251/95, 1995 O.J. (L 122) 1 (1995); Council Regulation 384/96, 1995 O.J. (L 56) 1 (1996); Council Regulation 2331/96, 1996 O.J. (L 317) 1 (1996); Council Regulation 3284/94, 1994 O.J. (L 349) 22 (1994), *as amended* Council Regulation 1252/95, 1995 O.J. (L 122) 2 (1995).

[295]Council Regulation 3283/94, *supra* note 294, at art. 11(2); Council Regulation 384/96, *supra* note 294, at art. 11(2); Council Regulation 3284/94, *supra* note 294, at art. 13(2). In practice, the Commission does not normally self-initiate reviews.

The EU requires the request for a review of an antidumping measure, for example, from "Community producers" to be substantiated in the following manner:

> an expiry review shall be initiated where the request contains sufficient evidence that the expiry of the measures would be likely to result in a continuation or recurrence of dumping and injury. Such a likelihood may, for example, be indicated by evidence of continued dumping and injury or evidence that the removal of injury is partly or solely due to the existence of measures or evidence that the circumstances of the exporters, or market conditions, are such that they would indicate the likelihood of further injurious dumping.[296]

Thus, requests for expiry reviews must be substantiated by evidence showing: (1) continued dumping or injury, (2) removal of injury due partly or solely to the existence of measures, or (3) other market evidence indicating the likelihood of further injurious dumping.

Likewise, the comparable provision for EU countervailing duty law also requires a substantiated request for an expiry review based on similar evidence:

> 3. An expiry review shall be initiated where the request contains sufficient evidence that the removal of measures would be likely to result in a continuation or recurrence of subsidization and injury. Such a likelihood may, for example, be indicated by evidence that the removal of injury is partly or solely due to the existence of measures or evidence that the circumstances of the exporters, or market conditions, are such that they would indicate the likelihood of further injurious subsidization.[297]

Upon receipt of a substantiated request, the Commission initiates an expiry review after consultation with the Advisory Committee.[298]

---

[296]Council Regulation 3283/94, *supra note* 294, at art. 11(2); Council Regulation 384/96, *supra* note 294, at art. 11(2); *see* Council Regulation 3284/94, *supra* note 294, at art. 13(3).

[297]Council Regulation 3284/94, *supra* note 294, at art. 13(3).

[298]Council Regulation 3283/94, *supra* note 294, at art. 11(6); Council Regulation 384/96, *supra* note 294, at art. 11(6); Regulation 3284/94, *supra* note 294, at art. 13(12). Although the EU is authorized to self-initiate an expiry review, the EU implementing legislation differs from post-Uruguay Round U.S. law in that it does did not provide for an expedited review based on the "adequacy" of questionnaire responses. *See infra* Chapter VI, Section A.1. The Advisory Committee consists of representatives of each

2. Judging the Adequacy of Responses

In its notice of initiation, the Commission will warn interested parties that non-cooperation with an information request during an expiry review will force the Commission to make its findings, affirmative or negative, on the basis of facts available.[299] According to post-Uruguay Round law, the Commission will resort to facts available in cases in which the interested party refuses access to, or otherwise does not provide, necessary information within the time limits or significantly impedes the investigation. Likewise, if the Commission finds that an interested party has supplied false or misleading information, the information will be disregarded and the Commission will resort to facts available. If an interested party does not cooperate or cooperates only partially, so that the relevant information is withheld, the Commission may choose a less favorable result for that party than if it had cooperated.

3. Simultaneous Reviews and Cumulation

The EU Regulations permit the Commission to consider the question of expiry if, at the end of the five year period, an interim review of measures is in progress.[300] During an interim review, the Commission conducts a review similar to a changed circumstance review by the U.S. DOC and ITC to determine the "need for the continued imposition of measures."[301] The Commission can initiate an interim review upon its own initiative, upon

---

Member State, with a representative of the Commission as chairman. Council Regulation 3283/94, *supra* note 294, at art. 15; Council Regulation 384/96, *supra* note 294, at art. 15; Council Regulation 3284/94, *supra* note 294, at art. 16; *see* Stanbrook & Bentley, *supra* note 37, at 157-58.

[299]Council Regulation 384/96, *supra* note 294, at art. 18; Council Regulation 3284/94, *supra* note 294, at art. 19; Synthetic Polyester Fibres Originating in Taiwan and in the Republic of Korea, Notice of Initiation of Review, para. 7, 1997 O.J. (C 321) (1997).

[300]Council Regulation 3283/94, *supra* note 294, at art. 11(7); Council Regulation 384/96, *supra* note 294, at art. 11(7); Council Regulation 3284/94, *supra* note 294, at art. 13(13).

[301]Council Regulation 3283/94, *supra* note 294, at art. 11(3); Council Regulation 384/96, *supra* note 294, at art. 11(3); Council Regulation 3284/94, *supra* note 294, at art. 13(6).

receipt of a request of a Member State, or upon the substantiated request of any exporter, importer, or Community producer. A substantiated request must contain "sufficient evidence that the continued imposition of the measure is no longer necessary to offset dumping[/countervailable subsidy] and/or the injury would be unlikely to continue or recur if the measure were removed or varied, or that the existing measure is not, or is no longer, sufficient to counteract the dumping[/countervailable subsidy] which is causing injury."[302]

In an interim review, the Commission will reopen the investigation to consider "whether the circumstances with regard to dumping[/subsidization] and injury have changed significantly, or whether existing measures are achieving the intended results in removing the injury. . . ."[303] Upon its conclusion of the interim review, the Commission can amend, repeal, or maintain its original decision, including increasing or decreasing the margins.[304]

According to Article 3(4) of Regulation 3283/94 and Article 5(4) of Regulation 3284/94, as amended, the Commission can cumulate imports for its injury determinations.[305] In practice, the Commission can conduct an investigation of the product from one country, an interim/expiry review

[302]Council Regulation 3283/94, *supra* note 294, at art. 11(3); Council Regulation 384/96, *supra* note 294, at art. 11(3); Council Regulation 3284/94, *supra* note 294, at art. 13(7).

[303]Council Regulation 3283/94, *supra* note 294, at art. 11(3); Council Regulation 384/96, *supra* note 294, at art. 11(3); Council Regulation 3284/94, *supra* note 294, at art. 13(9).

[304]*See* Stanbrook & Bentley, *supra* note 37, at 202-03.

[305]Council Regulation 3283/94, *supra* note 294, at art. 3(4); Council Regulation 384/96, *supra* note 294, at art. 3(4); Council Regulation 3284/94, *supra* note 294, at art. 5(4). The EU cumulation provision provides as follows:

> Where imports of a product from more than one country are simultaneously subject to [anti-dumping or countervailing] . . . investigations, the effects of such imports shall be cumulatively assessed only if it is determined that (a) the margin of dumping established in relation to the imports from each country is more than *de minimis* . . . and that the volume of imports from each country is not negligible; and (b) a cumulative assessment of the effects of the imports is appropriate in light of the conditions of competition between imported products and the conditions of competition between imported products and the conditions of competition between the imported products and the like Community product.

of the same product from another country, cumulate the imports, and render one decision.[306]

B. *THE EXPIRY REVIEW*

1. Deadlines

According to Regulations 3283/94 and 3284/94, as amended, a notice of expiry will be issued in the *Official Journal of the European Communities* during the fifth year of a measure regarding the impending expiry.[307] The deadline for filing a request for an expiry review would be no later than three months before the end of the five-year period. The Commission will then determine whether the request for an expiry review is sufficient to warrant initiation of a review and will issue a notice of initiation.[308]

In the notice of initiation, the Commission will request interested parties to make their views known in writing, provide supporting evidence, and request a hearing within 37 or 40 days of the notice of initiation, as specified in the notice.[309] If interested parties do not provide all necessary

---

[306]Council Regulation 384/96, *supra* note 294, at art. 3(4); Gas-Fuelled, Non-Refillable Pocket Flint Lighters Originating in Thailand, the Philippines and Mexico, Council Regulation 423/97, paras. 4-6, 11, 40-44, 1977 O.J. (L 65) (1997). In *Pocket Flint Lighters*, the Commission found that any decision to cumulate imports subject to an investigation and a review "should be made for each case on its merits, i.e. by examining the impact of the respective behavior of the exporting countries concerned." *Id.* at para. 43. In that case, the Commission found that the behavior of the exporting country subject to review was similar to the behavior of the exporting countries subject to the investigation in that the one subject to review was not prevented by outstanding measures from continued injurious dumping. *Id.*; *see* Fibre Building Board (Hardboard) Originating in Czechoslovakia, Poland and the USSR, Council Regulation 1786/89, para. 7, 1989 O.J. (L 176) (1989).

[307]Council Regulation 3283/94, *supra* note 294, at art. 11(2); Council Regulation 384/96, *supra* note 294, at art. 11(2); Council Regulation 3284/94, *supra* note 294, at art. 13(5).

[308]*See, e.g.*, Notice of Initiation of a Review of the Anti-Dumping Measures Applicable to Imports of Silicon Metal Originating in the People's Republic of China, 1995 O.J (C 193) 3 (1995).

[309]*Id.* at paras. 4, 6; Notice of Initiation of a Review of the Anti-Dumping Measure Applicable to Imports of Ferro-Silicon Originating in Poland and Egypt, paras. 4, 6, 1997 O.J. (C 204) (1997).

information or significantly impede the investigation, the Commission informs interested parties in its notice of initiation that it will make findings on the basis of facts available.[310] All expiry reviews normally shall be concluded within 12 months of the date of initiation.[311]

2. The Likelihood Tests

a. *The Commission's Determination of the Likelihood of Continuation or Recurrence of Dumping or Subsidization*

The EU Uruguay Round implementing legislation modified the standard used to determine whether or not a measure should be allowed to expire. Under pre-Uruguay Round law, Article 15 of the regulations required an inquiry into whether "expiry of the measure would lead again to injury or threat of injury."[312] Under post-Uruguay Round law, the regulations require the Commission to consider whether "expiry would be likely to lead to a continuation or recurrence of dumping [or subsidization] and injury."[313] Given that the Commission has not yet had the opportunity to apply its new regulations in many cases to date, it is not clear that the new language will necessitate any material change in analysis.[314] For example,

---

[310]*See, e.g.*, Notice of Initiation of a Review of the Anti-Dumping Measures Applicable to Imports of Sacks and Bags Made of Polyethylene or Polypropylene Originating in the People's Republic of China, para. 6, 1995 O.J. (C 271) (1995).

[311]Council Regulation 3283/94, *supra* note 294, at art. 11(5), Council Regulation 384/96, *supra* note 294, at art. 11(5); Council Regulation 3284/94, *supra* note 294, at art. 13(11). In the past, however, it has taken the EU as long as two years to complete an expiry review. *See, e.g.*, Polyester Yarn Originating in Taiwan and Turkey, Council Regulation 1074/96, para. 11, 1996 O.J. (L 141) (1996).

[312]Council Regulation 2423/88, *supra* note 294, at art. 15(3).

[313]Council Regulation 3283/94, *supra* note 294, at art. 11(2), Council Regulation 384/96, *supra* note 294, at art. 11(2); Council Regulation 3284/94, *supra* note 294, at art. 13(2).

[314]*See, e.g.*, Gas-Fuelled, Non-Refillable Pocket Flint Lighters Originating in Thailand, the Philippines and Mexico, Council Regulation 423/97, paras. 72-74, 1997 O.J. (L 65) (1997); Woven Polyolefin Sacks and Bags Originating in the People's Republic of China, Council Regulation 2003/97, paras. 13, 28, 1997 O.J. (L 284) 1 (1997).

even though the language of the pre-Uruguay Round regulation did not require an inquiry into the status of dumping or subsidization, the Commission would investigate imports during the one year prior to the notice of initiation of the expiry review.[315]

The Commission will not rely on pre-calculated margins but will recalculate those margins for an updated period. Under post-Uruguay Round law, the EU implementing legislation specifically directs the Commission to apply the same methodology as used in the original investigation provided that circumstances have not changed.[316] Measures will be repealed or maintained at the conclusion of the expiry review.[317]

In addition to margin information, the Commission will also consider evidence that the exporters have dumped in third countries as evidence of a propensity for dumping in expiry reviews.[318] The absence of or negligible imports into the EU, however, from a country subject to an expiry review can lead to exclusion from the review which results in the measure lapsing.[319] Finally, the Commission will also consider evidence of duty absorption[320] as favoring an affirmative finding that dumping is likely to recur.[321]

---

[315]*See, e.g.*, Polyester Yarn Originating in Taiwan and Turkey, Council Regulation 1074/96, para. 9, 1996 O.J. (L 141) (1996).

[316]*Compare* Council Regulation 2423/88, *supra* note 294, at art. 15, *with* Council Regulation 3283/94, *supra* note 294, at art. 11(9); Council Regulation 384/96, *supra* note 294, at art. 11(9).

[317]Council Regulation 384/96, *supra* note 294, at art. 11(6); Council Regulation 3284/94, *supra* note 294, at art. 13(12).

[318]*See, e.g.*, Monosodium Glutamate Originating in Indonesia, the Republic of Korea, Taiwan and Thailand, Council Regulation 81/96, para. 57, 1996 O.J. (L 15) (1996).

[319]Polyester Yarn Originating in Taiwan and Turkey, Council Regulation 1074/96, para. 4, 1996 O.J. (L. 141) (1996); Monosodium Glutamate Originating in Indonesia, the Republic of Korea, Taiwan and Thailand, Council Regulation 81/96, para. 57, 1996 O.J. (L 15) (1996).

[320]Under post-Uruguay Round law, the Commission will also reopen its investigation to address duty absorption based on evidence that measures have led to no movement, or insufficient movement, in resale prices or subsequent selling prices in the Community. *See* Council Regulation 384/96, *supra* note 294, at art. 12. The Commission will recalculate dumping margins in order to address duty absorption.

[321]Monosodium Glutamate Originating in Indonesia, the Republic of Korea, Taiwan and Thailand, Council Regulation 81/96, para. 57, 1996 O.J. (L 15) (1996). For ex-

b. *The Commission's Determination of the Likelihood of Continuation or Recurrence of Injury*

Due to the paucity of decisions applying post-Uruguay Round law, a review of the Commission's injury analysis under pre- and post-Uruguay Round law is necessary. The Commission's injury analysis has been divided into four parts. First, the Commission reconsiders the scope of the products investigated and the like product definitions, and defines the "Community industry" for purposes of review.[322]

Second, the Commission examines the current economic condition of the Community industry recognizing that the measure should normally have eliminated the injurious effects.[323] This analysis consists of three parts:

---

ample, in *Monosodium Glutamate*, the Commission found that reported export prices were unreliable because of their low resale prices which could only be explained by the existence of "compensatory arrangements." In *Woven Polyolefin Sacks and Bags*, the Commission considered, among other things, a formal finding of duty absorption. Woven Polyolefin Sacks and Bags Originating in the People's Republic of China, Council Regulation 2003/97, para. 1, 1997 O.J. (L 284) (1997).

[322]*See, e.g.*, Polyester Yarn Originating in Taiwan and Turkey, Council Regulation 1074/96, paras. 12-23, 1996 O.J. (L 141) 45, 46 (1996). The Commission has reasoned that it must reconsider the definition of like products in reviews because:

> [T]he design, production and marketing of particular product types often evolves over time, with new types still being essentially the same product . . . If the Commission were to be prevented from investigating new types of the same product in an Article 15 review, simply because those types had not yet been produced at the time of the original investigation, a new proceeding would have to be opened . . . If, following a review, existing measures could not be amended to include within the scope of those measures new types of the same product, the effectiveness of those measures would be impaired.

Plain Paper Photocopiers Originating in Japan, Council Regulation 2380/95, para. 15, 1995 O.J. L. 244 (1995).

[323]Ball Bearings With a Greatest External Diameter Exceeding 30 mm Originating in Japan, Council Regulation 2849/92, para. 26, 1992 O.J. (L 286) (1992); Silicon Carbide, Originating in the People's Republic of China, Poland, the Russian Federation, and Ukraine, Council Regulation 821/94, para. 14, 1994 O.J. (L 94) (1994) (Commission examines the present economic situation of the Community industry "to establish whether the expiry of the measures in force would lead again to dumping and injury or threat of injury. . . ."); Potassium Permanganate Originating in the People's Republic of China, Council Regulation 2819/94, para. 14, 1994 O.J. (L 298) (1994).

(1) brief consideration of the economic situation of the Community industry at the time of the original investigation, (2) detailed consideration of post-investigation developments in the economic situation of the Community industry, and (3) recent developments are compared with the situation at the time of the original investigation and a conclusion is made on the present state of the industry.[324] Thus, in order to determine the effect expiration of the measures would have, the Commission conducts what is tantamount to a new investigation of both dumping and injury.[325]

In order to discern the current situation of the industry, the Commission considers domestic production, production capacity and utilization, sales, stocks, employment, consumption, market share, price trends, profitability, investments, and other factors.[326] If the Commission finds that the imports continued to injure the domestic industry, the Commission presumes that "expiry of the measures would only lead to a further deterioration of an already weakened Community industry."[327] The fact, however, that the "imports are not currently causing injury is not by itself a reason for removing existing anti-dumping measures."[328] In the absence of current injury, the Commission's pre-Uruguay Round analysis would consider

[324]Plain Paper Photocopiers Originating in Japan, Council Regulation 2380/95, para. 27, 1995 O.J. (L 244) (1995).

[325]Ferro-Silicon Originating in Russia, Kazakhstan, Ukraine, Iceland, Norway, Sweden, Venezuela and Brazil, Council Regulation 3359/93, para. 72, 1993 O.J. (L 302) (1993) (Commission finds that the dumped imports are still causing material injury to the domestic industry). The Commission considers a recent annual period for purposes of calculating dumping margins and the previous four or five years for purposes of examining injury trends. *See, e.g.*, Monosodium Glutamate Originating in Indonesia, the Republic of Korea, Taiwan and Thailand, Council Regulation 81/96, paras. 8 & 34, 1996 O.J. (L 15) (1996); Plain Paper Photocopiers Originating in Japan, Council Regulation 2380/95, paras. 8, 27, 1995 O.J. (L 244) 3, 8 (1995).

[326]Potassium Permanganate Originating in the People's Republic of China, Council Regulation 2819/94, paras. 15-23, 1994 O.J. (L 298) (1994).

[327]Silicon Carbide, Originating in the People's Republic of China, Poland, the Russian Federation and Ukraine, Council Regulation 821/94, para. 40, 1994 O.J. (L 94) (1994); *see* Container Corner Fittings of Worked Cast Steel Originating in Austria, Comm. Decision 92/313/EEC, para. 31, 1992 O.J. (L 165) (1992); *see also* Woven Polyolefin Sacks and Bags Originating in the People's Republic of China, Council Regulation 2003/97, para. 43, 1997 O.J. (L 284) (1997).

[328]Certain Ball Bearings Originating in Japan and Singapore, Council Regulation 2553/93, para. 15, 1993 O.J. (L 235) (1993).

whether a "recurrence of injury to the Community industry caused by dumping would be foreseeable and imminent in the absence of measures."[329] Under the post-Uruguay Round analysis, the Commission considers whether "expiry would be likely to lead to a continuation or recurrence of dumping [or subsidization] and injury."[330] The term "injury" is defined as "material injury to the Community industry, threat of material injury to the Community industry or material retardation of the establishment of such an industry. . . ."[331]

Third, the Commission considers the "behavior of the exporters" as evidenced by their import volume, market share, market conditions, and sales prices.[332] With respect to volume, the Commission also analyzed the effect of excluding the imports of respondents excluded from the underlying measure.[333] With respect to sales prices, the Commission calculates the margin of price undercutting by the imports.[334] The Commission also relies on evidence of factors such as the vulnerability of the domestic industry, the existence of orders in other countries on the same merchandise, and the production capacity of foreign exporters to assess the possible effects of expiry of the order.[335] Finally, the Commission evaluates evidence that the orders have been

329 *Id.*

330 Council Regulation 3283/94, *supra* note 294, at art. 11(2); Council Regulation 384/96, *supra* note 294, at art. 11(2); Council Regulation 3284/94, *supra* note 294, at art. 13(2).

331 Council Regulation 384/96, *supra* note 294, at art. 3(1); Council Regulation 3284/94, *supra* note 294, at art. 5(1).

332 Potassium Permanganate Originating in the People's Republic of China, Council Regulation 2819/94, paras. 25-28, 1994 O.J. (L 298) (1994).

333 Polyester Yarn Originating in Taiwan and Turkey, Council Regulation 1074/96, para. 34, 1996 O.J. (L 141) 48 (1996).

334 *Id.* at para. 82.

335 Ball Bearings With a Greatest External Diameter Exceeding 30 mm Originating in Japan, Council Regulation 2849/92, para. 35, 39, 1992 O.J. (L 286) (1992); Potassium Permanganate Originating in the People's Republic of China, Council Regulation 2819/94, paras. 15-23, 1994 O.J. (L 298) (1994); Polyester Yarn Originating in Taiwan and Turkey, Council Regulation 1074/96, para. 43, 1996 O.J. (L 141) (1996); Ferro-Silicon Originating in Iceland, Norway, Sweden, Venezuela, or Yugoslavia, Council Regulation 341/90, para. 49, 1990 O.J. (L 38) (1990) ("in view of the development of new production units or the enlargement of existing units . . . it is realistic to expect an increase in those two countries' exports to the Community, even if, as certain of their exporters have claimed, this capacity is intended to serve the American and Japanese markets"); Propan-1-ol Originating in the United States of America, Commission Deci-

circumvented by, for example, switching the source of the imports to another country after imposition of measures.[336]

Fourth, the Commission considers whether the domestic industry's current injury or vulnerability is due to subject imports or other factors, such as imports from other countries and Community producers excluded from the definition of Community industry.[337] For example, the EU Commission has refused to allow a measure to expire based on evidence that the market was in a recession which caused the domestic industry to become much more vulnerable to dumped imports.[338] The Commission has also refused to allow a measure to expire when the recession was not shown to affect the product market which otherwise experienced an increase in ap-

---

sion 90/540/EEC, para. 16, 1990 O.J. (L 306) (1990) ("The increased demand in the US domestic market and the enlarged market in third countries for US exports reduce the possibility of a sharp increase of US exports being directed toward the Community. . . .").

[336]Certain Ball Bearings Originating in Japan and Singapore, Council Regulation 2553/93, para. 19-28, 1993 O.J. (L 235) (1993); *see* Light Sodium Carbonate Originating in Bulgaria, the German Democratic Republic, Poland and Romania, Council Regulation 1306/89, para. 26, 1989 O.J. (L 131) (1989) (Commission considers evidence of exporters pricing non-subject product with the same use at same price as subject product despite higher production costs and switching marketing policy to non-subject project as "an indication of their intention to retain a place on the Community market for this class of products.").

[337]Ferro-silicon Originating in Russia, Kazakhstan, Ukraine, Iceland, Norway, Sweden, Venezuela, and Brazil, Council Regulation 3359/93, paras. 72-80, 1993 O.J. (L 302) (1993) (the Commission considers whether current material injury was caused by the effects of dumping or other factors); Silicon Carbide, Originating in the People's Republic of China, Poland, the Russian Federation and Ukraine, Council Regulation 821/94, para. 43, 1994 O.J. (L 94) (1994) (the Commissions considers whether factors other than the low-priced imports might have contributed to the weak situation of the Community industry and especially whether imports from other countries may have contributed to this situation); Potassium Permanganate Originating in the People's Republic of China, Council Regulation 2819/94, para. 40, 1994 O.J. (L 298) (1994); Polyester Yarn Originating in Taiwan and Turkey, Council Regulation 1074/96, 1996 O.J. (L 141) (1996) (noting that the imports from third countries subject to anti-dumping investigations "may have exacerbated the already unfavorable situation of the Community industry").

[338]Ball Bearings With a Greatest External Diameter Exceeding 30 mm Originating in Japan Imposed by Regulation 1739/85, para. 35, 1992 O.J. (L 286) (1992).

parent consumption.[339] Likewise, the Commission will not allow a measure to expire due to imports from other countries if the subject imports remained an important factor which prevented the Community industry from improving its economic situation.[340]

In addition to the injury considerations, the Commission considers whether the Community interest would be served by retaining the measure.[341] In order to determine whether compelling reasons exist to make the measure unwarranted, the Commission considers the interests of the Community industry, consumers, and importers.[342] In assessing the Community interest in the measures, the Commission is required to give special consideration to "the need to eliminate the trade distorting effects of injurious dumping[/subsidization] and to restore effective competition."[343] Post-Uruguay Round law requires the Commission to accept timely submissions on the Community interest issue. The Commission, however, will not take into account information that is not supported by actual evidence which substantiates its validity.

In prior cases, the Commission has considered the level of industry investment in the context of whether the measures are in the Community's interest. For example, in *Woven Polyolefin Sacks and Bags*:

> The investigation has shown that the Community industry has made efforts to rationalize and to switch to production of more specialized types of sacks and bags (such as flexible intermediate bulk containers), indicating that the

---

[339]Polyester Yarn Originating in Taiwan and Turkey, Council Regulation 1074/96, para. 41, 1996 O.J. (L 141) (1996).

[340]Certain Electronic Weighing Scales Originating in Japan, Council Regulation 993/93, para. 86, 1993 O.J. (L 104) (1993); *see* Certain Glass Textile Fibres (Rovings) Originating in Czechoslovakia and the German Democratic Republic, Commission Decision 90/85/EEC, para. 8, 1990 O.J. (L 59) (1990) ("Concerning the foreseeable recurrence of injury or threat of injury after expiry of the anti-dumping measures, the consequences of expiry of the measures were considered in the light of their effectiveness during the period that the duty was in force.").

[341]*See* Council Regulation 384/96, *supra* note 294, at art. 21; Council Regulation 3284/94, *supra* note 294, at art. 22.

[342]Gas-Fuelled, Non-Refillable Pocket Flint Lighters Originating in Thailand, the Philippines and Mexico, paras. 75-78, 1997 O.J. (L 65) (1997); Woven Polyolefin Sacks and Bags Originating in the People's Republic of China, Council Regulation 2003/97, paras. 50-61, 1997 O.J. (L 284) (1997).

[343]Council Regulation 384/96, *supra* note 294, at art. 21; Council Regulation 3284/94, *supra* note 294, at art. 22.

industry can remain viable. *The significant investment made in order to achieve this rationalization would be wasted if the industry concerned is not protected against unfair and injurious imports.* Continuation of anti-dumping measures would serve to put the Community industry on a level playing field with imports . . . by counteracting unfair competitive practices.[344]

In order to determine consumers' interests, the Commission will calculate the cost increase for users.[345] The Commission will also consider whether a price increase would be absorbed by the distribution chain and whether the increase passed on to the consumer would be significant.[346] Finally, measures will be considered for expiration on a country-specific basis.

3. Summary of Affirmative Determinations

A summary of factors that typically weigh in favor of an affirmative EU expiry review is provided below:

- evidence of duty absorption
- third country dumping on the same merchandise
- current injury or vulnerability of the domestic industry
- significant investment in future production by domestic industry
- significant price undercutting by imports with current measures in force
- ample production capacity of exporters
- significant market share of imports
- significant rate of increased imports
- increased market share
- circumvention of the current measures
- Community interest would be served by retaining measure
- failure of respondents to participate in review
- affirmative finding that dumping continued
- market conditions and circumstances of exporters
- level of current dumping margins
- affirmative finding that dumping margins have increased

[344]Woven Polyolefin Sacks and Bags Originating in the People's Republic of China, Council Regulation 2003/97, para. 55, 1997 O.J. (L 284) (1997) (emphasis added).

[345]*Id.* at para. 58.

[346]Gas-Fuelled, Non-Refillable Pocket Flint Lighters Originating in Thailand, the Philippines and Mexico, Council Regulation 423/97, para. 77, 1997 O.J. (L 65) (1997).

C. *SUBSEQUENT SUNSET REVIEWS*

If the Commission decides to continue the measure after an expiry review, the measure will expire again five years from the date of the conclusion of the most recent review which has covered both dumping and injury.[347] In order for a measure to survive, the Commission must determine in another expiry review that expiry would be likely to lead to a continuation or recurrence of dumping or subsidization and injury.

D. *APPEALS OF EXPIRY REVIEW DETERMINATIONS*

Council decisions are appealable to the Court of First Instance and then to the European Court of Justice.[348]

E. *A POST-URUGUAY ROUND EXPIRY REVIEW*

In order to gain a more complete understanding of how the Commission conducts its expiry reviews, a description of one recent post-Uruguay Round expiry review is provided as an example.

1. The Expiry Review Schedule

On October 13, 1997, the Commission issued its determination to impose definitive antidumping duties on woven polyolefin sacks and bags

---

[347]Council Regulation 384/96, *supra* note 294, at art. 11(2); Council Regulation 3284/94, *supra* note 294, at art. 13(2). Under pre-Uruguay Round law, however, the Commission had occasion to alter the expiration deadline for a subsequent review. *See* Stanbrook & Bentley, *supra* note 37, at 205. For example, in *Plain Paper Photocopiers*, the Commission published its notice of expiry in August 1991 and completed its determination continuing the measures in October 1995. Due to the length of the proceedings, the Commission continued the measures for only an additional two years, rather than five additional years. Plain Paper Photocopiers Originating in Japan, Council Regulation 2380/95, paras. 3, 103, 1995 O.J. (L 244) (1995).

[348]Stanbrook & Bentley, *supra* note 37, at 14; Montag & Fiebig, supra note 34, at 118-19, *citing* Council Decision 93/350, 1993 O.J. (L 144) 21 (1993), *as amended* Council Decision, 1994 O.J. (L 66) 29 (1994).

from the People's Republic of China.[349] The original regulation had imposed definitive antidumping duties on November 17, 1990. The Commission issued a notice of the impending expiry of the measures on April 19, 1995. In response, the Commission received a request for an expiry review as well as an interim review from the European Association for Textile Polyolefins on behalf of eight Community producers allegedly representing a major proportion of the total production of the product in the European Community. On October 17, 1995, the Commission issued its notice of initiation of an expiry/interim review and requested comments within 10 days on the appropriateness of Turkey as an appropriate market economy third country to establish normal value. In addition, the notice required interested parties to present their views and information within 37 days as well as request a hearing.[350]

During the review, the Commission received comments from a number of importers and one organization representing importers. In addition, questionnaire responses were received from four Community producers and two importers. The Commission noted, however, that its investigation was hampered by the fact that no Chinese exporters replied to the Commission's questionnaire or made their views known in writing.[351] The Commission conducted an on-site investigation at seven companies, including producers, exporters, and importers.[352]

2. A Seven-Part Decision

The Commission's decision in *Woven Polyolefin Sacks and Bags* is divided into seven parts. The procedural section provides a brief summary of the scope of the original decision and background to the review which is followed by sections on the like product, likelihood of continuation or recurrence of dumping, the Community industry, the likelihood of recur-

[349]Woven Polyolefin Sacks and Bags Originating in the People's Republic of China, Council Regulation 2003/97, 1997 O.J. (L 284) 1 (1997).

[350]Notice of Initiation of a Review of the Anti-Dumping Measures Applicable to Imports of Sacks and Bags Made of Polyethylene or Polypropylene Originating in the People's Republic of China, 1995 O.J. (C 271) 3-4 (1995).

[351]Woven Polyolefin Sacks and Bags Originating in the People's Republic of China, Council Regulation 2003/97, para. 6, 1997 O.J. (L 284) (1997).

[352]*Id.* at para. 7.

rence or continuation of injury, the Community interest, and antidumping measures.

In the review, the Commission reconsidered its like product determination and found that imported sacks and bags produced and sold in Turkey, the analogue market economy, constituted a like product to those exported from the People's Republic of China and to those produced and sold by the Community industry.[353] The Commission also considered whether Community producers supporting the request for review and cooperating with the investigation represented a major proportion of total Community production.[354] In this review, the Commission found that four producers that had cooperated with the review manufactured a major share (at least 65%) of the Community's total output. Therefore, the Commission found that the four producers constituted the "Community industry" for purposes of the investigation.

3. The Decision

The Commission's analysis in the *Woven Polyolefin Sacks and Bags* expiry review covered the period January 1 to September 30, 1995, in its dumping investigation and the period January 1, 1992, to September 30, 1995, in its injury investigation.[355] With respect to the likelihood of continuation or recurrence of dumping, the Commission considered whether dumping continued to take place based on a calculation of normal values and export prices. Because no Chinese producer responded to the questionnaire, the Commission was forced to use importer pricing data as best evidence available to establish the export price.[356] As a result, the Commission calculated a weighted-average dumping margin of 102.4%.

With respect to the injury analysis, the Commission was required to make two determinations due to the fact that it was conducting simultaneous expiry and interim reviews. First, the Commission was required to determine whether expiry of the measures would be likely to lead to a continuation or recurrence of injury for the expiry review, and, second, whether the measures were either no longer necessary or were no longer sufficient to

[353] *Id.* at para. 12.

[354] *Id.* at para. 27, *citing* Council Regulation 384/96, *supra* note 294, at art. 4(1).

[355] *Id.* at para. 8.

[356] *Id.* at paras. 13-26.

counteract the dumping which is causing injury for the interim review. The Commission considered Community consumption, volume and market share of dumped imports, prices of dumped imports, factors relating to the Community industry, and price undercutting in the event of expiry. [357]

In its decision, the Commission noted that despite declines in Chinese import volume and market share, the Chinese imports retained a significant market share of 6.1% in 1995. The Commission further observed the Chinese producers' ability to undercut Community producers even with antidumping measures in place contributed to the downward pressure on prices in the Community market.[358] The Commission calculated an average margin of undercutting of Community producers' prices by Chinese prices of 15.3%.[359] The Commission made a second calculation of undercutting of 52.9% which was the threatened level of undercutting in the event of expiry of the measures.[360]

With respect to factors relating to the Community industry, the Commission noted the falling production, sales volumes, sales values, and increasing losses and concluded that the industry was in a "weakened state" which would be exacerbated in the event of undercutting on the scale which would arise should the measures against imports from China expire.[361] Therefore, the Commission concluded that the level of undercutting would be dramatically increased if the measures were to expire, providing a strong incentive for Chinese producers to increase their exports to the Community and creating further downward pressure on Community producers' prices. As a result, the Commission decided that expiry of the measures would be likely to lead to a recurrence of injury.[362]

With respect to the issue of Community interest, the Commission noted that no users of sacks and bags made submissions in the investigation which was a sign that the antidumping measures had a limited effect on their interests.[363] The Commission also observed that the market for sacks and bags had increased even though Chinese imports had declined demonstrating a lack of short supply. Finally, the Commission found it relevant

---

[357] *Id.* at paras. 28-49.
[358] *Id.* at paras. 31-32.
[359] *Id.* at para. 37.
[360] *Id.* at para. 44.
[361] *Id.* at paras. 38-43.
[362] *Id.* at paras. 46-48.
[363] *Id.* at para. 50.

that Community producers had made efforts to rationalize and to switch to production of more specialized types of bags and sacks to remain viable. The Commission refused to jeopardize this investment by subjecting Community producers to unfair and injurious imports. The Commission also anticipated that the effect on the competitiveness of Community users as compared to third country users would be minimal because of the small cost increase caused by the measures. Further, the Commission noted that importers were able to switch to other sources of supply and did not expect the impact of any increase in duties on importers to be substantial.

For these reasons, the Commission found that there were "no compelling reasons not to maintain the measures in force, amended according to the outcome of the review, in order to restore a competitive regime of fair pricing and to remove the threat of injury to the Community industry which would result if the measures were allowed to expire."[364] The Commission, therefore, repealed the original regulation imposing antidumping duties and enacted a new regulation imposing definitive antidumping duties for a five year period. As part of the interim review portion of the investigation, the Commission then recalculated the antidumping duty margins.[365]

---

[364]*Id.* at paras. 51, 55, 57-58, 60-61.

[365]*Id.* at para. 65, art. 1.

CHAPTER IV

Canadian Sunset Reviews: Legislation and Practice

A. *INITIATING EXPIRY REVIEWS*

In order to implement the Antidumping and Subsidies Agreements, Canada enacted the World Trade Organization Agreement Implementation Act in 1994.[366] Although Canada enacted implementing legislation and regulations to reflect Uruguay Round changes in the antidumping and countervailing duty law, Canada did not revise Section 76 of the Special Import Measures Act which provides for the automatic expiration of antidumping and countervailing duty orders after five years unless the CITT has initiated a review before expiration of the five year period. The review period was, however, extended to five years for undertakings in the WTO implementing legislation.[367] The CITT also issued special guidelines on November 20, 1996, regarding changes in the CITT's practice in expiry reviews. The following sections, therefore, will review CITT practice in light of pre- and post-Uruguay Round expiry reviews.

---

[366]*See* Steger, *supra* note 55, at 244, *citing* Stats. Can. 1994, c. 47.

[367]An Act to Implement the Agreement Establishing the World Trade Organization, ch. 47, §§175, 186, 1994 S.C. (Can.), *reprinted in* WTO Committee on Anti-Dumping and Practices & Committee on Subsidies and Countervailing Measures, *Notification of Laws and Regulations Under Articles 18.5 and 32.6 of the Agreements: Canada*, G/ADP/N/1/CAN/1, G/SCM/N/1/CAN/1.

1. Grouping Sunset Reviews and Cumulation

With respect to grouping reviews, the CITT issued guidelines in November 1996 which adopted the following practice:

> Where there are orders or findings with dates of expiry up to one year apart concerning identical goods, or goods which the Tribunal considers to closely resemble each other, the Tribunal has adopted the following practice:
>
> - The Tribunal intends to issue a single notice of expiry in respect of the various orders or findings inviting persons or governments to make submissions requesting or opposing the review of each order or finding.
> - The Tribunal will make a separate decision as to whether a review of each order or finding is warranted.
> - If the Tribunal decides to review one or more of the orders or findings, it intends, where circumstances of fairness permit, to conduct a single review.
> - With respect to orders or findings concerning goods that closely resemble each other, the notice of expiry will invite the views of persons or governments on whether the orders or findings should not be joined in a single review.[368]

Thus, the CITT will group orders with anniversary dates up to one year apart. If the CITT decides to conduct a review, the CITT will issue a notice of review which states whether or not a single review will be conducted.[369]

The CITT will also make a cumulative assessment of the threat of dumping in expiry review proceedings. For example, in *Certain Carbon Steel Welded Pipe,* the CITT rejected foreign interested parties' argument that the CITT should not cumulatively assess the effects of a threat of dumping of Romanian goods with those of other countries subject to the order because Romanian goods were "negligible" because they had not been exported to Canada in the last five years. The CITT found, however, that the negligibility requirement did not apply to expiry reviews and that its cu-

---

[368]CITT, *Guideline: Changes in the Tribunal's Practice in Proceedings Related to the Expiry of Orders and Findings and To Reviews Under Section 76 of the "Special Import Measures Act"* 3 (Nov. 20, 1996).

[369]*See, e.g.,* Notice of Review of Finding Concerning Certain Carbon Steel Plate and Alloy Steel Plate, Review No.: RR-97-006, at 1 (Nov. 20, 1997).

mulative assessment of the threat of dumping in an expiry review was consistent with the Canadian statute and the WTO Agreement.[370]

2. Self-Initiation and Requests for Expiry Reviews

Pursuant to Section 76(2) of the SIMA, the CITT may on its own initiative or at the request of the Deputy Minister or any other person or government review an order or finding and rehear any matter before deciding it. According to Section 76(3), however, the CITT shall not initiate a review at the request of any person or government "unless the person or government satisfies the Tribunal that a review is warranted."[371] Thus, the CITT conducts a full expiry review only if a request for review contains adequate information and is found to be "warranted." If the CITT finds that a request for review asking for continuation of an order is inadequate, the CITT concludes that a review is "not warranted." There does not appear to be any expedited review procedure.

In order to determine whether a review is "warranted," the CITT issues a notice of expiry not later than eight months before the expiry of an order or finding.[372] According to the CITT rules, the notice shall contain the following information:

> (a) the date on which the order or finding will be deemed to be rescinded;
> (b) the date on or before which any written submission must be filed by interested parties requesting or opposing the initiation of a review of the order or finding;
> (c) the number of copies of each written submission that must be filed;
> (d) instructions with respect to the filing or confidential information;
> (e) the address to which written submissions or correspondence may be sent or delivered and at which information may be obtained; and
> (f) such other information as the Tribunal specifies.[373]

---

[370]Certain Carbon Steel Welded Pipe Originating In or Exported From Argentina, India, Romania, Taiwan, Thailand, Venezuela and Brazil, Review No.: RR-95-002, at 8-9 (July 25, 1996).

[371]Special Import Measures Act, ch. 25, §76(2) & (3), 1996 S.C. (Can.).

[372]CITT, *Guideline: Changes in the Tribunal's Practice in Proceedings Related to the Expiry of Orders and Findings and To Reviews Under Section 76 of the "Special Import Measures Act"* 1 (Nov. 20, 1996); CITT Rules, Can. Gaz. Pt. II, §72 (1991).

[373]CITT Rules, Can. Gaz. Pt. II, §72 (1991).

In its notice of expiry for an antidumping review, for example, the CITT will also ask interested parties to submit information concerning:

- the likelihood of the resumption of dumped imports if the finding were allowed to expire, with supporting information, including information relating to exporters in [countries] with regard to their activities in the Canadian market, their domestic market and other markets;
- the likely volumes and price ranges of dumped imports if they were to resume;
- the domestic industry's performance since the findings, including trends in its production, sales, market share and profits;
- the likelihood of material injury to the domestic industry if the findings were allowed to expire, having regard to the anticipated effects of a resumption of dumped imports on the industry's future performance;
- other developments affecting, or likely to affect, the performance of the domestic industry; and
- any other change in circumstances, domestically or internationally, including changes in the supply and demand for [the product], as well as changes in trends and sources of imports into Canada.[374]

Persons and governments have approximately one month to make submissions requesting or opposing a review of the order or finding. If the CITT receives opposing submissions, the CITT will circulate all submissions to each person or government that has filed a submission for rebuttal comments within one week. The CITT makes its adequacy determination on the basis of those submissions.

When the CITT receives response(s) in support of continuation, the CITT will determine whether the request for review is adequate based on a consideration of the party's response to its request for information. The issue is whether the party requesting a review has provided sufficient information to justify initiation of a review; the adequacy of submissions from parties opposing the review and continuation of the finding is not consid-

---

[374]Notice of Expiry of Findings Preformed Fibreglass Pipe Insulation With a Vapour Barrier, Expiry No.: LE-97-006, at 1 (Feb. 18, 1998). As shown below, the information requested by the CITT is similar to the information that will be requested by the U.S. International Trade Commission.

ered.[375] For example, in *Flat Wooden Toothpicks*, the CITT rejected the request from the sole domestic producer for a review when the producer failed to submit information supporting claims of excess capacity; import prices; domestic prices, production, sales, margins, or profits; exports of subject goods into other markets; import competition; or other information requested in the notice.[376] Likewise, the CITT refused to initiate a review in *Butt Weld Fittings* where insufficient information was provided to support the allegation that dumping in Canada would resume and no information was provided to assess the conditions of the domestic market and domestic industry since the last review.[377] In *Alpine Ski Poles*, the CITT explained that "a relatively broad range of information is required" to support a request for review, such as data on the activities of exporters in their own and other markets:

> Mere allegations do not provide an adequate basis to address the question of dumping in a review . . . Even if the submission had satisfied the need for meaningful information on dumping, to initiate a review, the Tribunal needs a basis to assess the likelihood of material injury resulting from the dumping . . . In the absence of data such as volumes and values of production, and financial and market information, the Tribunal does not consider that it has sufficient information to determine that a review is warranted.[378]

---

[375]*See, e.g.*, Statement of Reasons, Alpine Ski Poles of Aluminum Alloy Originating In or Exported from France and Italy, Expiry No.: LE-91-001, at 1-2 (July 25, 1991); Statement of Reasons, Rubber Hockey Pucks, With The Exception of Sponge Rubber Pucks, Originating In or Exported from Czechoslovakia and the German Democratic Republic, Expiry No.: LE-90-006, at 2 (Dec. 19, 1990).

[376]Statement of Reasons, Flat Wooden Toothpicks Originating In or Exported From the United States of America and Produced by or on Behalf of Forster Mfg. Co. Inc. of Wilton, Maine, Its Successors and Assigns, Expiry No.: LE-96-003, at 1-2 (Oct. 22, 1996); *see* Rubber Hockey Pucks, With The Exception of Sponge Rubber Pucks, Originating In or Exported from Czechoslovakia and the German Democratic Republic, Expiry No. LE-90-006, at 2 (Dec. 19, 1990) (CITT refused to initiate review when request did not include information regarding exports to other markets and did not include comprehensive information on levels and trends in domestic production, sales, prices and profits.).

[377]Statement of Reasons, Butt Weld Fittings Originating In or Exported from Japan, Expiry No.: LE-91-004 (Dec. 6, 1991).

[378]Statement of Reasons, Alpine Ski Poles of Aluminum Alloy Originating In or Exported from France and Italy, Expiry No.: LE-91-001, at 3 (July 25, 1991).

In addition, information should be provided concerning the marketing practices of foreign exporters that would show how they would respond to rescission of the finding.[379]

B. *THE EXPIRY REVIEW*

1. Deadlines

If the CITT decides to conduct a review, the CITT issues a notice of review which states whether or not a single review will be conducted.[380] The notice of review also includes a schedule for the conduct of the review including deadlines for the filing of briefs and a hearing. A recent review established the following deadlines:[381]

Day	*Event*
1	Notice of Expiry of Findings
35	Comments
42	Rebuttal Comments
106	Notice of Review of Finding and Schedule
131	Distribution of Questionnaires
131	Notice of Appearances, Declarations and Undertakings
168	Replies to all Questionnaires
204	Distribution of Tribunal Exhibits, Including the Research Staff Report
217	Manufacturers' Cases
To be confirmed	Interrogatories by Importers, Exporters, and Other Parties, and Replies by Manufacturers
229	Importers', Exporters', and Other Parties' Cases
To be confirmed	Interrogatories by Manufacturers and Replies by Importers, Exporters and Other Parties
239	Manufacturers' Reply Submissions
251	Public Hearing
272	Order and Statement of Reasons Issued

[379] *See* Statement of Reasons, Plain Hardboard Sheets or Panels Originating In or Exported from the Union of Soviet Socialist Republics and Poland, Expiry No.: LE-90-005, at 2 (Aug. 31, 1990).

[380] *See, e.g.,* Notice of Review of Finding Concerning Certain Carbon Steel Plate and Alloy Steel Plate, Review No.: RR-97-006, at 1 (Nov. 20, 1997).

Thus, an expiry review will normally be completed well within a year of initiation. During a review, the CITT issues questionnaires to the domestic industry, sales agencies, importers, and/or purchasers.[382] Based on those questionnaires, the CITT's research staff prepares a pre-hearing staff report. In addition, interested parties have the ability to seek responses to interrogatories from opposing parties.[383] The CITT conducts hearings and, like the EU Commission, issues one, final decision. The CITT also conducts meetings with interested parties to obtain additional information.[384]

In the 1996 CITT Guidelines for expiry reviews, the CITT suggests that interested parties should "endeavour to base their submissions exclusively on public information" because expiry proceedings are expected to deal primarily with issues raised in the CITT's public statement of reasons.[385] If necessary, the CITT will accept confidential submissions and provides for the filing of those documents. The CITT also allows anyone to have access to the public record of an expiry proceeding.

2. No Early Expiry of Orders or Findings

When the CITT does not receive any responses to its notice of expiry, the CITT allows the order or finding to expire if it decides not to self-initiate a review.[386] The CITT will not, however, allow the order or finding to expire prior to the fifth year anniversary in the absence of a showing of

---

[381] Notice of Expiry of Findings Concerning Certain Carbon Steel Plate and Alloy Steel Plate, Expiry No.: LE-97-003 (Aug. 6, 1997); Notice of Review of Finding Concerning Certain Carbon Steel Plate and Alloy Steel Plate, Review No.: RR-97-006 (Nov. 20, 1997).

[382] *See, e.g.,* Fresh, Whole, Yellow Onions, Originating In or Exported From the United States of America, For Use or Consumption in the Province of British Columbia, Review No.: RR-96-005, at 1 (May 21, 1997).

[383] *See, e.g., id.* at 2 (CITT grants motion of foreign interested parties seeking a response to interrogatories served on domestic industry.).

[384] Photo Albums with Self-Adhesive Leaves, Imported Together or Separately, and Self-Adhesive Leaves, Originating In or Exported from the Republic of Korea, Hong Kong, the People's Republic of China, Singapore, Malaysia, Taiwan, Indonesia, Thailand and the Philippines, Review No.: RR-94-006, at 2 (Aug. 25, 1995).

[385] CITT, *Guideline: Changes in the Tribunal's Practice in Proceedings Related to the Expiry of Orders and Findings and to Reviews Under Section 76 of the "Special Import Measures Act"* 1 (Nov. 20, 1996).

[386] *See* Notice of Expiry of Findings Concerning Certain Carbon Steel Plate and Alloy Steel Plate, Expiry No.: LE-97-003, at 2 (Aug. 6, 1997) ("If the Tribunal decides that

significant changed circumstances. For example, in *Subsidized Grain Corn*, submissions from a number of agricultural and industrial corn users requested the expiry of the finding prior to the fifth year anniversary.[387] The CITT, however, concluded that "[i]n the absence of any significantly changed circumstances, the Tribunal is not satisfied that a review to consider this matter is warranted, also keeping in mind the opposition to early expiry by two of the initial complainants."[388]

3. The Likelihood Tests

As explained above, Canada did not substantively revise its sunset review provisions in response to Uruguay Round changes. According to Section 76(5) of the Special Import Measures Act, an antidumping or countervailing duty order or finding would be revoked as of the expiration of five years without the initiation of a review. Based on a review of recent post-Uruguay Round cases, it appears that the CITT has not changed the substantive review standard developed during the course of pre-Uruguay Round expiry reviews. Therefore, this section discusses pre- and post-Uruguay Round expiry reviews without distinction.

To determine whether to continue an order, the CITT engages in a two-part inquiry. First, the CITT would determine whether there exists a likelihood that dumping[389] or subsidization will resume[390] if the order is re-

---

a review is not warranted, an order, with reasons, will be issued. An order or finding will expire unless a review is initiated before its expiry date."); Gasoline Powered Chain Saws Originating In or Exported From the Federal Republic of Germany, Sweden and the United States of America, Expiry No.: LE-91-006 (Feb. 17, 1992); CITT Rules, Can. Gaz. Pt. II, §72(1991).

[387]Subsidized Grain Corn in All Forms, Excluding Seed Corn, Sweet Corn and Popping Corn, Originating in or Exported from the United States of America, Expiry No.: LE-91-003, at 2 (Jan. 15, 1992).

[388]*Id.*

[389]*See, e.g.*, Certain Carbon Steel Welded Pipe Originating In or Exported From Argentina, India, Romania, Taiwan, Thailand, Venezuela, and Brazil, Review No.: RR-95-002, at 10 (July 25, 1996).

[390]Boneless Manufacturing Beef Originating in or Exported from the European Economic Community in Respect of Which Subsidies Have Been Paid Directly or Indirectly By the European Economic Community and/or the Government of a Member State, Review No.: RR-90-006, at 13, 15-16 (July 22, 1991).

scinded. Second, the CITT would determine whether the resumption of dumped or subsidized imports would be likely to cause material injury.[391] In making these determinations, the CITT will consider the relevant economic indicators in the market over the five year period, including apparent consumption, volume and values of imports and domestic shipments, relative market shares, number of producers, domestic production capacity, capacity utilization, and employment.[392]

a. *The CITT's Determination of Likelihood of Continuation or Recurrence of Dumping or Subsidization*

In order to determine whether exporters have a high propensity to dump, the CITT would consider "enforcement data" provided by Revenue Canada regarding dumping margins during the five year review period.[393] The "fact that anti-dumping duties have been collected while an anti-dumping duty action is in force is an indicator of a likelihood of resumed

---

[391]*Id. Compare* Deep Tillage Sweeps, Field Cultivator Sweeps, Reversible Points, Reversible Heavy Duty Chisels, Reversible Twisted Chisels and Reversible Furrow Shovels, Known as Tillage or Earth Engaging Tools, Used on Chisel Plows and Field Cultivators, Originating in or Exported from Brazil, Review No. RR-93-001, at 7 (Nov. 23, 1993), *with* Aluminum Coil Stock and Steel Head and Bottom Rails, for Use in the Production of Horizontal Venetian Blinds, Originating in or Exported from Sweden, Review No. RR-96-002, at 7 (Feb. 6, 1997). The SIMA does not define the term "material injury." Nevertheless, the CITT typically considers evidence of serious price erosion or suppression, loss of market share, underutilization of capacity, and decreased profitability to support a finding of material injury. Shane B. Brown, Richard S. Gottlieb & Darrel H. Pearson, 5 INTERNATIONAL TRADE LAWS OF CANADA: SPECIAL IMPORT MEASURES 34 (R.S. Gottlieb & D.H. Peason eds., 1992); *see* CITT Rules, Can. Gaz. Pt. II, §61 (1991).

[392]Certain Oil and Gas Well Casing Made of Carbon Steel Originating in or Exported from the Republic of Korea and the United States of America, Review No.: RR-95-001, at 12 (July 5, 1996); Fresh Iceberg (Head) Lettuce Originating in or Exported from the United States of America, Review No.: RR-97-002, at 5 (Nov. 28, 1997).

[393]*See, e.g.*, Machine Tufted Carpeting with Pile Predominantly of Nylon, Other Polyamide, Polyester or Polypropylene Yarns, Excluding Automotive Carpeting and Floor Coverings of an Area Less Than Five Square Metres, Originating in or Exported from the United States of America, Review No.: RR-96-004, at 13-14 (May 8, 1997) ("The Tribunal can only conclude that, if these exporters are not pricing up to normal values while the finding is being enforced, there is every likelihood that they will continue to dump machine tufted carpeting in the absence of the finding.").

dumping."[394] The CITT will also consider, among other things, the length of time measures have been in place in deciding whether an order should be rescinded.[395] For example, in *Twisted Polypropylene and Nylon Rope Originating in or Exported from the Republic of Korea*, the CITT noted that "past performance can, in some instances, provide an indication of future intentions, the dumping of the subject [merchandise] . . . by the [foreign manufacturers] . . . occurred many years ago."[396] Therefore, the CITT considered it "more appropriate to draw conclusions based on the [foreign manufacturers'] . . . behavior in the more recent past."[397]

The fact that antidumping or countervailing duties were collected after the order was in place is not determinative.[398] In addition to enforcement data, the CITT will consider whether the past, recent, and current behavior of exporters and market conditions in the countries of origin, Canada, and elsewhere made it likely that dumping or subsidization would resume in the foreseeable future (within the next year or two).[399] In order to determine whether exporters would resume dumping in the "foreseeable future," the CITT "looks for persuasive evidence that the recent behavior of exporters and market conditions in the countries of origin, Canada and elsewhere make it likely that dumping will resume in the foreseeable future." [400] Therefore, the CITT "typically focuses on circumstances in the next year or two and places considerably less weight on the possibility of dumping sometime later in the five-year period during which a finding might be continued." The CITT has considered evidence of other factors including the pricing of sub-

[394]Certain Waterproof Rubber Footwear Originating in or Exported from Czechoslovakia, Poland, the Republic of Korea, Taiwan, Hong Kong, Malaysia, Yugoslavia and the People's Republic of China, Review No.: RR-97-001, at 11 (Oct. 20, 1997).

[395]*See* Twisted Polypropylene and Nylon Rope Originating in or Exported from the Republic of Korea, Review No.: RR-96-003, at 7 (Feb. 21, 1997).

[396]*Id.* at 8.

[397]*Id.*

[398]*See id.;* Photo Albums With Self-Adhesive Leaves, Imported Together or Separately, and Self-Adhesive Leaves Originating In or Exported From the Republic of Korea, Hong Kong, the People's Republic of China, Singapore, Malaysia, Taiwan, Indonesia, Thailand and the Philippines, Review No.: RR-94-006, at 9 (Aug. 25, 1995).

[399]*See* Stainless Steel Bars and Stainless Steel Wire in Cut Lengths, Originating In or Exported From Brazil, the Federal Republic of Germany, France, Japan, the Republic of Korea, and Spain, Review No.: RR-89-009, at 9 (July 20, 1990).

[400]Stainless Steel Bars and Stainless Steel Wire in Cut Lengths, Originating in or Exported from Brazil, the Federal Republic of Germany, France, Japan, the Republic of Korea, and Spain, Review No.: RR-89-009, at 9 (July 20, 1990).

ject goods by the named countries in other foreign countries or the pricing of other related products produced by those same countries.[401] The CITT has also relied on evidence, *inter alia*, of excess production capacity of foreign exporters and dumping actions against imports in other countries and orders against related products in Canada to support a finding that dumping would be likely in the absence of the order.[402] According to the CITT, exporters that have lost market share in their domestic market are likely to attempt to regain lost market share elsewhere, including Canada.[403]

---

[401]*See* Photo Albums With Pocket, Slip-In or Flip-Up Style Sheets (Imported Together or Separately), and Refill Sheets Thereof, Originating in or Exported from Japan, the Republic of Korea, the People's Republic of China, Hong Kong, Taiwan, Singapore, Malaysia and the Federal Republic of Germany, Review No.: RR-92-003, at 9 (Feb. 25, 1993).

[402]*Id.* at 10-11; *see* Deep Tillage Sweeps, Field Cultivator Sweeps, Reversible Points, Reversible Heavy Duty Chisels, Reversible Twisted Chisels and Reversible Furrow Shovels, Known as Tillage or Earth Engaging Tools, Used on Chisel Plows and Field Cultivators, Originating in or Exported from Brazil, Review No.: RR-93-001, at 8 (Nov. 23, 1993); Paint Brushes Using Natural Hog Bristle as the Filament Material, and the Components Thereof Known as "Heads," Originating in or Exported from the People's Republic of China, Review No.: RR-93-003, at 11 (Jan. 18, 1994); Women's Leather Boots and Shoes Originating in or Exported from Brazil, the People's Republic of China and Taiwan; Women's Leather Boots Originating in or Exported from Poland, Romania and the [Former] Yugoslavia; and Women's Non-Leather Boots and Shoes Originating in or Exported From the People's Republic of China and Taiwan, Review No.: RR-94-003, at 20 (May 16, 1995); Carbon Steel Welded Pipe in the Nominal Size Range 12.7 mm to 406.4 mm (1/2 in. to 16 in.) Inclusive, In Various Forms and Finishes, Usually Supplied to Meet ASTM A53, ASTM A120, ASTM A252, ASTM A589 or AWWA C200-80 or Equivalent Specifications, Including Water Well Casing, Piling Pipe, Sprinkler Pipe and Fencing Pipe, But Excluding Oil and Gas Line Pipe Made to API Specifications Exclusively, Originating In or Exported From the Republic of Korea, Review No.: RR-94-004, at 8-9 (June 5, 1995). If a review of normal values has not been conducted for several years prior to the expiry review, the CITT will then consider a number of different factors, including the pricing of subject goods by the named countries in foreign countries or the pricing of other related products produced by those same countries. *See* Photo Albums With Pocket, Slip-In or Flip-Up Style Sheets (Imported Together or Separately), and Refill Sheets Thereof, Originating in or Exported from Japan, the Republic of Korea, the People's Republic of China, Hong Kong, Taiwan, Singapore, Malaysia and the Federal Republic of Germany, Review No.: 92-003, at 7-9 (Feb. 25, 1993).

[403]Machine Tufted Carpeting with Pile Predominantly of Nylon, Other Polyamide, Polyester or Polypropylene Yarns, Excluding Automotive Carpeting and Floor Coverings

Finally, the CITT has considered evidence of "circumvention" in deciding whether dumping or subsidization was likely to resume.[404] In the case of *Whole Potatoes from the State of Washington*, the CITT found that evidence of U.S. producers circumventing the antidumping order by shipping non-subject grades of potatoes at times when the U.S. price for those potatoes was below established normal values supported a finding of the likelihood of resumed dumping. Likewise, in *Carbon Steel Welded Pipe from the Republic of Korea*, the CITT relied on evidence that Korean exporters had attempted to circumvent the antidumping order by describing the subject goods as non-subject goods at the time of entry into Canada.[405] And in *Photo Albums*, the CITT based its finding of a strong likelihood of resumed dumping on its observation that the sourcing of dumped imports shifted from country to country as new findings were issued ("country switching"). Therefore, the CITT in that case refused to allow the findings to expire on some countries and not on others.[406]

---

of an Area Less Than Five Square Metres, Originating in or Exported from the United States of America, Review No.: RR-96-004, at 18 (May 8, 1997).

[404]Whole Potatoes With Netted or Russeted Skin, Excluding Seed Potatoes, in Non-Size A, Also Commonly Known as Strippers, Originating In or Exported From the State of Washington, United States of America, For Use or Consumption In the Province of British Columbia, Review No.: RR-89-010, at 10-11 (Sept. 14, 1990).

[405]Carbon Steel Welded Pipe in the Nominal Size Range 12.7 mm to 406.4 mm (1/2 in. to 16 in.) Inclusive, In Various Forms and Finishes, Usually Supplied to Meet ASTM A53, ASTM A120, ASTM A252, ASTM A589 or AWWA C200-80 or Equivalent Specifications, Including Water Well Casing, Piling Pipe, Sprinkler Pipe and Fencing Pipe, But Excluding Oil and Gas Line Pipe Made to API Specifications Exclusively, Originating In or Exported From the Republic of Korea, Review No.: RR-94-004, at 9 (June 5, 1995).

[406]*See* Photo Albums With Self-Adhesive Leaves, Imported Together or Separately, and Self-Adhesive Leaves, Originating In or Exported From the Republic of Korea, Hong Kong, the People's Republic of China, Singapore, Malaysia, Taiwan, Indonesia, Thailand, and the Philippines, Review No.: RR-94-006, at 10-11 (Aug. 25, 1996); *see also* Waterproof Rubber Footwear Originating In or Exported from Czechoslovakia, Poland, the Republic of Korea, Taiwan, Hong Kong, Malaysia, Yugoslavia and the People's Republic of China, Review No.: RR-92-001, at 10 (Oct. 21, 1992).

b. *The CITT's Determination of the Likelihood of Continuation or Recurrence of Injury*

If the evidence suggested a high propensity to dump or to receive subsidies, the CITT would consider whether such dumping or subsidization was likely to be materially injurious. In the context of its injury determination, the CITT will also reconsider regional industry and like product determinations.[407] In order to determine whether the domestic industry is vulnerable and that injury would prove to be material, the CITT has considered factors including changes in import shares, the health of the domestic industry, market conditions, marketing practices of importers, idle capacity,[408] and any other changes in circumstances that might render the domestic industry more or less vulnerable than at the time of the original finding.[409] In particular, the CITT considers evidence of supply and de-

---

[407]*See, e.g.*, Fresh, Whole, Yellow Onions, Originating in or Exported from the United States of America, For Use or Consumption in the Province of British Columbia, Review No.: RR-96-005, at 7 (May 21, 1997) (regional industry determination); Machine Tufted Carpeting with Pile Predominantly of Nylon, Other Polyamide, Polyester or Polypropylene Yarns, Excluding Automotive Carpeting and Floor Coverings of an Area Less Than Five Square Metres, Originating in or Exported from the United States of America, Review No.: RR-96-004, at 12 (May 8, 1997) (like product determination).

[408]Photo Albums With Pocket, Slip-In or Flip-Up Style Sheets (Imported Together or Separately), and Refill Sheets Thereof, Originating in or Exported from Japan, the Republic of Korea, the People's Republic of China, Hong Kong, Taiwan, Singapore, Malaysia and the Federal Republic of Germany, Review No.: RR-92-003, at 12-13 (Feb. 25, 1993).

[409]Stainless Steel Bars and Stainless Steel Wire in Cut Lengths, Originating in or Exported from Brazil, the Federal Republic of Germany, France, Japan, the Republic of Korea, and Spain, Review No.: RR-89-009, at 11-13 (July 20, 1990); Certain Dumped Integral Horsepower Induction Motors, One Horsepower (1 HP) to Two Hundred Horsepower (200 HP) Inclusive, With Exceptions, Originating in or Exporting from the United States of America, Review No.: RR-89-013 (Oct. 10, 1990); *see* Carbon Steel Welded Pipe in the Nominal Size Range 12.7 mm to 406.4 mm (1/2 in. to 16 in.) Inclusive, In Various Forms and Finishes, Usually Supplied to Meet ASTM A53, ASTM A120, ASTM A252, ASTM A589 or AWWA C200-80 or Equivalent Specifications, Including Water Well Casing, Piling Pipe, Sprinkler Pipe and Fencing Pipe, But Excluding Oil and Gas Line Pipe Made to API Specifications Exclusively, Originating In or Exported From the Republic of Korea, Review No.: RR-94-004, at 10 (June 5, 1995). The CITT would consider the market, production, and pricing developments since the last review. *See* Paint Brushes Using Natural Hog Bristle as the Filament Material, and the Components

mand conditions in the domestic market and conditions of competition.[410] For example, the CITT has considered evidence that recessions affected customer purchases and adversely affected market conditions for the domestic industry.[411]

That the cause of an industry's current difficulties was due to factors unrelated to dumping would not preclude the CITT from finding that resumption of dumping would cause material injury. For example, in *Twisted Polypropylene and Nylon Rope Originating in or Exported from the Republic of Korea*,[412] the CITT explained:

> It is evident that the industry's current difficulties are the result of a variety of competitive and economic factors unrelated to dumping. Nevertheless, these difficulties have weakened the industry to such an extent that a resumption of dumping could quickly put at least one major producer out of business. Indeed, the testimony of industry witnesses representing this producer revealed that the company has been given two years to improve its performance or face drastic restructuring. This suggests that, whether or not this finding is continued, the industry of today may be quite different from the industry of two years from now. Given the ongoing restructuring of the Canadian industry, a continuation of the injury finding would be appropriate in the circumstances.

The CITT then noted that it would contemplate a review of its decision in two years if circumstances so warranted. The CITT has also found an industry to be vulnerable despite the fact that the industry has made, or was in the process of making, "considerable investments to expand . . . production capacities in order to better serve" domestic and export markets.[413] In the case of new

---

Thereof Known as "Heads," Originating in or Exported from the People's Republic of China, Review No.: RR-93-003, at 11 (Jan. 18, 1994).

[410]*See* Hydraulic Turbines Originating in the Union of Soviet Socialist Republics; Hydraulic Turbines Originating in or Exported from Japan, or from the People's Republic of China and Introduced into the Commerce of Canada by or on Behalf of a Manufacturer, Producer, Vendor or Exporter in Japan, and Alternating Current Electric Generators Originating in or Exported from Italy and Japan, Review No.: RR-89-004, at 20-21 (June 19, 1990).

[411]*See* Twisted Polypropylene and Nylon Rope Originating in or Exported from the Republic of Korea, Review No.: RR-91-003, at 8-9 (Feb. 25, 1992).

[412]*Id.*

[413]*See* Certain Stainless Steel Welded Pipe Originating In or Exporting From Taiwan, Review No.: RR-96-001, at 11 (Sept. 12, 1996).

investment, the CITT was reluctant to allow the order to expire because the "resumption of dumping would threaten not only that new investment but also the viability of the production facilities that are already in place."[414]

Injury or vulnerability of the domestic industry, however, is not a prerequisite to an affirmative finding. For example, in *Certain Oil and Gas Well Casing*, the CITT noted that a "reasonable financial performance today does not, in and of itself, preclude the industry from being injured in the face of dumped imports."[415] In that case, the CITT continued the order based on evidence that, *inter alia*, 10 percent of the underutilized capacity in the United States would be more than enough to supply the entire Canadian market.

Finally, the CITT has considered the duration of an order in the context of an expiry review. Despite a five-year expiration deadline, the CITT interpreted article 9 of the Tokyo Round Agreement as not requiring any specific limit to an order:

> In our view, it is clear . . . that there are no specific limits on the duration of a finding. It is incumbent on the Tribunal to examine each case on its own merits and to decide, based on the evidence, whether circumstances warrant continuing or rescinding the finding. If this examination leads to the conclusion that there is an ongoing risk of injurious dumping, then the finding should be continued. If not, the finding should be rescinded.[416]

More recently, however, the CITT has noted that it imposes a higher burden of proof for "old" orders:

> The Tribunal was mindful of the fact that a finding or order has now been in place for 10 years and that continuing the order would, absent an interim review, extend anti-dumping protection to the industry until the year 2001.

---

[414] *Id.; see* Photo Albums With Pocket, Slip-In or Flip-Up Style Sheets (Imported Together or Separately), and Refill Sheets Thereof, Originating in or Exported from Japan, the Republic of Korea, the People's Republic of China, Hong Kong, Taiwan, Singapore, Malaysia and the Federal Republic of Germany, Review No.: RR-92-003, at 12 (Feb. 25, 1993).

[415] Certain Oil and Gas Well Casing Made of Carbon Steel Originating in or Exported from the Republic of Korea and the United States of America, Review No.: RR-95-001, at 15 (July 5, 1996).

[416] Waterproof Rubber Footwear Originating in or Exported from Czechoslovakia, Poland, the Republic of Korea, Taiwan, Hong Kong, Malaysia, Yugoslavia and the People's Republic of China, Review No.: RR-92-001, at 7-8 (Oct. 21, 1992).

> The Tribunal recognizes that the evidence must be particularly compelling to warrant continuation of the order.[417]

The CITT's view, however, was not based on any particular language of the Final Act but on its own construction of the law.

4. Summary of Affirmative Determinations

A summary of factors that typically weigh in favor of an affirmative Canadian expiry review is provided below:

- current injury or vulnerability of the domestic industry
- significant production capacity and inventories of exporters
- increasing production capacity of exporters
- worldwide overcapacity
- export orientation of the foreign producers
- price attractiveness of Canadian market
- easy transportation distance to the Canadian market
- inability of domestic producers to meet demand of market
- third country dumping on same or related merchandise
- continued dumping
- level of continued dumping or subsidization
- evidence of sales below cost by exporters
- strong price competition in the Canadian market

[417]Certain Oil and Gas Well Casing Made of Carbon Steel Originating In or Exported From the Republic of Korea and the United States of America, Review No.: RR-95-001, at 13 (July 5, 1996); *see* Deep Tillage Sweeps, Field Cultivator Sweeps, Reversible Points, Reversible Heavy Duty Chisels, Reversible Twisted Chisels and Reversible Furrow Shovels, Known as Tillage or Earth Engaging Tools, Used on Chisel Plows and Field Cultivators, Originating in or Exported from Brazil, Review No. RR: 93-001, at 7-8 (Nov. 23, 1993) ("The Tribunal is of the view that, in conducting a second review of a finding that has been in place for almost a decade, the burden on the domestic industry to demonstrate that these criteria [for an expiry review] have been satisfied is clearly a heavy one.").

- significant investment in future production by domestic industry
- exporters' Canadian market share (stable or increased)
- continued existence of subsidy program
- significant rate of increased imports
- exporters have lost market share in their domestic market
- declining demand in exporters' domestic market
- exporters' domestic market unable to absorb growth in production and capacity
- high degree of dependence on export markets by exporters
- weak demand in Canadian market
- shrinking Canadian market
- circumvention of the current measures
- elimination of imports after finding

C. *SUBSEQUENT EXPIRY REVIEWS*

According to Section 76(5) of SIMA, an order or finding shall be deemed to have been rescinded as of the expiration of five years after the day on which the last order was made if one or more orders continuing the order or finding have been made pursuant to a review, the day on which the last such order was made.[418] In order for the order or finding to survive, the CITT must determine in another expiry review whether the resumption of dumped or subsidized imports would be likely to cause material injury.

D. *APPEALS OF EXPIRY REVIEW DETERMINATIONS*

According to Section 76(1) of SIMA, an application for judicial review of an order or finding of the CITT can be made to the Federal Court of Appeal on any ground set out in subsection 18.1(4) of the Federal

[418]Special Import Measures Act, ch. 25, §76(5), 1996 S.C. (Can.).

Court Act.[419] Subsequent appeals may be made to the Supreme Court of Canada.[420]

E. *A POST-URUGUAY ROUND EXPIRY REVIEW*

In order to gain a more complete understanding of how the CITT conducts its expiry reviews, a description of one recent post-Uruguay Round expiry review is provided as an example.

1. The Expiry Review Schedule

On November 28, 1997, the CITT issued its determination continuing the antidumping finding on fresh iceberg lettuce from the United States.[421] The original antidumping finding had been issued on November 30, 1992.[422] The CITT issued its notice of expiry on March 8, 1997, notifying all interested parties and governments that the finding was scheduled to expire over eight months later on November 28, 1997.[423]

Upon receipt of submissions requesting and opposing the review and responses thereto, the CITT found that a review was warranted and issued

---

[419]*Id.* §76(1); Federal Court Act, ch. F-7, §§18.1(4), 28(1)(e), 1996 S.C. (Can.). Section 18.1(4) permits an appeal if the CITT:

> (a) acted without jurisdiction, acted beyond its jurisdiction or refused to exercise its jurisdiction;
> (b) failed to observe a principle of natural justice, procedural fairness or other procedure that it was required by law to observe;
> (c) erred in law in making a decision or an order, whether or not the error appears on the face of the record;
> (d) based its decision or order on an erroneous finding of fact that it made in a perverse or capricious manner or without regard for the material before it;
> (e) acted, or failed to act, by reason of fraud perjured evidence; or
> (f) acted in any other way that was contrary to law.

Id. §18.1(4).

[420]CITT, *Introductory Guide on the Canadian International Trade Tribunal* at 3.

[421]*See* Fresh Iceberg (Head) Lettuce Originating in or Exported from the United States of America, Review No.: RR-97-002 (Nov. 28, 1997).

[422]*See id.* at 1 n.2.

[423]*See id.* at 1 n.3.

its notice of review on May 9, 1997.[424] The CITT also sent letters to parties with a known interest in the review and provided the review schedule. On May 22, 1997, the CITT sent questionnaires to the BC Vegetable Marketing Commission (BCVMC), sales agencies, growers, importers, and purchasers of iceberg lettuce. Interested parties were required to file notices of appearances, declarations and undertakings by June 4, 1997, and questionnaire responses by June 13, 1997. Based on those questionnaire responses, the CITT's research staff prepared public and protected pre-hearing staff reports by July 24, 1997.[425] The record before the CITT included the original 1992 finding and the public pre-hearing staff report for the 1992 finding. Public and *in camera* hearings were held on October 8 and 9, 1997. In its final determination, the CITT noted that the only party to participate or submit evidence in the review was the domestic interested party, BCVMC.

2. An Eight-Part Decision

The CITT's decision in *Fresh Iceberg Lettuce* is divided into eight parts. The background section provides the review schedule which is followed by a summary of the 1992 antidumping inquiry, a description of the product, a description of the domestic industry,[426] a review of economic indicators for the domestic industry, a summary of the BCVMC's position, an analysis of whether to continue or rescind the finding, and a conclusion.

In the original inquiry, the CITT found that British Columbia (BC) constituted a separate regional market in accordance with Article 4 of the GATT Anti-Dumping Code.[427] Specifically, the CITT observed that BC growers sold most of their production of iceberg lettuce in British Columbia. The original finding excluded the period from January 1 to May 31 and

---

[424]Notice of Review, Review No.: 97-002 at 1 (May 9, 1997).

[425]*See* Notice of Review, Review No.: 97-002 at 1, 3 (May 9, 1997); Fresh Iceberg (Head) Lettuce Originating in or Exported from the United States of America, Review No.: RR-97-002, at 1 (Nov. 28, 1997).

[426]In its published decisions, the CITT does not review its "like product" determination from the original finding or consider the percentage of the domestic industry in support of continuation.

[427]Fresh Iceberg (Head) Lettuce Originating in or Exported from the United States of America, Review No.: RR-97-002, at 2 (Nov. 28, 1997).

from October 16 to December 31 in each calendar year because BC growers had not traditionally supplied the marketplace during those periods.

Based on a review of the 1988-1992 period, the CITT found in the original inquiry that the dumping of U.S. iceberg lettuce had caused, was causing, and was likely to cause material injury to BC production of like goods. The CITT noted that U.S. imports dumped during 1991 had caused an erosion of BC selling prices which led to severe financial losses for the industry. In crop year 1992, however, both U.S. and BC selling prices recovered and BC industry returned to profitability.[428]

In the expiry review, the CITT analyzed economic indicators, such as the number of growers, production volumes, harvested acreage, yields, sales volumes, and market shares, for the year of the finding and post-finding period of 1992 to 1996.[429] The CITT reviewed the trends over the course of the five-year period and noted the adverse weather conditions in 1996 and 1997 and the six-week strike in 1996 which affected domestic market share. The CITT found, however, that despite the atypical 1996 period due to factors beyond their control, BC growers had been able to regain a large part of the market share lost during the 1998-92 period. "For example, in 1995, BC growers had almost 51 percent of the market, compared to 50 percent in 1989."[430]

3. The Decision

The CITT's analysis in the *Fresh Iceberg Lettuce* expiry review was divided into three parts. First, the CITT found that a regional industry for iceberg lettuce continued to exist in British Columbia.[431] Second, the CITT considered whether there was a likelihood of resumption of dumping. Third, the CITT considered whether a resumption of dumping was likely to

[428] *Id.*

[429] *Id.* at 5.

[430] *Id.* at 6.

[431] *Id.* at 7. According to Section 2(1.1) of SIMA, the CITT considers whether: (a) the producers in the market sell all or almost all of their production of like goods in the market, and (b) the demand in the market is not, to any substantial degree, supplied by producers of like goods located elsewhere in Canada. Special Import Measures Act, ch. 25, §2(1.1), 1996 S.C. (Can.); An Act to Implement the Agreement Establishing the World Trade Organization, ch. 47, §144(4), 1994 S.C. (Can.).

cause material injury to production in the regional market.[432] According to Section 42(5) of SIMA, the CITT will not make an affirmative injury finding unless: (1) there is a concentration of those goods into the regional market; and (2) the dumping or subsidizing of those goods has caused injury or retardation or is threatening to cause injury to the producers of all or almost all of the production of the like goods in the regional market.[433]

With respect to the likelihood of resumption of dumping issue, the CITT made the following observations. The CITT noted that the BC market was a traditional export market for the United States, which had an enormous production capacity.[434] Based on a review of production volumes and acreage, the CITT observed that annual levels of U.S. production were unlikely to decline rapidly.[435] The CITT further noted that, during the 1993-96 period, U.S. export values were below normal values for most of the period and significant antidumping duties were collected.[436] Even with the payment of significant antidumping duties, however, the CITT found that U.S. exporters were able to maintain their market share.[437]

Finally, the CITT explained that BC would remain a price taker and the United States a price setter given that California alone produced 200 times the volume of lettuce grown in BC.[438] The CITT concluded that U.S. prices were likely to be lower than the normal values established by Revenue Canada and that dumping was likely to resume if the finding were rescinded.[439]

With respect to the likelihood of material injury issue, the CITT found that dumping would likely be concentrated in the regional market if the finding were rescinded. The CITT also found that injury would be caused to producers of all or almost all of the production of the like goods within

---

[432]Fresh Iceberg (Head) Lettuce Originating in or Exported from the United States of America, Review No.: RR-97-002, at 8 (Nov. 28, 1997).

[433]Special Import Measures Act, ch. 25, §42(5), 1996 S.C. (Can.); An Act to Implement the Agreement Establishing the World Trade Organization, ch. 47, §144(4), 1994 S.C. (Can.).

[434]Fresh Iceberg (Head) Lettuce Originating in or Exported from the United States of America, Review No.: RR-97-002, at 8-10 (Nov. 28, 1997).

[435]*Id.* at 9.

[436]*Id.* at 10.

[437]*Id.* at 8.

[438]*Id.* at 9.

[439]*Id.* at 10.

the regional market.[440] The CITT commented on the fact that, but for the existence of the antidumping duties during the period, BC prices would have been forced to meet U.S. selling prices. Therefore, the CITT concluded that BC prices would decline to U.S. levels in the absence of protection which would likely cause material injury in the form of price erosion and reduced revenues.[441] In this regard, the CITT found particularly compelling the domestic industry's calculations as to what grower returns would have been in the absence of antidumping duties during the period. The CITT concluded that the magnitude of the likely reductions in grower revenue but for continuation of the finding would be significant and would materially affect the profitability of the industry.[442]

Finally, the CITT observed the benefits of the 1992 finding which had provided a "certain level of stability to the domestic industry."[443] The CITT commented on the significant efforts made by the domestic industry during the period to meet the demands of the market by investing in agricultural operations. The CITT noted that the growers had taken advantage of the protection afforded by the antidumping duties by making the effort to increase their competitiveness not only in growing iceberg lettuce but also in improving their overall agricultural operations. The CITT acknowledged that those investments would be at risk if dumping were to resume if the finding were rescinded. Therefore, the CITT decided to continue the finding on iceberg lettuce from the United States for use or consumption in the province of British Columbia.

---

[440] *Id.* at 13.
[441] *Id.* at 11.
[442] *Id.* at 12.
[443] *Id.* at 11-12.

CHAPTER V

Australian Sunset Reviews: Legislation and Practice

A. *INITIATING CONTINUATION INQUIRIES*

In order to implement the Antidumping and Subsidies Agreements, Australia enacted the Customs Legislation (World Trade Organization Amendments) Act of 1994[444] which amended Section 8A of the Anti-Dumping Authority Act of 1988, effective January 1, 1995. Significantly, the 1994 amendments inserted a substantive standard of review not previously included in the law governing continuation inquiries. According to the new standard, Section 8A prohibits the Authority from recommending the continuation of a measure unless it is satisfied that the expiration of the notice would lead, or would be likely to lead, to a continuation of, or recurrence of the material injury that the measure is intended to prevent.[445] Because the first continuation inquiry report was issued in December 1994, this section reviews all continuation inquiries without regard to whether they were issued before or after the Uruguay Round.[446]

---

[444]Customs Legislation (World Trade Organization Amendments) Act 1994.

[445]Anti-Dumping Authority Act of 1988, as amended, §8A(7A), *reprinted in* AUSTRALIAN CUSTOMS LAW AND PRACTICE (CCH) ¶ 91,874. According to the ADA, "the measure continues in force after the specified expiry date for a period of five years in the case of dumping and countervailing duties unless the relevant notice is revoked before the end of that period. In the case of an undertaking, provision can be made for it to expire after a period of less than five years." Expandable Polystyrene from the Republic of Korea and Singapore, Anti-Dumping Authority Report No. 178, at 5 (Sept. 1997).

[446]*See* Bulk Brandy from France, Anti-Dumping Authority Report No. 141, at 20 (Dec. 1994). In its first report, the ADA applied the same standard as provided in the

1. Applications for Continuation Inquiries

Section 8A of the Anti-Dumping Authority Act of 1988, as amended, provides the requirements for initiating sunset reviews in Australia. Not later than 8 months before an antidumping measure expires, the ADA publishes a notice informing interested parties that the dumping or countervailing duty notice or undertaking is due to expire and inviting applications for continuation of the measure within 60 days.[447] According to the statute, the application must be in writing, in an approved form, contain such information as the form requires, and be signed in the manner indicated in the form.[448] There is no provision for the ADA to self-initiate a continuation inquiry.

2. Grouping Continuation Inquiries

The ADA has reviewed multiple measures, whether or not antidumping or countervailing, from various countries covering the same product and the same expiry date.[449] Although the ADA will issue one report to the Minister covering multiple orders, the ADA supplies a recommendation for each measure. In at least one continuation inquiry to date, however, the ADA attempted to combine inquiries with similar products, expiry dates, and countries: canned pears from the People's Republic of China and canned peaches from Greece, Spain, and the People's Republic of China. Therefore, the ADA informed the applicant that the continuation inquiries could be combined if the application for continuation of antidumping measures on canned peaches was received by a certain date. Because the applicant failed to submit its application by the earlier receipt date, "the Authority had no alternative but to initiate the inquiry regarding canned pears as a separate inquiry as it had to meet the statutory deadline for that inquiry."[450]

Uruguay Round implementing legislation. Specifically, the ADA analyzed whether the continued application of the countervailing duty was necessary to prevent the continuation or recurrence of injury by subsidized imports. *Id.*

[447]Australian Anti-Dumping Authority Act 1988, as amended, §8A(1), *reprinted in* Australian Customs Law and Practice (CCH) ¶91,873.

[448]*Id.* §8A(3).

[449]Canned Peaches from Greece, Spain and People's Republic of China, Anti-Dumping Authority Report No. 163, at 1 (Dec. 1996).

[450]*Id.* at 34.

B. *THE CONTINUATION INQUIRY*

1. Deadlines

If the ADA receives a satisfactory application for continuation of a measure, the ADA must issue, within 120 days or such other period as is prescribed, a report to the Minister recommending whether the measure should be continued.[451] In order to prepare the report, the ADA must hold an inquiry into the matter.[452] The ADA is required to consider all timely submissions received during an inquiry.[453] The ADA is also required to place on the public record a statement of the essential facts on which it proposes to base its report.[454] Interested parties are then able to comment within 7 days on the statement of essential facts.[455] A recent continuation inquiry established the following deadlines:[456]

Day	*Event*
1	announcement of expiry
60	deadline for applications for continuation
85	notice of continuation inquiry
126	deadline for interested party comments
187	ADA submits statement of essential facts for record
194	deadline for comments on statement of essential facts
201	ADA deadline for report to Minister
243	expiration deadline for product

[451]Australian Anti-Dumping Authority Act of 1988, as amended, §8A(4), *reprinted in* AUSTRALIAN CUSTOMS LAW AND PRACTICE (CCH) ¶91,873.

[452]*Id.* §8A(5).

[453]*Id.* §8A(7).

[454]*Id.* §23A(8)

[455]Automotive Lead-Acid Storage Batteries from Indonesia, the Republic of Korea, Malaysia, the Philippines, and Taiwan, Anti-Dumping Authority Report No. 152, at 22 (May 1996); Plaster of Paris Bandages from Germany, Anti-Dumping Authority Report No. 154, at 7-8 (Aug. 1996); Glace Cherries from France and Italy, Anti-Dumping Authority Report No. 167, at 7 (Feb. 1997), *citing* Australian Anti-Dumping Authority Act of 1988, as amended, §7(7), *reprinted in* AUSTRALIAN CUSTOMS LAW AND PRACTICE (CCH) ¶91,852.

[456]Canned Tomatoes from Italy, Spain and the People's Republic of China, Anti-Dumping Authority Report No. 169, at 7, Attachment 3 (March 1997).

2. The Likelihood Tests

a. The ADA's Determination of Likelihood of Continuation or Recurrence of Dumping or Subsidization

In a continuation inquiry, the ADA will first reconsider its domestic industry[457] and like product definitions.[458] Although the statute is focused on material injury,[459] the ADA has observed:

> It is important to note that the test to be applied by the Authority is a positive one; in other words, the Authority needs to be satisfied that certain events (e.g. dumping) are likely to occur. It is not the case that the Authority could recommend that measures continue on the basis that it cannot be satisfied that these events will not occur (i.e. a negative test).[460]

---

[457]The ADA will determine whether the application satisfies the local content requirement of the Customs Act which specifies that for goods, other than non-manufactured raw products, to be regarded as produced in Australia: (1) they must be wholly or partially manufactured in Australia; (2) not less than one quarter of the factory or works cost of the goods must be represented by the sum of the value of Australian labour, material, and factory overheads; and (3) where the goods have been partly manufactured in Australia, then at least one substantial process in the manufacture of the goods must be carried out in Australia. *See, e.g.,* Expandable Polystyrene from the Republic of Korea and Singapore, Anti-Dumping Authority Report No. 178, at 10 (Sept. 1997), *citing* Customs Act 1901, as amended, §268T(2)-(4).

[458]Dioctyl Phthalate from Belgium, France, the Federal Republic of Germany, the Republic of Korea and Venezuela, Anti-Dumping Authority Report No. 156, at 10 (Oct. 1996); Canned Ham from Denmark, the Republic of Ireland, and the Netherlands, Anti-Dumping Authority Report No. 165, at 11 (Jan. 1997). The Customs Act of 1901, as amended, defines "like goods" as "goods that are identical in all respects to the goods under consideration or that, although not alike in all respects to the goods under consideration, have characteristics closely resembling those of the goods under consideration." Customs Act 1901, as amended, §269T(1), *reprinted in* AUSTRALIAN CUSTOMS LAW AND PRACTICE (CCH) ¶74,321.

[459]Anti-Dumping Authority Act 1988, as amended, §8A(7A), *reprinted in* AUSTRALIAN CUSTOMS LAW AND PRACTICE (CCH) ¶91,874. The statute, however, does not define "material injury." See Customs Act 1901, as amended, §269TAE, *reprinted in* AUSTRALIAN CUSTOMS LAW AND PRACTICE (CCH) ¶74,473; *see also* Hollander & Gruen, *supra* note 88, at 6. Instead, the statute provides a list of factors that the Minister may have regard to such as margins, import volumes, and import prices.

[460]Automotive Lead-Acid Storage Batteries from Indonesia, the Republic of Korea, Malaysia, the Philippines, and Taiwan, Anti-Dumping Authority Report No. 152, at 22

Second, the ADA considers whether the subject imports continue to be dumped or subsidized, whether dumping or subsidies are likely to continue,[461] the level of dumping or subsidies,[462] and whether, in the absence of duties, exporters are likely to export to Australia dumped or subsidized imports.[463] To do so, the ADA has visited major importers and verified their sales prices.[464] The ADA will also consider whether or not Customs has collected duties on imports since their imposition.[465]

The ADA has found a likelihood of future dumping based, in part, on evidence that imports from exporters "under reference" virtually stopped after the imposition of measures when there was also evidence of third country dumping.[466] Even if imports and dumping duties collected are insignificant during the five-year period, the Authority will find evidence of export prices below domestic prices and excess capacity to support a continuation finding.[467] The ADA, however, has noted that over-capacity, by itself, was insufficient to indicate the likelihood of future dumping.[468]

(May 1996); Plaster of Paris Bandages from Germany, Anti-Dumping Authority Report No. 154, at 21 (Aug. 1996).

461 Canned Peaches from Greece, Spain and the People's Republic of China, Anti-Dumping Authority Report No. 163, at 10 (Dec. 1996).

462 Canned Ham from Denmark, the Republic of Ireland and the Netherlands, Anti-Dumping Authority Report No. 165, at 31 (Jan. 1997).

463 *See* Dioctyl Phthalate from Belgium, France, the Federal Republic of Germany, the Republic of Korea and Venezuela, Anti-Dumping Authority Report No. 156, at 17 (Oct. 1996).

464 Automotive Lead-Acid Storage Batteries from Indonesia, the Republic of Korea, Malaysia, the Philippines, and Taiwan, Anti-Dumping Authority Report No. 152, at 16 (May 1996).

465 Plaster of Paris Bandages from Germany, Anti-Dumping Authority Report No. 154, at 23 (Aug. 1996); Clear Float Glass from the People's Republic of China, Belgium, Germany, Indonesia, the Philippines, and Thailand, Anti-Dumping Authority Report No. 177, at 29 (Sept. 1997) (ADA considers dumping duties collected during previous five year period based on Customs' commercial database).

466 Dioctyl Phthalate from Belgium, France, the Federal Republic of Germany, the Republic of Korea, and Venezuela, Anti-Dumping Authority Report No. 156, at 1, 15, 18 (Oct. 1996). The ADA relied on evidence of excess capacity and potentially dumped sales in third country markets to support its continuation finding. *Id.* at 18-19; *but see* Canned Pears from the People's Republic of China, Anti-Dumping Authority Report No. 157, at 3, 17-18 (Oct. 1996); Canned Peaches from Greece, Spain and the People's Republic of China, Anti-Dumping Authority Report No. 163, at 26 (Dec. 1996).

467 Polyvinyl Chloride Homopolymer Resin from the Federative Republic of Brazil, Mexico, and the United States of America, Anti-Dumping Authority Report No. 160, at

Like Canada and the EU, the existence of measures in other countries against the subject merchandise "suggests a propensity on the part of the exporters to dump into markets where anti-dumping measures are not in place."[469] Likewise, the ADA will also consider evidence, in the absence of outstanding measures, that foreign exporters are exporting to third countries at dumped prices.[470] However, dumping in third countries when there can be no dumping liability because, for example, both countries are part of the EU, is insufficient evidence to support a finding of a likelihood to dump in Australia.[471]

The fact that exporters have been found to have dumped in Australia, however, is also insufficient for a likelihood finding:

22-23 (Nov. 1996); Dibutyl Phthalate from the People's Republic of China and Italy, Anti-Dumping Authority Report No. 162, at 19-20 (Dec. 1996). Evidence of "low" third country prices, however, is insufficient to support a likelihood of dumping finding. *See* Canned Pears from the People's Republic of China, Anti-Dumping Authority Report No. 157, at 3, 17-18 (Oct. 1996). For example, in *Canned Pears*, the ADA required applicants to support their claim of third country dumping with evidence of normal values: "The Authority's view is that it is up to the applicant to make a case and the Authority will confine itself to inquiring into the claims made by the applicants and by other parties." *Id.* at 18.

[468]Automotive Lead-Acid Storage Batteries from Indonesia, the Republic of Korea, Malaysia, the Philippines, and Taiwan, Anti-Dumping Authority Report No. 152, at 24 (May 1996); Clear Float Glass from the People's Republic of China, Belgium, Germany, Indonesia, the Philippines and Thailand, Anti-Dumping Authority Report No. 177, at 32 (Sept. 1997) ("The Authority considers the existence of spare production capacity in a country does not mean that manufacturers in that country will necessarily export CFG to Australia at dumped prices.").

[469]Polyvinyl Chloride Homopolymer Resin from the Federative Republic of Brazil, Mexico, and the United States of America, Anti-Dumping Authority Report No. 160, at 22 (Nov. 1996).

[470]Plaster of Paris Bandages from Germany, Anti-Dumping Authority Report No. 154, at 15-16 (Aug. 1996); *see* Dioctyl Phthalate from Belgium, France, the Federal Republic of Germany, the Republic of Korea and Venezuela, Anti-Dumping Authority Report No. 156, at 18-19 (Oct. 1996).

[471]Canned Peaches from Greece, Spain and the People's Republic of China, Anti-Dumping Authority Report No. 163, at 26 (Dec. 1996) ("Even if the dumping margin were correct, dumping in Germany by Greek canners, of itself, would not indicate that they would also dump in Australia — as the Greek canners know that the Australian canning industry would seek anti-dumping action.").

> [C]ontinuation inquiries are conducted when anti-dumping measures that have been in place for five years are about to expire under sunset provisions of Australia's anti-dumping legislation. It follows that in every continuation inquiry, one will find that injurious dumping occurred five years or so ago. If the Authority were to accept injurious dumping that occurred five years or more ago as a reliable predictor of future injurious dumping, then every anti-dumping measure would be continued indefinitely.
>
> The Authority must judge each case on the basis of the evidence provided. However, it is not satisfied that past dumping, in itself, is a good reason to continue measures.[472]

In addition, the likelihood determination can also depend on the country's (or countries') historic share of the Australian market. For example, in *Canned Peaches*, the ADA found that both Greek and Spanish canners received a countervailable subsidy. The ADA, however, only continued the order for Greek peaches because, *inter alia*, Greece was a major exporter of canned peaches and held a significant share of the Australian market until duties were imposed whereas Spanish exporters never had a significant share of the Australian market.[473]

b. The ADA's Determination of Likelihood of Continuation or Recurrence of Injury

According to the Section 8A(7A) of the statute, the ADA must not recommend continuation of a measure "unless it is satisfied that the expiration of the notice would lead, or would be likely to lead, to continuation of, or recurrence of the material injury that the antidumping measure is intended to prevent."[474] In order to make that determination, the ADA will consider (1) the history of imports during the five year period, (2) the recent eco-

---

[472]Canned Pears from the People's Republic of China, Anti-Dumping Authority Report No. 157, at 20 (Oct. 1996); *see* Canned Peaches from Greece, Spain and the People's Republic of China, Anti-Dumping Authority Report No. 163, at 34 (Dec. 1996).

[473]Canned Peaches from Greece, Spain and the People's Republic of China, Anti-Dumping Authority Report No. 163, at 35 (Dec. 1996).

[474]Australian Anti-Dumping Authority Act of 1988, as amended, §8A(7A), *reprinted in* AUSTRALIAN CUSTOMS LAW AND PRACTICE (CCH) ¶91,874.

nomic performance of the domestic industry, and (3) the likely effect on the economic performance of the industry if the measure were to expire.[475]

In order to determine the domestic industry's economic performance and whether the industry has experienced material injury "from some cause or causes"[476] since the measure was imposed, the ADA analyzes data concerning volume trends, market shares, price trends (including price undercutting, suppression, and depression),[477] profits, and profitability, production, and capacity utilization.[478] The ADA has considered the current economic performance of an industry and compared it to its performance three years immediately preceding the imposition of duties.[479]

A finding that the domestic industry is currently experiencing material injury does not guarantee continuation of an order.[480] For example, in *Dried Egg Whites*, the ADA refused to continue a countervailing duty measure despite continued subsidization of egg whites when the domestic industry's poor condition was mostly attributable to imports from third countries.[481] A finding that the domestic industry is not currently experi-

---

[475]Bulk Brandy from France, Anti-Dumping Authority Report No. 141, at 6 (Dec. 1994); Automotive Lead-Acid Storage Batteries from Indonesia, the Republic of Korea, Malaysia, the Philippines and Taiwan, Anti-Dumping Authority Report No. 152, at 5 (May 1996).

[476]Polyvinyl Chloride Homopolymer Resin from the Federative Republic of Brazil, Mexico, and the United States of America, Anti-Dumping Authority Report No. 160, at 16 (Nov. 1996); Dried Egg Whites from the Netherlands, Anti-Dumping Authority Report No. 168, at 21 (March 1997); High Density Polyethylene from the Republic of Korea, Saudi Arabia and Singapore, Anti-Dumping Authority Report No. 172, at 19 (June 1997).

[477]Polyvinyl Chloride Homopolymer Resin from the Federative Republic of Brazil, Mexico, and the United States of America, Anti-Dumping Authority Report No. 160, at 12-15 (Nov. 1996).

[478]Bulk Brandy from France, Anti-Dumping Authority Report No. 141, at 16-19 (Dec. 1994); Automotive Lead-Acid Storage Batteries from Indonesia, the Republic of Korea, Malaysia, the Philippines, and Taiwan, Anti-Dumping Authority Report No. 152, at 18-21 (May 1996); *see* Automotive Lead-Acid Storage Batteries from Indonesia, the Republic of Korea, Malaysia, the Philippines, and Taiwan, Anti-Dumping Authority Report No. 152, at 20 (May 1996).

[479]Plaster of Paris Bandages, Anti-Dumping Authority Report No. 154, at 1 (Aug. 1996).

[480]Dried Egg White from the Netherlands, Anti-Dumping Authority Report No. 168, at 21, 27 (March 1997).

[481]*Id.* at 26.

encing material injury does not preclude continuation of an order.[482] Instead, the Authority will determine whether or not expiration would lead or would be likely to lead to a recurrence of material injury.[483] In such a case, the ADA will rely on evidence of continued dumping or subsidized imports and significant market share to support a continuation finding.[484] If the Authority decides to continue an order, it will determine whether recalculation of the amount of duty is necessary.[485]

3. Summary of Affirmative Determinations

A summary of factors that typically weigh in favor of an affirmative Australian expiry review is provided below:

- increased or significant market share for imports
- significant rate of increased imports
- elimination of imports after measure
- evidence of third country dumping
- existence of price undercutting by imports
- significant production capacity of exporters
- continued dumping or subsidization
- current injury
- failure of respondents to participate in review

[482] *See, e.g.*, Dibutyl Phthalate from the People's Republic of China, Anti-Dumping Authority Report No. 162, at 2, 15-16 (Dec. 1996).

[483] Bulk Brandy from France, Anti-Dumping Authority Report No. 141, at 19, 21, 24 (Dec. 1994); Canned Tomatoes from Italy, Spain and the People's Republic of China, Anti-Dumping Authority Report No. 169, at 18, 29, 31 (March 1997).

[484] *See, e.g.*, Canned Tomatoes from Italy, Spain, and the People's Republic of China, Anti-Dumping Authority Report No. 169, at 29 (March 1997).

[485] Bulk Brandy from France, Anti-Dumping Authority Report No. 141, at 24 (Dec. 1994); Glace Cherries from France and Italy, Anti-Dumping Authority Report No. 167, at 23 (Feb. 1997).

C. *SUBSEQUENT CONTINUATION INQUIRIES*

Section 8A(11) of the Anti-Dumping Authority Act of 1988, as amended, provides that a measure will continue in force for a period of five years after the specified expiry day if continued unless: (a) the dumping or countervailing duty notice is revoked before the end of that period; or (b) provision is made for an earlier expiration in the case of an undertaking.[486] In order for the measure to survive, the ADA must determine in another continuation inquiry whether the expiration of the notice would lead, or would be likely to lead to, a continuation or recurrence of the material injury that the measure is intended to prevent.[487]

D. *APPEALS OF CONTINUATION INQUIRIES*

The Minister's determinations in continuation inquiries can be appealed to the Federal Court.[488]

E. *A POST-URUGUAY ROUND CONTINUATION INQUIRY*

In order to gain a more complete understanding of how the ADA conducts its continuation inquiries, a description of one recent post-Uruguay Round continuation inquiry is provided as an example.

1. The Continuation Inquiry Schedule

The antidumping measures resulted from a decision on October 15, 1992.[489] On February 26, 1997, the ADA announced that the duties were

[486]Anti-Dumping Authority Act 1988, as amended, §8A(11), *reprinted in* AUSTRALIAN CUSTOMS LAW AND PRACTICE (CCH) ¶91,874.

[487]*Id.* §8A(7A).

[488]Administrative Decisions (Judicial Review) Act 1977; Judiciary Act 1903; *see* ANTI-DUMPING AUTHORITY, ANNUAL REPORT 1994-95, at 2; H. Keith C. Steele, *The Australian Antidumping System, in* ANTIDUMPING LAW AND PRACTICE: A COMPARATIVE STUDY, *supra* note 236, at 223, 237-38.

[489]Expandable Polystyrene from the Republic of Korea and Singapore, Anti-Dumping Authority Report No. 178, at 4, Attachment 1 (Sept. 1997).

scheduled to expire on November 3, 1997, and invited interested parties to apply for continuation of the duties.[490] The ADA received an application for continuation of the measures on April 24, 1997. Based on that application, the ADA decided to hold an inquiry into the matter and published a notice of inquiry on May 21, 1997, inviting interested parties to submit comments no later than June 30, 1997.[491] During the course of the inquiry, the ADA visited eleven companies.[492] On September 5, 1997, the ADA placed on the public file a statement of essential facts and requested comments by September 15, 1997.[493]

2. A Nine-Part Decision

On October 15, 1997, the Commonwealth of Australia Gazette included a notice of the ADA's determination to continue the dumping duties on exports of expandable polystyrene from the Republic of Korea and to take no action to continue the dumping duties on exports of expandable polystyrene from Singapore, and the Minister's acceptance of those recommendations.[494] The ADA's decision in *Expandable Polystyrene* is divided into nine parts. A brief summary and conclusion section is followed by a list of abbreviations used in the report. The introduction provides a procedural summary of the continuation inquiry. A background section is then followed by a description of the industry and market; including like goods, industry structure, and market structure; a description of the economic performance of the industry; the ADA's assessment of dumping; the ADA's assessment of the case, including the local industry and importers' claims; and the ADA's recommendation.

In the original inquiry, the ADA found that dumped imports from Korea and Singapore had caused and threatened to cause material injury to the Australian industry.[495] The Minister accepted the ADA's recommendation and imposed dumping duties on certain exporters in Korea and Singapore. Based on subsequent Customs reviews, the measures on Korean imports

---

[490] *Id.* at Attachment 3.

[491] *Id.* at 1 & Attachment 1.

[492] *Id.* at 7.

[493] *Id.*

[494] Commonwealth of Australia Gazette, No. GN 41, at 2977 (Oct. 15, 1997).

[495] Expandable Polystyrene from the Republic of Korea and Singapore, Anti-Dumping Authority Report No. 178, at 8 (Sept. 1997).

were extended to encompass all exporters in Korea and the measure on Singapore was extended to include an additional exporter.[496]

In the continuation inquiry, the ADA confirmed its like product definition and satisfied itself that the applicant, Huntsman, produced expandable polystyrene that met the local content requirements.[497] The ADA also concluded that Huntsman and its affiliate, which imported expandable polystyrene, conducted day-to-day operations independently.

The ADA also considered the economic performance of the local industry since the duties were put into place from 1992 to 1997.[498] The ADA's assessment consisted of a review of volume trends, market shares, price trends, price undercutting, price depression, price suppression, profits, and profitability. The ADA noted that during the period, the local industry's domestic sales declined and one of the two producers ceased production in 1995.[499] The remaining domestic producer's sales, however, increased as did sales from Korea and third countries. Sales from Singapore were erratic. While local market share declined, the market share of third country exporters rose significantly.[500]

With respect to prices, the ADA noted that any analysis of the price effects of imports from Korea and Singapore was of limited use given that Australia's prospective system allowed those imports to enter at the lower of either undumped prices or non-injurious prices. The ADA, however, found that Huntsman suffered price undercutting and depression and suppression by imports. Finally, the ADA found that Huntsman was suffering losses by 1996-97.[501]

In the ADA's assessment of dumping, the ADA noted that Korean producers continued to pay increasing amounts of dumping duties during the period. The ADA also reviewed evidence that the Korean producers were also operating well below full capacity and that the export prices to Australia were significantly higher than those to third countries or the average Korean export price.[502] The ADA further noted that Singapore had less

---

[496] *Id.* at 4, 8.

[497] *Id.* at 10-11.

[498] *Id.* at 12.

[499] *Id.* at 13.

[500] *Id.* at 14.

[501] *Id.* at 14-16.

[502] *Id.* at 18-19.

production capacity than Korea and that Singapore had dumped in three of the five years since the measures were imposed, but dumped duties paid were not significant.[503] The ADA also reviewed evidence demonstrating that the price of Singapore expandable polystyrene in third countries was, on average, lower than the price to Australia. Finally, the ADA reviewed data concerning the volume and value of dumped product from the two countries for the 1992-97 period.[504]

3. The Decision

The ADA's analysis in *Expandable Polystyrene* was divided into four parts. First, the ADA provided an introduction to frame the issue as to (1) whether, in the absence of duties, exporters to which the current measures apply are likely to export to Australia at dumped prices, and if so, (2) whether the dumping of itself, is likely to lead to a recurrence of material injury to the Australian industry. Second, the ADA reviewed the applicant's claims as well as the claims of importers, exporters, and users of the merchandise.[505]

Third, the ADA assessed those claims in light of the applicable likelihood standard. The ADA did not find it relevant that the applicant also imported expandable polystyrene from Korea. The ADA noted that there was nothing "untoward about the fact that Huntsman imports EPS to supplement its supply from local production. There is no requirement that the Australian industry must be able to satisfy a certain proportion of the Australian market before anti-dumping measures can be imposed or continued."[506] Further, the ADA noted that it was not "required to pass judgement on the technical or economic efficiency of Australian companies."[507]

With respect to Korean imports, the ADA found that there was substantial scope for Korean producers to increase exports to Australia. Given that the domestic price of expandable polystyrene from Korea was significantly above the average Korean export prices, the ADA concluded that

[503] *Id.* at 19-20.
[504] *Id.* at 20-21.
[505] *Id.* at 22-23.
[506] *Id.* at 24.
[507] *Id.*

there is a likelihood that Korean exports will be made at dumped prices and, in the absence of measures, the volume and price of Korean exports would be such as to cause the recurrence of material injury to the Australian industry.

With respect to Singaporean imports, the ADA concluded that there was little scope for the Singaporean producer to increase exports. The ADA further noted that the domestic Singapore prices were below the export price and, therefore, the ADA was not satisfied that future exports would be at dumped prices. Finally, the ADA stated that it was not satisfied that in the absence of measures, the volume and price of Singaporean exports would be such as to cause a recurrence of material injury to the Australian industry. Therefore, the ADA recommended the continuation of duties only on exports from Korea.[508]

F. *AUSTRALIA ANNOUNCES REFORMS*

On February 24, 1998, the Australian Ministers for Industry, Science & Tourism and Customs & Consumer Affairs announced a comprehensive reform of Australia's antidumping and countervailing duty system.[509] The reforms were based, in part, on a September 1996 report prepared by Mr. Lawrie Willet AO at the request of the Minister of Small Business and Consumer Affairs and the Minister of Responsible for Customs.[510]

In that report, Mr. Willet addressed the need for expediting the Australia's antidumping and countervailing duty procedures as well as making other substantive changes.[511] The report proposed replacing the two-stage antidumping and countervailing investigation process with a 155 day, single-stage system which would consist of an investigation period of 100 days and a 55 day review period.[512] The report further suggested that Customs be the administrating agency, rather than Customs and the ADA.[513] Under the proposed scheme, Customs would conduct the investigation and imple-

---

[508]*Id.* at 24-25.

[509]Hon. John Moore MP & Hon. Warren Truss MP, JOINT PRESS RELEASE (036/98) (Feb. 24, 1998).

[510]*See* Willet *supra* note 79.

[511]*Id.* at 5.

[512]*Id.* at 9.

[513]*Id.* at 9, 15-16.

ment an internal review process. The ADA would be abolished. With respect to continuation inquiries, the report further suggested extending the time frame from 120 days to 155 days in order to facilitate the internal review mechanism.[514]

According to the February 24, 1998, announcement, the Australian government intends to adopt the expedited 155 day investigation procedure and will abolish the ADA.[515] As of this writing, it was unclear whether or not the deadline for continuation inquiries would be changed.

---

[514]*Id.* at 16-17, 107.

[515]Hon. John Moore, MP & Hon. Warren Truss, MP, JOINT PRESS RELEASE (036/98) (Feb. 24, 1998).

CHAPTER VI

United States Sunset Reviews: Legislation and Practice

A. *PROCEDURAL PROVISIONS IN THE URUGUAY ROUND AGREEMENTS ACT*

The Uruguay Round Agreements Act (URAA) implements changes made by the Uruguay Round Agreements on Antidumping and Subsidies as well as addresses the administrative requirements necessary to implement those changes. In addition, the URAA; its legislative history, as contained in the Senate Report, House Report, and Statement of Administrative Action (SAA); and the agencies' regulations and policy bulletin provide guidance as to how the new U.S. law should be applied in individual cases. [516] As with

[516]S. REP. NO. 103-412 (1994); H.R. REP. NO. 103-826(I) (1994), *reprinted in* 1994 U.S.C.C.A.N. 3773; Statement of Administration Action, *reprinted in* H.R. Doc. No. 103-316, vol. 1, at 656, 807, 911 (1994) [hereinafter SAA]. On October 23, 1997, the ITC issued proposed regulations, and on March 20, 1998, the DOC issued interim final rules governing the conduct of sunset reviews. Notice of Proposed Amendments to Rules of Practice and Procedure, 62 Fed. Reg. 55,185 (ITC 1997) [hereinafter *Proposed Regulations*]; Procedures for Conducting Five-year ("Sunset") Reviews of Antidumping and Countervailing Duty Orders, 63 Fed. Reg. 13,516 (Dep't Comm. 1998) [hereinafter *Interim Regulations*]. On April 16, 1998, the DOC issued its policy bulletin regarding the conduct of sunset reviews and requested comments. Policies Regarding the Conduct of Five-year ("Sunset") Reviews of Antidumping and Countervailing Duty Orders; Policy Bulletin 98:3, 63 Fed. Reg. 18,871 (Dep't Comm. 1998) [hereinafter *Policy Bulletin*]. Finally, on June 5, 1998, the ITC issued its final regulations. Rules of Practice and Procedure, 63 Fed. Reg. 30,599 (ITC 1998) [hereinafter *Final Regulations*].

original investigations, the administrative agencies charged with conducting sunset reviews of orders or suspension agreements are the Department of Commerce (DOC) and the International Trade Commission (ITC).

1. Initiating Sunset Reviews

Consistent with Uruguay Round Agreements, the URAA requires the DOC and the ITC to commence a sunset review five years after the date of publication of the following orders and suspended investigations:

> (A) a countervailing duty order (other than a countervailing duty order to which subparagraph (B) applies or which was issued without an affirmative determination of injury by the Commission under section 1303 of this title), an antidumping duty order, or a notice of suspension of investigation, described in section (a)(1) of this section,
>
> (B) a notice of injury determination under section 1675b of this title with respect to a countervailing duty order, or
>
> (C) a determination under this section to continue an order or suspension agreement. . . . [517]

The Uruguay Round provisions contain a transition clause which allows member states to treat existing measures or "transition orders" as having been imposed on January 1, 1995, the date the WTO Agreement entered into force with respect to the United States.[518] Thus, the URAA provides for the commencement of sunset reviews for transition orders between July 1998 and December 1999.[519]

As explained below, in light of the task of conducting the first round of sunset reviews with approximately 325 transition orders,[520] Congress re-

---

[517] 19 U.S.C. §1675(c)(1) (1980 & Supp. 1998). All references to the U.S. Code in Chapter VI will be to the 1998 supplement unless otherwise specified.

[518] Antidumping Agreement, *supra* note 5, at art. 18.3.2; Subsidies Agreement, *supra* note 5, at art. 32.4; 19 U.S.C. §§1675(c)(6)(C), (D), (notes).

[519] *Proposed Regulations, supra* note 516, at 55,185; 19 U.S.C. §1675(c)(6)(A)(i); *see* 19 C.F.R. §351.218(c)(4); *see Policy Bulletin, supra* note 516, at 18,872.

[520] *Interim Regulations, supra* note 516, at 13,517. The URAA defines "transition order" in the following manner:

> (i) a countervailing duty order under this subtitle or under section 1303 of this title,
>
> (ii) an antidumping duty order under this subtitle or a finding under the Antidumping Act, 1921, or
>
> (iii) a suspension of an investigation under section 1671c or 1673c of this title,

quired the administrative agencies to initiate reviews and allowed them to organize those reviews by grouping reviews, eliminating needless reviews, expediting some reviews, and allowing waiver of other reviews. Expedited reviews will be conducted when aggregate interested party responses to the agencies' requests for information are found to be inadequate. The underlying rationale for resort to an expedited review is that if parties provide no or inadequate information at the outset, they are unlikely to provide adequate information in a full sunset review.[521]

Notwithstanding the abbreviated schedule, the agencies apply the same substantive likelihood test to the available facts in an expedited review as in a full review. Although the Agreements do not expressly provide for expedited reviews, as shown below, the URAA and agency regulations provide procedural and evidentiary protections in expedited reviews which conform to the Agreements' requirements.[522] For example, the regulations governing expedited and full reviews provide for the notification of interested parties of the initiation of the sunset review and any final determination. Interested parties will have 30 days to submit responses to the DOC's notice of initiation, 50 days to submit responses to the ITC's notice of institution, and additional opportunities to file written comments on the agencies' decisions. The information submitted and relied upon by the agencies in both reviews will be certified as to its accuracy. Finally, reliance on facts available in an expedited review is consistent with the Agreements' provisions permitting resort to facts available when interested parties do not provide necessary information.

a. Grouping Reviews and Cumulation

An antidumping or countervailing duty order or suspension agreement can cover imports of one or multiple products from one country. As a result, there can be multiple orders or suspension agreements covering the

---

which is in effect on the date the WTO Agreement enters into force with respect to the United States.

19 U.S.C. §1675(c)(6)(C). Transition orders will be treated as if they were issued on the date the WTO Agreement entered into force for the United States. *Id.* §1675(c)(6)(D). The date the WTO Agreement entered into force with respect to the United States was January 1, 1995. *See id.* (notes).

[521] 19 U.S.C. §1675(c)(3); *see* SAA, *supra* note 516, at 880.

[522] *See infra* Chapter VI, Section A.1.c & .2.

same or similar products from multiple countries. Thus, foreign producers from one country can also produce products covered by multiple orders or suspension agreements.

Pursuant to Section 751(c)(5)(D) of the Tariff Act of 1930, as amended (19 U.S.C. §1675(c)(5)(D)), the ITC, in consultation with the DOC, has the discretion to group orders or suspended investigations for sunset reviews if the ITC considers that such grouping is appropriate and will promote administrative efficiency.[523] According to the legislative history, grouping would be appropriate if the reviews involve the same domestic like product and may also be considered when the reviews involve related like products or identical or related producers.[524] Grouping reviews should promote administrative efficiency by reducing the number of times information is requested and permitting use of a single administrative record for grouped reviews.[525] Grouping of reviews involving identical or related producers, however, would also appear to be geared to reducing the burdens of foreign producers in participating in multiple reviews.[526]

Just as U.S. law permits cumulation of imports in making injury determinations in original investigations, U.S. law permits the ITC to cumulate imports in making injury determinations in sunset reviews. Specifically, Sec-

---

[523]19 U.S.C. §1675(c)(5)(D).

[524]H.R. REP. NO. 103-826(I) at 58 (1994); SAA, *supra* note 516, at 881. "Domestic like product" is defined as "a product which is like, or in the absence of like, most similar in characteristics and uses with, the article subject to an investigation under this subtitle." 19 U.S.C. §1677(10). There is no definition, however, for "related like products." In its proposed schedule of October 9, 1997, however, the agencies grouped orders and suspended investigations involving the same or related like products. For example, the agency apparently concluded that tapered roller bearings and other antifriction bearings were related like products and that steel pipes, tubes, and tubular goods were related like products. Transition Orders; Schedule and Grouping of Five-year Reviews, 62 Fed. Reg. 52,686, 52,689 (Dep't Comm. 1997).

[525]H.R. REP. NO. 103-826(I) at 58 (1994); SAA, *supra* note 516, at 881.

[526]Potential foreign interested parties have argued that the ITC should not cumulate imports covered by an expedited review with those in a full review. They suggested that the ITC conduct a full review even if there is not adequate interest shown for the review of one of the orders in a grouping. *See* Stewart and Stewart Rebuttal Comments at 17-18, 29 (1/21/98). In response, the ITC stated in its comments on the final regulations that it would normally conduct full reviews for all countries in a grouped review even where domestic interested party responses are not inadequate and responses from foreign interested parties are mixed. *See Final Regulations, supra* note 516, at 30,604.

tion 752(a)(7) of the Tariff Act of 1930, as amended (19 U.S.C. §1675a(a)(7)), gives the ITC the discretion to cumulate imports from all countries with respect to which sunset reviews were initiated *on the same day*:

> For purposes of this subsection, the Commission may cumulatively assess the volume and effect of imports of the subject merchandise from all countries with respect to which reviews under section 1675(b) or (c) of this title were initiated *on the same day*, if such imports would be *likely to compete* with each other and with the domestic like products in the United States market. The Commission shall not cumulatively assess the volume and effects of imports of the subject merchandise in a case in which it determines that such imports are likely to have no discernible adverse impact on the domestic industry.[527]

The statute, however, requires the DOC to initiate sunset reviews for non-transition orders or suspended investigations by a deadline which is thirty days before the fifth anniversary date.[528] For subsequent sunset reviews for

---

[527]19 U.S.C. §1675a(a)(7) (emphasis added). In contrast, the ITC cumulates imports to determine material injury or threat thereof in original investigations if such imports *compete* with each other and with domestic like products in the United States market. 19 U.S.C. §§1677(7)(G)(i), (H). In order to determine whether imports compete with each other and the domestic like product, the ITC has generally considered the following four factors:

> (1) the degree of fungibility between the imports from different countries and between imports and the domestic like product;
> (2) the presence of sales or offers to sell in the same geographical markets of imports from different countries and the domestic like product;
> (3) the existence of common or similar channels of distribution for imports from different countries and the domestic like product; and
> (4) whether the imports are simultaneously present in the market.

See U.S. Steel Group v. United States, 873 F. Supp. 673, 685 (CIT 1994), *aff'd*, 96 F.3d 1352 (Fed. Cir. 1996); Fundicao Tupy, S.A. v. United States, 678 F. Supp. 898 (CIT 1988), *aff'd*, 859 F.2d 915 (Fed. Cir. 1988). According to the legislative history, "[t]he Committee recognizes that the Commerce Department will control the date of initiation of sunset reviews, and hence could preclude cumulation simply by initiating reviews of the same products from different countries on different days where there are no legitimate reasons for doing so. The Committee intends to monitor Commerce Department practice closely to ensure that such manipulation does not occur." S. REP. NO. 103-412, at 51 (1994).

[528]19 U.S.C. §1675(c)(1) & (2); 19 C.F.R. §351.218(c) (1997); *see* SAA, *supra* note 516, at 881-82.

non-transition orders, the DOC will initiate a sunset review by a deadline which is not later than thirty days before the fifth anniversary of the date of the last determination by the ITC to continue the order or suspended investigation.[529] According to the legislative history, the DOC expects to initiate a sunset review shortly before the thirty-day period begins.[530] Given that orders and suspension agreements covering the same merchandise can have different anniversary dates,[531] the grouping provision permits the DOC to initiate a sunset review for orders or suspension agreements with different anniversary dates on the same date permitting cumulation.[532] According to the legislative history and the DOC's regulations, a domestic interested party can request an earlier initiation date if it demonstrates that early initiation would promote administrative efficiency.[533]

In contrast, the statute provides for a different initiation schedule for transition orders between July 1998 and December 1999 or "the date of the determination to continue such orders."[534] According to the URAA, the

---

[529]19 U.S.C. §1675(c)(2); 19 C.F.R. §351.218(c)(2) (1997).

[530]SAA, *supra* note 516, at 882.

[531]For example, the DOC issued its antidumping duty orders on furfuryl alcohol from the People's Republic of China and South Africa on June 21, 1995, and the order on furfuryl alcohol from Thailand on July 25, 1995, despite the fact that all three cases were initiated on the same day. Furfuryl Alcohol from the People's Republic of China, 60 Fed. Reg. 32,302 (Dep't Comm. 1995) (Order); Furfuryl Alcohol from South Africa, 60 Fed. Reg. 32,302 (Dep't Comm. 1995) (Order); Furfuryl Alcohol from Thailand, 60 Fed. Reg. 38,035 (Dep't Comm. 1995) (Order); Furfuryl Alcohol from the People's Republic of China, the Republic of South Africa, and Thailand, 59 Fed. Reg. 32,953 (Dep't Comm. 1994) (Notice of Initiation). Although these orders were issued under pre-Uruguay Round law, it is not clear that orders under post-Uruguay Round law covering the same merchandise would necessarily have the same anniversary date.

[532]*See* Antidumping Duties; Countervailing Duties, 61 Fed. Reg. 7308, 7319 (Dep't Comm. 1996) (Proposed Regulations) (Comments on §351.218). In its interim regulations, the DOC clarified that sunset review proceedings before the DOC would be subject merchandise- and country-specific (*i.e.*, order-specific). *Interim Regulations, supra* note 516, at 13,517.

[533]SAA, *supra* note 516, at 882; 19 C.F.R. §351.218(c)(3) (1997). The DOC may decline to initiate a review early if the request is filed by a domestic interested party that is a related party or an importer within the meaning of Section 771(4)(B) of the Tariff Act of 1930, as amended (19 U.S.C. §1677(4)(B)) or 19 C.F.R. §351.203(e)(4) (1997).

[534]19 U.S.C. §1675(c)(6)(A)(i) & (iii).

DOC and the ITC are instructed to consult with each other to determine the sequence of reviews of transition orders with the oldest orders generally being reviewed first.[535] The choice of selecting the oldest orders to review first appears to have been primarily a means to promote "administrative efficiency."[536] According to the legislative history, the entire scheduling process is subject to administrative discretion although the DOC will publish a proposed schedule for review of transition orders, including the Commission's intended grouping, for public comment.[537]

On October 9, 1997, the DOC issued a proposed schedule for the conduct of the review of transition orders and the ITC's proposal for grouping reviews. The proposal first grouped orders and suspended investigations involving the same domestic like product or related like products. An average date for each group was then determined based on the effective date of each order within a group and then listed in chronological order.[538] The DOC and ITC received comments on the proposed schedule and grouping of transition orders in December 1997.[539] After receiving comments on

---

[535]19 U.S.C. §1675(c)(6)(B); *see* SAA, *supra* note 516, at 882 ("To accommodate special problems that may arise where reviews of transition orders are grouped, Commerce may initiate reviews out of chronological sequence.").

[536]SAA, *supra* note 516, at 882. The Final Act does not impose any presumption that imports subject to older orders are less likely to be continuing to cause injury. One commentator, however, explained the Administration's approach in the following manner:

> The Administration determined that the most sensible approach was to generally organize the reviews on a chronological basis, with the oldest orders being reviewed first. The reason for this was twofold: (1) it seemed probable that imports subject to older orders would be less likely to be continuing to cause injury; and (2) from the point of view of respondents, it seemed fairest to conduct initial reviews for potential revocation on those orders in existence for the longest period of time.

Barbara R. Stafford & Linda S. Chang, *The Sunset Provisions: Mortality and the Uruguay Round, in* 1 THE COMMERCE DEPARTMENT SPEAKS ON INTERNATIONAL TRADE AND INVESTMENT 721, 743 (PLI, 1994).

[537]SAA, *supra* note 516, at 882-83.

[538]Transition Orders; Schedule and Grouping of Five-year Reviews, 62 Fed. Reg. 52,686, 52,686 (Dep't Comm. 1997).

[539]A significant number of comments objected to the fact that orders covering arguably related like products would be grouped or argued that the ITC should not cumulate related like products. *See, e.g.,* Japan Bearing Industrial Association Public Comments at 1 (12/8/97); Ad Hoc Committee of Domestic Nitrogen Producers Public

their proposed schedule, the DOC made only minor changes and published the final schedule and grouping on May 14, 1998, less than two months before the initiation of the first sunset review.[540]

b. Automatic Initiation of Sunset Reviews

The language of Article 11.3 of the Antidumping Agreement and Article 21.3 of the Subsidies Agreement gave member states two options for initiating sunset reviews: (1) an agency self-initiation, or (2) a domestic industry request.[541] The United States opted to self-initiate all sunset reviews. According to the Statement of Administrative Action, the Administration concluded that automatic initiation would reduce the burden on both the domestic industry and the agencies.[542] The automatic initiation process fixes the date of initiation for sunset reviews for non-transition or-

---

Comments at 1-2 (12/8/97); Lehigh Portland Cement Company Public Comments at 1, 3 (12/8/97); Mississippi Potash Corp. Public Comments at 1-2 (12/8/97); Cookware Manufacturers Association Public Comments at 1 (12/5/97); Canadian Embassy Public Comments at 1-2 (12/8/97); General Housewares Corp. Public Comments at 5 (12/8/97). Potential domestic interested parties also requested that their procedural rights to present their case not be compromised by grouping the reviews. The Torrington Company Public Comments at 1 (12/5/97); The Timken Company Public Comments at 2 (12/5/97).

[540]Transition Orders; Final Schedule and Grouping of Five-Year Reviews, 63 Fed. Reg. 26,779 (Dep't Comm. 1998), *republished at* Transition Orders; Final Schedule and Grouping of Five-Year Reviews, 63 Fed. Reg. 29,372 (Dep't Comm. 1998).

[541]The Antidumping Agreement states:

> [A]ny definitive anti-dumping duty shall be terminated on a date not later than five years from its imposition . . . , unless the authorities determine, *in a review initiated before that date on their own initiative or upon a duly substantiated request made by or on behalf of the domestic industry* within a reasonable period of time prior to that date, that the expiry of the duty would be likely to lead to continuation or recurrence of dumping and injury.

Antidumping Agreement, *supra* note 5, at art. 11.3 (emphasis added).

[542]SAA, *supra* note 516, at 879.

> Automatic initiation will avoid placing an unnecessary burden on the domestic industry and promote efficiency of administration by: (1) combining into a single

ders to not later than 30 days before the fifth anniversary date and for transition orders according to the agencies' published schedule.[543]

Although reviews are self-initiated, the agencies will decide to conduct an expedited or full review based on the adequacy of interested party responses, including those of the domestic industry. Consistent with the Agreements' requirements to provide ample notice,[544] the URAA requires a notice to be published in the *Federal Register* each time the DOC initiates a sunset review. The notice must request the following information.[545] First, interested parties are required to state their willingness to participate in the review by providing information requested by the DOC and ITC. Second, interested parties are required to make a statement concerning the likely effects of revocation of the order or termination of the suspended investigation. Finally, interested parties must submit such other information or industry data as the DOC or ITC specify.[546] According to the SAA, the DOC and ITC may request such "other information" as data regarding sales, prices, imports, and market conditions.[547] Consistent with the Agreements, both the DOC and the ITC's regulations provide interested parties 30 and 50 days, respectively, to supply requested information.[548]

i. The DOC's Notice of Initiation

Not later than 15 days after the notice of initiation, the DOC's regulations require domestic interested parties to file a notice of intent to partici-

---

> action notification to all parties of the upcoming five-year review; and (2) providing an effective means of evaluating the level of interest of all affected parties and the need for a full-fledged review.

Id.

[543] 19 U.S.C. §§1675(c)(2), 1675(c)(6)(A)(i), (D); 19 C.F.R. §351.218(c)(1), (4) (1997).

[544] Antidumping Agreement, *supra* note 5, at arts. 12.1, 12.3; Subsidies Agreement, *supra* note 5, at arts. 22.1, 22.7.

[545] 19 U.S.C. §1675(c)(2).

[546] *Id.*

[547] SAA, *supra* note 516, at 879.

[548] *See* Antidumping Agreement, *supra* note 5, at art. 6; *Subsidies Agreement, supra* note 5, at art. 12.

pate in the sunset review.[549] The purpose of the notice of intent requirement is to alleviate the burden of all other potential interested parties in responding to a request for information when there is no domestic industry interest.[550] If no domestic interested party files a notice of intent to participate in the sunset review, the DOC will treat the failure as a non-response, notify the ITC within 20 days of the notice of initiation, and issue a final determination revoking the order or terminating the suspended investigation not later than 90 days after the date of publication of the notice of initiation.[551] If the DOC does receive a notice of intent to participate and the review progresses, any domestic interested party that did not file such a notice will be considered "not willing to participate," and the DOC will not accept or consider any unsolicited submissions from that party during the course of the review.[552]

Within 30 days from the notice of initiation, all interested parties must file a substantive response to the DOC's request for information.[553] According to the DOC's regulations, interested parties, except foreign governments in a countervailing duty review, must file the following information in their substantive response to the notice of initiation:[554]

---

[549]*Interim Regulations, supra* note 516, §351.218(d). The notice of intent to participate will include, *inter alia*, a brief statement expressing an intent to participate; the name, address, and telephone number of the party and counsel; and a statement indicating whether the domestic producer is related to a foreign producer or exporter or imports or is related to an importer. *Id.*

[550]*Id.* at 13,517. As explained *infra*, the DOC is instructed to revoke or terminate within 90 days of the notice of initiation in the absence of a response from a domestic interested party to the notice of initiation. 19 U.S.C. §1675(c)(3)(A).

[551]*Interim Regulations, supra* note 516, §351.218(d)(1)(iii)(B).

[552]*Id.* §351.218(d)(1)(iii)(A).

[553]*Id.* §351.218(d)(3)(i).

[554]In addition to the required responses, the DOC's regulations also require interested parties to submit any information or evidence showing "good cause" to consider other factors in addition to required factors or any other relevant information in deciding whether or not revocation or termination is likely to lead to continuation or recurrence of dumping or countervailable subsidies. *Interim Regulations, supra* note 516, §351.218(d)(3)(iv); 19 U.S.C. §§1675a(b)(2), (c)(2). See Section B.1, *infra*, for a description of the factors the DOC will consider in making its determination in a sunset review.

DOC Reporting Requirements for Interested Parties Except Foreign Governments in CVD Reviews[555]

Regulation	*Provision*
§351.218(d)(3)(ii)(A)	The name, address, and phone number of the interested party (and its members, if applicable) that intends to participate in the sunset review and the statutory basis (under section 771(9) of the Act) for interested party status;
§351.218(d)(3)(ii)(B)	The name, address, and phone number of legal counsel or other representative, if any;
§351.218(d)(3)(ii)(C)	The subject merchandise and country subject to the sunset review;
§351.218(d)(3)(ii)(D)	The citation and date of publication in the **Federal Register** of the notice of initiation;
§351.218(d)(3)(ii)(E)	A statement expressing the interested party's willingness to participate in the review by providing information requested by the Department, which must include a summary of that party's historical participation in any segment of the proceeding before the Department related to the subject merchandise;
§351.218(d)(3)(ii)(F)	A statement regarding the likely effects of revocation of the order or termination of the suspended investigation under review, which must include any factual information, argument, and reason to support such statement;
§351.218(d)(3)(ii)(G)	Factual information, argument, and reason concerning the dumping margin or countervailing duty rate, as applicable, that is likely to prevail if the Secretary revokes the order or terminates the suspended investigation, that the Department should select for a particular interested party(s);
§351.218(d)(3)(ii)(H)	A summary of the Department's findings regarding duty absorption, if any, including a citation to the **Federal Register** notice in which the Department's findings are set forth; and
§351.218(d)(3)(ii)(I)	A description of any relevant scope clarification or ruling, including a circumvention determination, or changed circumstances determination issued by the Department during the proceeding with respect to the subject merchandise.

[555] *See Interim Regulations, supra* note 516.

In addition, respondent interested parties must file the following required information:

DOC Reporting Requirements for Respondent Interested Parties[556]

Regulation	*Provision*
§351.218(d)(3)(iii)(A)	That party's individual weighted average dumping margin or countervailing duty rate, as applicable, from the investigation and each subsequent completed administrative review, including the final margin or rate, as applicable, where such margin or rate was changed as a result of a final and conclusive court order;
§351.218(d)(3)(iii)(B)	For each of the five calendar years (or fiscal years, if more appropriate) preceding the year of publication of the notice of initiation, that party's volume and value (normally on an FOB basis) of exports of the subject merchandise to the United States;
§351.218(d)(3)(iii)(C)	As applicable, for the calendar year (or fiscal year, if more appropriate) preceding the year of initiation of the dumping investigation, that party's volume and value (normally on an FOB basis) of exports of subject merchandise to the United States;
§351.218(d)(3)(iii)(D)	For each of the five calendar years (or fiscal years, if more appropriate) preceding the year of publication of the notice of initiation, on a volume basis (or value basis, if more appropriate), that party's percentage of the total exports of subject merchandise (defined in section 771(25) of the Act) to the United States; and
§351.218(d)(3)(iii)(E)	For each of the three most recent years, including the year of publication of the notice of initiation, that party's volume and value (normally on an FOB basis) of exports of subject merchandise to the United States during the two fiscal quarters as of the month preceding the month in which the notice of initiation was published.

[556]*See Interim Regulations, supra* note 516.

According to 19 C.F.R. §351.218(d)(3)(ii) of the DOC's regulations, the general reporting requirements apply to all interested parties except for the foreign government of a country subject to a countervailing duty (CVD) sunset review as described in §351.218(d)(3)(v)(A).[557] Foreign governments have the following reporting requirements:

DOC Reporting Requirements for Foreign Governments in CVD Reviews[558]

Regulation	*Provision*
§351.218(d)(3)(ii)(A)	The name, address, and phone number of the interested party (and its members, if applicable) that intends to participate in the sunset review and the statutory basis (under section 771(9) of the Act) for interested party status.
§351.218(d)(3)(ii)(B)	The name, address, and phone number of legal counsel or other representative, if any.
§351.218(d)(3)(ii)(C)	The subject merchandise and country subject to the sunset review.
§351.218(d)(3)(ii)(D)	The citation and date of publication in the **Federal Register** of the notice of initiation.
§351.218(d)(3)(ii)(E)	A statement expressing the interested party's willingness to participate in the review by providing information requested by the Department, which must include a summary of that party's historical participation in any segment of the proceeding before the Department related to the subject merchandise.
If the original investigation was conducted on an aggregate basis, the foreign government must also submit:	
§351.218(d)(3)(ii)(F)	A statement regarding the likely effects of revocation of the order or termination of the suspended investigation under review, which must include any factual information, argument, and reason to support such statement.

557 *Id.* §351.218(d)(3)(v)(A), (B).

558 *See id.*

DOC Reporting Requirements for Foreign Governments in CVD Reviews ***(Continued)***

Regulation	*Provision*
§351.218(d)(3)(ii)(G)	Factual information, argument, and reason concerning the dumping margin or countervailing duty rate, as applicable, that is likely to prevail if the Secretary revokes the order or terminates the suspended investigation, that the Department should select for a particular interested party(s).
§351.218(d)(3)(ii)(I)	A description of any relevant scope clarification or ruling, including a circumvention determination, or changed circumstances determination issued by the Department during the proceeding with respect to the subject merchandise.
§351.218(d)(3)(v)(B)(2)	The countervailing duty rate from the investigation and each subsequent completed administrative review, including the final rate where such rate was changed as a result of a final and conclusive court order.
§351.218(d)(3)(v)(B)(3)	For each of the five calendar years (or fiscal years, if more appropriate) preceding the year of publication of the notice of initiation, the volume and value (normally on an FOB basis) of exports of subject merchandise to the United States.

Section 777(h) of the Tariff Act of 1930, as amended (19 U.S.C. §1677f(h)), requires the DOC (and the ITC) to allow industrial users of the subject merchandise and, if the merchandise is sold at the retail level, representative consumer organizations to submit relevant information in their proceedings.[559] Therefore, any industrial users of the subject merchandise or representative consumer organizations that intend to participate in the sunset review must submit the following information:

[559] 19 U.S.C. §1677f(h).

DOC Reporting Requirements for Industrial Users and Consumers[560]

Regulation	*Provision*
§351.218(d)(3)(ii)(A)	The name, address, and phone number of the interested party (and its members, if applicable) that intends to participate in the sunset review and the statutory basis (under section 771(9) of the Act) for interested party status.
§351.218(d)(3)(ii)(B)	The name, address, and phone number of legal counsel or other representative, if any.
§351.218(d)(3)(ii)(C)	The subject merchandise and country subject to the sunset review.
§351.218(d)(3)(ii)(D)	The citation and date of publication in the **Federal Register** of the notice of initiation.

Finally, all interested parties and industrial users and consumers have the option of submitting the following information in response to the notice of initiation:

Optional Information To Be Filed With Substantive Response[561]

Regulation	*Provision*
§351.218(d)(3)(iv)(A)	An interested party may submit information or evidence to show good cause for the Secretary to consider other factors under section 752(b)(2) (CVD) or section 752(c)(2) (AD) of the Act and paragraph (e)(2)(ii) of this section. Such information or evidence must be submitted in the party's substantive response to the notice of initiation under paragraph (d)(3) of this section.
§351.218(d)(3)(iv)(B)	A substantive response from an interested party under paragraph (d)(3) of this section also may contain any other relevant information or argument that the party would like the Secretary to consider.

[560] *See Interim Regulations, supra* note 516.

[561] *See id.*

Within five days of the date the substantive response is filed, any interested party that filed a substantive response to the DOC's notice of initiation may file rebuttal comments. The rebuttal comment deadline will also serve as the deadline for considering any additional information unless the DOC requests additional information after deciding to proceed to a full review.[562]

ii. The ITC's Notice of Institution

The ITC's regulations require interested parties to respond within 50 days from the ITC's notice of institution.[563] The notice will request the following information: (1) a statement expressing the party's willingness to participate in the review by providing information; (2) a statement regarding the likely effects of revocation or termination; and (3) such information or industry data as specified in the notice.[564] In addition, the ITC proposes to request the following information:

ITC Reporting Requirements for All Interested Parties[565]

1. The name and address of your firm or entity (including World Wide Web address if available) and name, telephone number, fax number, and E-mail address of the certifying official.
2. A statement indicating whether your firm/entity is a U.S. producer of the DOMESTIC LIKE PRODUCT, a U.S. union or worker group, a U.S. importer of the SUBJECT MERCHANDISE, a foreign producer or exporter of the SUBJECT MERCHANDISE, a U.S. or foreign trade or business association, or another interested party (including an explanation). If you are a union/worker group or trade/business association, identify the firms in which your workers are employed or which are members of your association.
3. A statement indicating whether your firm/entity is willing to participate in this review by providing information requested by the Commission.

[562]*Id.* §351.218(d)(4).

[563]*Final Regulations, supra* note 516, §207.61(a).

[564]*Id.*

[565]*See Final Regulations, supra* note 516, at Annex A.

ITC Reporting Requirements for All Interested Parties (Continued)

4. A statement of the likely effects of the revocation of the countervailing duty order/antidumping duty order/termination of the suspension agreement on the DOMESTIC INDUSTRY in general and/or your firm/entity specifically. In your response, please discuss the various factors specified in section 752(a) of the Act (19 U.S.C. §1675a(a)) including the likely volume of subject imports, likely price effects of subject imports, and likely impact of imports of SUBJECT MERCHNAIDSE on the DOMESTIC INDUSTRY.
5. A list of all known and currently operating U.S. producers of the DOMESTIC LIKE PRODUCT. Identify any known related parties and the nature of the relationship as defined in section 771(4)(B) of the Act (19 U.S.C. §1677(4)(B)).
6. A list of all known and currently operating U.S. importers of the SUBJECT MERCHANDISE and producers of the SUBJECT MERCHANDISE in [INSERT COUNTRY] that currently export or have exported SUBJECT MERCHANDISE to the United States or other countries since [INSERT YEAR OF PETITION].
7. Identify significant changes, if any, in the supply and demand conditions or business cycle for the DOMESTIC LIKE PRODUCT that have occurred in the United States or in the market for the SUBJECT MERCHANDISE in SUBJECT COUNTRY since the ORDER DATE, and significant changes, if any, that are likely to occur within a reasonably foreseeable time. Supply conditions to consider include technology; production methods; development efforts; ability to increase production (including the shift of production facilities used for other products and the use, cost, or availability of major inputs into production); and factors related to the ability to shift supply among different national markets (including barriers to importation in foreign markets or changes in market demand abroad). Demand conditions to consider include end uses and applications; the existence and availability of substitute products; and the level of competition among the DOMESTIC LIKE PRODUCT produced in the United States, SUBJECT MERCHANDISE produced in the SUBJECT COUNTRY, and [INSERT PRODUCT DESCRIPTION] from other countries.
8. (OPTIONAL) A statement of whether you agree with the above definitions of the DOMESTIC LIKE PRODUCT and DOMESTIC INDUSTRY; if you disagree with either or both of these definitions, please explain why and provide alternative definitions.

ITC Reporting Requirements for U.S. Producers, Importers, and Foreign Producers Requesting Information for the Preceding Year[566]

U.S. Producers	*Importers*	*Foreign Producers*
(a) Production (*quantity*) and, if known, an estimate of the percentage of total U.S. production of the DOMESTIC LIKE PRODUCT accounted for by your firm's (s') production; and	(a) The *quantity* and *value* of U.S. imports, if known, an estimate of the percentage of total U.S. imports of SUBJECT MERCHANDISE from [INSERT COUNTRY] accounted for by your firm's (s') imports; and	(a) Production (*quantity*) and, if known, an estimate of the percentage of total production of SUBJECT MERCHANDISE in [INSERT COUNTRY] accounted for by your firm's (s') production; and
(b) the *quantity* and *value* of U.S. commercial shipments of the DOMESTIC LIKE PRODUCT produced in your U.S. plant(s).	(b) the *quantity* and *value* of U.S. commercial shipments of SUBJECT MERCHANDISE imported from [INSERT COUNTRY].	(b) the *quantity* and *value* of your firm's exports to the United States of *Subject Merchandise* and, if known, an estimate of the percentage of total exports to the United States of SUBJECT MERCHANDISE from [INSERT COUNTRY] accounted for by your firm's (s') exports.

c. *Judging the Adequacy of Substantive Responses for a Full Review*

There are three possible "responses" to the notice of initiation: (1) no response; (2) an inadequate response; or (3) an adequate response. The agencies will independently determine whether interested parties have responded

566 *See id.* According to Annex A of the ITC's regulations, union/worker groups or trade/business associations should provide the same information as requested from producers/importers for the firms in which they are employed or which are members of their association. *Id.*

adequately to the notice of initiation.[567] The purpose of assessing the adequacy of interested party responses is to determine whether interested parties will participate fully in a sunset review by providing the information necessary to make a substantiated determination. The SAA explains that, if parties fail to submit adequate responses to the agencies' requests for information in the notices of initiation, it is likely that those parties will not respond or submit adequate or usable responses to more comprehensive questionnaires.[568] Absent a reasonable likelihood of collecting necessary additional information, the agencies are not required to extend the sunset review.

i. The DOC's Regulations

The DOC's regulations provide criteria that the agency will use to evaluate substantive responses for adequacy. Although adequacy determinations will be made on a case-by-case basis, the DOC will normally find that an interested party has provided an adequate response if they submit a complete substantive response to the questions identified above and found in 19 C.F.R. §351.218(d)(3).[569] The DOC may disregard a response from a domestic producer (1) related to a foreign producer or to a foreign exporter, or (2) that is an importer of the subject merchandise or is related to such an importer.[570] To avoid needless reviews, the DOC will revoke the order or ter-

---

[567] *See* SAA, *supra* note 516, at 879-80 ("Because Commerce and the Commission may require different information from different sources to conduct reviews, the agencies may decide separately whether the responses are inadequate and whether to issue a determination based on the facts available without further fact-gathering."). The Senate Report further indicates that the adequacy of responses should be conducted by the two agencies independently because "each agency will be relying on different information from different sources to conduct its reviews." S. REP. NO. 103-412, at 46 (1994).

[568] *See* SAA, *supra* note 516, at 880.

[569] *Interim Regulations*, *supra* note 516, §§351.218(e)(1)(i)(A), (ii)(A). The DOC may also consider a substantive response that does not contain all the required information to be complete where the party is unable to report certain information and provides a reasonable explanation as to why it is unable to provide the information. *Id.* at 13,518.

[570] *Id.* §351.218(e)(1)(i)(B). Section 771(4)(B) of the Tariff Act of 1930, as amended (19 U.S.C. §1677(4)(B)), defines "related parties" in the following manner:

> (i) If a producer of a domestic like product and an exporter or importer of the subject merchandise are related parties, or if a producer of the domestic like product is also an importer of the subject merchandise, the producer may, in appropriate circumstances, be excluded from the industry.

minate the suspended investigation within 90 days of initiating the review if no domestic interested party responds to the notice of initiation.[571]

Likewise, according to the DOC's regulations, if no domestic interested party(s)' response is adequate for any reason and no other domestic interested party has filed a complete substantive response, the DOC will treat the response as a non-response. The DOC will then notify the ITC within 40 days after the notice of initiation and issue a final determination revoking the order or terminating the suspended investigation not later than 90 days after the notice of initiation.[572] The interim regulations thus appear to merge "no response" and "inadequate response" into a single category of "no response." In contrast, if respondent interested parties have provided inadequate responses to the notice of initiation, the DOC will notify the ITC normally not later than 50 days after the date of initiation and conduct an expedited review.[573]

In cases involving review of countervailable subsidies, the legislative history confirms that the DOC would require a response from the foreign government before initiating a full sunset review.[574] In a countervailing

---

(ii) For purposes of clause (i), a producer and an exporter or importer shall be considered to be related parties, if—
   (I) the producer directly or indirectly controls the exporter or importer,
   (II) the exporter or importer directly or indirectly controls the producer,
   (III) a third party directly or indirectly controls the producer and the exporter or importer, or
   (IV) the producer and the exporter or importer directly or indirectly control a third party and there is reason to believe that the relationship causes the producer to act differently than a nonrelated producer.

For purposes of this subparagraph, a party shall be considered to directly or indirectly control another party if the party is legally or operationally in a position to exercise restraint or direction over the other party.

[571]19 U.S.C. §1675(c)(3)(A); 19 C.F.R. §351.221(c)(5)(ii) (1997) ("The Secretary, without issuing preliminary results of review, may issue final results of review under paragraphs (3) or (4) of subsection 751(c) of the Act if the conditions of those paragraphs are satisfied."); SAA, *supra* note 516, at 880; H.R. REP. NO. 103-826(I), at 56 (1994); S. REP. NO. 103-412, at 46 (1994). In comments on the proposed regulations, the DOC has warned that "parties will receive no further notice of the review unless and until they provide" a response to a request for information in the notice of initiation. 61 Fed. Reg. at 7319.

[572]*Interim Regulations, supra* note 516, §351.218(e)(1)(i)(C).

[573]*Id.* §351.218(e)(1)(ii)(C).

[574]SAA, *supra* note 516, at 880; S. REP. NO. 103-412, at 46 (1994).

duty case, the "participation of the foreign government is indispensable, because only that government is in a position to explain its actions and intentions with respect to present and future subsidization."[575] In the absence of a response from the foreign government, the DOC will conduct an expedited review and rely on evidence provided by the domestic industry or that is otherwise available.[576]

ii. The ITC's Regulations

The ITC will generally consider the adequacy of responses to the notice of institution and make a decision whether or not to conduct an expedited review for each individual order or suspension agreement. If a particular order covers multiple domestic like products, then the ITC will consider the adequacy issue for each domestic like product.[577]

Section 782(d) of the Tariff Act of 1930, as amended (19 U.S.C. §1677m(d)), permits the DOC or ITC to disregard all or part of a questionnaire response if the agency has informed the person submitting the information of the nature of the deficiency and provided, to the extent practicable, the person with an opportunity to remedy or explain the deficiency and the subsequent response is not satisfactory or is untimely.[578] Consistent with Section 782(d), therefore, the ITC staff will review each response to the notice of institution for completeness and, to the extent practicable, will attempt to notify the submitter and provide a brief period of time (between 5 to 10 days) to remedy or explain the deficiency.[579]

In comments on the ITC's regulations, the agency has indicated that it could exercise its discretion to conduct a full review notwithstanding inadequate interested party responses in two circumstances. First, the ITC will normally conduct full reviews for all countries in a grouped review where aggregate domestic interested party responses are not inadequate and responses from foreign interested parties are adequate with respect to some of the countries in the group, but inadequate with respect to others. Second, the ITC may decide to conduct a full review if there is a need to re-examine

---

[575]SAA, *supra* note 516, at 880.

[576]*Id.*; *Interim Regulations, supra* note 516, §351.218(e)(1)(ii)(B).

[577]*Final Regulations, supra* note 516, §207.62(a).

[578]19 U.S.C. §1677m(d).

[579]*Final Regulations, supra* note 516, at 30,603.

the domestic like product definition made in the original determination even when domestic and/or foreign interested party responses are inadequate.[580]

iii. An Expedited Review Based on "Facts Available"

When interested parties, whether foreign or domestic, provide in the aggregate an inadequate response to a notice of initiation, the DOC, within 120 days, and the ITC, within 150 days, have the discretion to issue a final determination based on the "facts available" in an expedited review without further investigation.[581] Otherwise, the agencies will conduct full reviews on the basis of adequate responses.[582] The DOC has made it clear in its regulations that it will normally only conduct a full review if it receives adequate responses from both domestic and respondent interested parties.[583]Appendix

---

[580]*Final Regulations, supra* note 516, at 30,604. According to comments on the final regulations:

> In appropriate circumstances, the Commission may revisit its original domestic like product and domestic industry determinations in five-year reviews. For example, the Commission may revisit its like product determination when there have been significant changes in the products at issue since the original investigation or when domestic like product definitions differed for individual orders within a group concerning similar products.

Id. at 30,602.

[581]19 U.S.C. §1675(c)(3)(B); *see* SAA, *supra* note 516, at 879 ("if there is inadequate response to a notice of initiation by foreign and domestic interested parties, Commerce and the Commission will conduct an expedited review based on the facts available"). Notably, the statute states that the DOC "shall" revoke or terminate the order or suspended investigation when receiving no response to its notice of initiation, but both DOC and the ITC "may" issue a final determination based on facts available when receiving an inadequate response. *Compare* 19 U.S.C. §1675(c)(3)(A) *with* 19 U.S.C. §1675(c)(3)(B). Thus, the agencies have the discretion to conduct a full review even when the response to the notice of initiation is inadequate. *See Final Regulations, supra* note 516, at 30,604. According to the ITC's regulations, the response to the notice of institution of the sunset review becomes the only opportunity for interested parties to submit factual information if the ITC determines that the response rate is inadequate. *Final Regulations, supra* note 516, at 30,601 ("the Commission will reach an expedited determination 'without further investigation,' and will not generate additional factual information if it decides to conduct an expedited review.").

[582]*See id.* §351.218(e)(1)(ii)(C)(2).

[583]*Id.* §351.218(e)(2).

II contains charts detailing the proposed schedule for expedited and full reviews.

Although the Agreements do not specifically require an assessment of the adequacy of interested party responses when a sunset review is initiated, the URAA' s reliance on resort to facts available in expedited reviews is consistent with the Agreements' requirements. Not only do the Agreements encourage "expeditious" reviews, but the Agreements permit resort to facts available in the absence of necessary information requested from interested parties.[584] Pursuant to Section 776 of the Tariff Act of 1930, as amended (19 U.S.C. §1677e), therefore, the statute permits the DOC or ITC to make determinations based on the "facts otherwise available." The agencies may rely on the following information in making adverse inferences based on "facts otherwise available": (1) the petition; (2) the final determination in the investigation; (3) any previous review; or (4) any other information placed on the record in making its adverse inference.[585]

The DOC has adopted regulations to guide its application of facts otherwise available in sunset reviews. According to 19 C.F.R. §351.308, the DOC will normally rely on the following data when issuing its final results based on facts available: (1) calculated countervailing duty rates or dumping margins, as applicable, from prior determinations, and (2) information contained in parties' substantive responses to the notice of initiation consistent with Section 752(b) or 752(c).[586] According to the ITC's comments on its final regulations, "facts available" may include: (1) information submitted on the record in the sunset review by parties and non-parties; (2) other information the ITC may compile before the record closes; (3) material from the record of the original investigation and subsequent ITC reviews, if any; and (4) available information from the DOC's proceedings.[587]

The agencies may invoke adverse inferences when an interested party has failed to cooperate by not acting to the best of its ability to comply with

---

[584]Antidumping Agreement, *supra* note 5, at arts. 6.8, 11.4; Subsidies Agreement, *supra* note 5, at arts. 12.7, 21.4.

[585]19 U.S.C. §1677e(b); *see* SAA, *supra* note 516, at 879 ("The facts available may include prior agency determinations involving the subject merchandise as well as information submitted on the record by parties in response to the notice of initiation.").

[586]As discussed *infra* in Section B, Section 752(b) and 752(c) of the Tariff Act of 1930, as amended (19 U.S.C. §§1675a(b), (c)) provide guidance to the DOC in making its determination as to whether revocation or termination would be likely to lead to the continuation or recurrence of dumping or countervailing subsidies.

[587]*Final Regulations, supra* note 516, at 30,606.

an information request.[588] Adopting an adverse inference, however, is discretionary. If the agency finds, for example, that the domestic industry expressed a willingness but not the ability to comply with information requests sufficient to warrant a full review, the agency would not be required to invoke an adverse inference against the domestic industry.[589] According to the legislative history, "[t]he standard for judging the adequacy of information should not be so high as to lead the agencies to disregard fairly complete information submitted by parties clearly willing to participate."[590]

d. Judging the Adequacy of Response Rates for a Full Review

In addition to responding to substantive questions in the notice of initiation, the agencies will impose an additional adequacy requirement before conducting a full sunset review in cases where some, but not all, interested parties submitted responses. According to the SAA, the agencies would determine the adequacy of an initial response by considering the "proportion of parties that respond and their likely share of the market if the order were revoked or the suspended investigation terminated."[591] In addition, the DOC was instructed to "consider the effect of the order or suspension agreement, taking into account the possible impact of the different dumping margins or net countervailable subsidies for individual exporters on import volumes."[592] The SAA left the determination regarding adequacy of initial responses to the agencies' discretion with the stated intention that they would "develop guidelines, either through regulation or practice, for making the decision called for by new section 751(c)(3)(B)."[593]

The lack of any specific statutory standing requirement, however, indicates that Congress did not intend to impose a heavy burden on interested parties to prove entitlement to a full sunset review during the

---

[588] 19 U.S.C. §1677e(b); *see, e.g., Final Regulations, supra* note 516, at 30,602, §207.62(e).

[589] *See* SAA, *supra* note 516, at 880.

[590] S. Rep. No. 103-412, at 46 (1994).

[591] SAA, *supra* note 516, at 880; S. Rep. No. 103-412, at 46 (1994).

[592] SAA, *supra* note 516, at 880.

[593] *Id.*

initiation phase.[594] For instance, Congress did include a specific statutory standing requirement to determine domestic industry standing in an original investigation.[595] In order to file an antidumping or countervailing duty petition in an original investigation, the petitioner must affirmatively establish the support of a petition which is filed "by or on behalf of the domestic industry" as defined in the statute and regulations. According to Sections 702 and 732 of the Tariff Act of 1930, as amended (19 U.S.C. §§1671a(c)(4)(A) and 1673a(c)(4)(A)), the URAA requires that the DOC find that a petition has been filed "by or on behalf of a domestic industry" under the following circumstances:

> (i) the domestic producers or workers who support the petition account for at least 25 percent of total production of the domestic like product, and
> (ii) the domestic producers or workers who support the petition account for more than 50 percent of the production of the domestic like product produced by that portion of the industry expressing support for or opposition to the petition.

The DOC is required to poll the industry or rely on other information to determine support for the petition if the petition does not establish support of domestic producers or workers accounting for more than 50 percent of the total production of the domestic like product.[596]

---

[594]*See* Stewart and Stewart Comments at 34 (12/22/97). Indeed, U.S. negotiators fought to establish a self-initiation provision for sunset reviews. *Id.*

[595]"It is well established that where Congress has included specific language in one section of a statute but has omitted it from another, related section of the same Act, it is generally presumed that Congress intended the omission." Ad Hoc Committee of AZ-NM-TX-FL Producers of Cement v. United States, 13 F.3d 398, 401 (Fed. Cir. 1994), *citing* Russello v. United States, 464 U.S. 16, 23 (1983).

[596]19 U.S.C. §§1671a(c)(4)(D), 1673a(c)(4)(D). These new URAA standing requirements are in sharp contrast with the standing requirement under the pre-URAA law whereby the DOC presumed that the petitioner had filed the petition on behalf of the domestic industry. *See* Suramerica de Aleaciones Laminadas, C.A. v. United States, 966 F.2d 660 (Fed. Cir. 1992); NTN Bearing Corp. v. United States, 757 F. Supp. 1425 (CIT 1991), *aff'd,* 972 F.2d 1355 (Fed. Cir. 1992); Comeau Seafoods, Ltd. v. United States, 724 F. Supp. 1407 (CIT 1989); Florex v. United States, 705 F. Supp. 582, 587-88 (CIT 1989). A majority of the domestic industry would have to oppose the petition to overcome the presumption of standing. *See* Minebea Co., Ltd. v. United States, 984 F.2d 1178 (Fed. Cir. 1993); Mitsubishi Heavy Indus., Ltd. v. United States, Slip Op. 97-153, at 6 (CIT Nov. 19, 1997).

In contrast, the sunset review provisions require the agencies to initiate a review and receive some response to the notice of initiation from domestic interested parties to proceed further.[597] In evaluating the market shares to determine the adequacy of responses, the Senate Report specifically cautioned that the "Committee does not intend to establish a strict numerical test for determining adequacy. Rather, the agencies should evaluate the responses on a case-by-case basis."[598]

i. The DOC's Regulations

The DOC's regulations state how the agency will determine whether there has been an adequate showing of "market share" to support a full sunset review. According to comments on the DOC's regulations, the agency will determine separately the adequacy of domestic and respondent interested parties' responses.[599] In assessing responses in the aggregate, the DOC will consider only those responses that are individually considered adequate.[600]

With respect to domestic interested party responses, the DOC will normally consider receipt of one adequate domestic interested party response to be adequate.[601] With respect to respondent interested party responses, the DOC will normally find that respondent interested parties have provided an adequate response when it receives responses from parties accounting on average for more than 50 percent, on a volume basis (or value basis, if appropriate), of the total exports of subject merchandise to the United States over the five calendar years preceding the year of publication of the notice of initiation.[602] The difference in the adequacy standards is presumably due to the fact that the information relevant to the DOC's determination is within the control of foreign producers or exporters.

---

[597] 19 U.S.C. §1675(c)(3)(A).

[598] S. Rep. No. 103-412, at 46 (1994).

[599] *Interim Regulations,* supra note 516, at 13,518.

[600] *Id.*

[601] *Id.* §351.218(e)(1)(i)(A).

[602] *Id.* §351.218(e)(1)(ii)(A).

ii. The ITC's Regulations

The ITC's regulations indicate that the agency will consider separately whether the responses from domestic interested parties and foreign interested parties are adequate on a case-by-case basis. The fact that a single domestic or foreign interested party has filed an adequate response to the notice of institution will not, per se, be considered a sufficient indication that either pertinent group of interested parties as a whole is interested in a full review. [603] According to comments on the final regulations, the ITC will consider several factors in determining the adequacy of responses on an aggregate basis, including:

> (1) the level of interested parties' responses, including examination of the responding parties' share of domestic production, foreign production, subject imports, or exports for the most recent calendar year;
> (2) the structure of the industries in question (*e.g.*, whether or not fragmented);
> (3) the prevalence of related parties;
> (4) the ability of particular foreign producers to export to the United States;
> (5) the extent to which subject imports appear to have been excluded from the U.S. market by the order or suspension agreement under review.[604]

In its proposed regulations, the ITC tentatively identified a range of percentiles that would indicate an adequate response rate for domestic producers/unions, on the one hand, and foreign producers/importers, on the other hand. For example, responses accounting for more than 50 percent of domestic production, 50 percent of subject imports, or 50 percent of pro-

---

[603] *Final Regulations, supra* note 516, at 30,603.

[604] *Id.* at 30,603-04. According to the final regulations, the ITC will consider a response from either U.S. importers or foreign producers to constitute an adequate response from "foreign producers/importers." *Id.* at 30,603. Adequate responses by unions or worker groups that are interested parties will be counted as being equal to the production of the domestic like product of the firms at which the workers in the group or union are employed. *Id.* The ITC will also evaluate the significance of non-responses of related parties on a case-by-case basis. *Id.* at 30,604. According to the ITC, the ability of foreign exporters to export to the United States could be relevant in a case where particular foreign producers do not manufacture a version of the subject merchandise that can be exported to the United States. *Id.*

duction of the subject merchandise will normally be considered to be a strong indication of an adequate response rate for domestic producers/ unions or foreign producers/importers.[605] In contrast, responses accounting for less than 25 percent will normally be considered to be a strong indication of an inadequate response rate for domestic producers/unions or foreign producers/importers.[606]

The ITC's proposed sunset standard, however, appeared to be as or more onerous than the standing requirement in original investigations. Therefore, in response to comments on the proposed regulations, the ITC decided not to adopt numerical guidelines for adequacy rates. The ITC further clarified that it had not intended to equate adequacy guidelines with industry representation requirements.[607]

e. *Request for Simultaneous Expedited Review and Injury Investigation for Certain Countervailing Duty Orders*

As explained above in Chapter II, Section A.4.c, by the end of the Uruguay Round, all outstanding U.S. countervailing duty orders were not issued with the benefit of an injury test. According to the WTO Agreement and Subsidies Agreement, however, all WTO member states are entitled to an injury test in countervailing duty investigations and prior to levying duties pursuant to existing orders.[608] The URAA, therefore, not only repeals Section 303 but also provides a mechanism for domestic interested parties to request an injury investigation for outstanding countervailing duty orders that did not benefit from an injury test.[609]

So that the ITC can cumulate imports in its injury analysis, the URAA also allows interested parties to request an expedited sunset review of orders involving the same or comparable subject merchandise at the same time as requesting an injury investigation of outstanding countervailing

---

[605] *Proposed Regulations, supra* note 516, at 55,190.

[606] *Id.*

[607] *Final Regulations, supra* note 516, at 30,603.

[608] SAA, *supra* note 516, at 923, 942.

[609] 19 U.S.C. §1675b(a)(1); *see Final Regulations, supra* note 516, §207.46(g).

duty orders.[610] If an expedited sunset review is initiated, the sunset review will be treated as having been initiated on the same day as the investigation, and the ITC may cumulatively assess the volume and effect of imports of the subject merchandise from all countries with respect to which such investigations are treated as initiated on the same day.[611]

Regardless of whether the ITC decides to cumulate imports subject to the simultaneous sunset review and injury investigation, the ITC must apply two different legal standards for injury to determine whether to continue the orders.[612] In the injury investigation, the ITC is required to determine whether an industry in the United States is likely to be materially injured if the order is revoked.[613] In contrast, in the sunset review, the ITC will determine whether material injury would be likely to continue or recur if the order was revoked.[614] Section 753(e) of the Tariff Act of 1930, as amended (19 U.S.C. §1675b(e)(3)), further requires the ITC to issue final determinations in the injury investigation and sunset review at the same time. In all other respects, the ITC is required to conduct the sunset review in accordance with applicable statutory standards governing the conduct of sunset reviews.[615]

f. Waiver of Reviews

Pursuant to Section 751(c)(4) of the Tariff Act of 1930, as amended (19 U.S.C. §1675(c)(4)), foreign interested parties may waive the DOC's portion of the sunset review.[616] Waiver of the DOC's portion of the sunset

---

[610] 19 U.S.C. §1675b(e)(1)(A). The DOC may decline to initiate a sunset review if the interested party who requested the investigation is a related party or an importer within the meaning of 19 U.S.C. §1677(4)(B). See *supra* note 570 for the definition of "related parties" within the meaning of 19 U.S.C. §1677(4)(B).

[611] 19 U.S.C. §1675b(e)(2).

[612] SAA, *supra* note 516, at 944.

[613] *Id.*

[614] The URAA defines "material injury" as harm which is not inconsequential, immaterial, or unimportant. 19 U.S.C. §1677(7)(A).

[615] 19 U.S.C. §1675b(e)(3).

[616] 19 U.S.C. §1675(c)(4); *see Interim Regulations, supra* note 516, §351.218(d)(2). According to 19 U.S.C. §1677(9)(A) and (B), a foreign interested party is defined as:

review automatically results in an affirmative finding that revocation of the order or termination of the suspended investigation would be likely to lead to continuation or recurrence of dumping or a countervailable subsidy with respect to that interested party.[617]

If a foreign government files for a waiver of the DOC's sunset review, the DOC will find that respondent interested parties have provided an inadequate response and will notify the ITC and will conduct an expedited review. The final results of the review will normally include a determination that revocation or termination would be likely to lead to continuation or recurrence of a countervailable subsidy for all respondent interested parties.[618]

According to the DOC's interim regulations, a respondent interested party may waive participation by filing a statement of waiver not later than 30 days after the date of publication of the notice of initiation.[619] An interested party that files a waiver will not be permitted to submit unsolicited information in the DOC's portion of the sunset review.[620] The DOC will also consider the failure of a respondent interested party to file a complete substantive response to a notice of initiation as a waiver of participation.[621] The waiver provision is a straightforward way to reduce the burden of all parties in otherwise needless administrative proceedings when there is little doubt that dumping or subsidization is likely to continue or recur.[622]

(A) a foreign manufacturer, producer, or exporter, or the United States importer, of subject merchandise or a trade or business association a majority of the members of which are producers, exporters, or importers of such merchandise,

(B) the government of a country in which such merchandise is produced or manufactured or from which such merchandise is exported. . . .

19 U.S.C. §§1677(9)(A), (B).

[617] 19 U.S.C. §1675(c)(4)(B).

[618] SAA, *supra* note 516, at 881; H.R. Rep. No. 103-826(I), at 57 (1994); *Interim Regulations, supra* note 516, §§351.218(d)(2)(iv), (e)(1)(ii)(B).

[619] *Interim Regulations, supra* note 516, §351.218(d)(2). According to the DOC's interim regulations, a statement of waiver must include (1) the name, address, and phone number of the respondent interested party and their legal counsel or other representative, (2) the subject merchandise and country subject to review, and (3) the citation to the *Federal Register* of the notice of initiation. *Id.* §351.218(d)(2)(ii).

[620] *Id.* §351.218(d)(2)(i).

[621] *Id.* §351.218(d)(2)(iii).

[622] *See* S. Rep. No. 103-412, at 46 (1994); H.R. Rep. No. 103-826(I), at 57 (1994).

2. Conducting an Expedited or Full Review: Procedures and Deadlines

The DOC and ITC will conduct simultaneous sunset reviews. An outline of anticipated deadlines for the conduct of expedited and full sunset reviews is provided in Appendix II. The schedules permit the agencies to satisfy the substantive and procedural requirements of the Agreements in expedited and full sunset reviews. Consistent with the procedural and evidentiary requirements in the Agreements, the regulations permit a full 30 or more days to respond to the notices of initiation as well as to submit comments on whether a review should be expedited and whether an order or suspended investigation should be revoked or terminated.[623] Both the URAA and the agencies' regulations: (1) require interested parties to serve their submissions on other interested parties and certify to their accuracy;[624] (2) provide for the protection of confidential information;[625] and (3) permit consideration of information from industrial users and consumer organizations.[626] The URAA requires the DOC to verify all information relied upon in making a revocation.[627] The DOC's regulations also provide for the disclosure of calculations performed, if any, in connection with a final determination consistent with the Agreements.[628] In addition to

---

[623]Antidumping Agreement, *supra* note 5, at art. 6; Subsidies Agreement, *supra* note 5, at art. 12; *see* 19 U.S.C. §§1675(e) & 1677m(g); *Interim Regulations, supra* note 516, §351.218(d)(3); *Final Regulations, supra* note 516, §207.61; Appendix II.

[624]*See* Antidumping Agreement, *supra* note 5, at art. 6; Subsidies Agreement, *supra* note 5, at art. 12; 19 U.S.C. §§1677f(d) & 1677m(b); *Final Regulations, supra* note 516, §207.3, Annex A; 19 C.F.R. §§351.303(f), (g) (1997).

[625]Antidumping Agreement, *supra* note 5, at art. 6; Subsidies Agreement, *supra* note 5, at art. 12; 19 U.S.C. §1677f; Antidumping and Countervailing Duty Proceedings: Administrative Protective Order Procedures: Procedures for Imposing Sanctions for Violations of a Protective Order, 63 Fed. Reg. 24,391 (Dep't Comm. 1998) (Final Regulations); 19 C.F.R. §207.7 (1997).

[626]Antidumping Agreement, *supra* note 5, at art. 6; Subsidies Agreement, *supra* note 5, at art. 12; 19 U.S.C. §1677f(h); *Final Regulations, supra* note 516, §207.61(d); *Interim Regulations, supra* note 516, §351.218(d)(3)(vi).

[627]Antidumping Agreement, *supra* note 5, at art. 6; Subsidies Agreement, *supra* note 5, at art. 12; 19 U.S.C. §1677m(i).

[628]Antidumping Agreement, *supra* note 5, at art. 6; Subsidies Agreement, *supra* note 5, at art. 12; 19 C.F.R. §351.224(b) (1997); *see Final Regulations, supra* note 516, §207.68.

the submission of briefs on the merits, the URAA provides for the conduct of a hearing upon request.[629]

a. *Expedited Reviews*

Upon receipt of inadequate substantive responses to the notice of initiation from either domestic or respondent interested parties, the DOC will conduct an expedited review. Within five days of the submission of substantive responses, the DOC's regulations provide for a submission of rebuttal comments. In addition, interested parties are free to submit comments on the issue of whether the DOC should conduct an expedited review within 70 days after initiation.[630] If the DOC decides against conducting a full review, a final determination will be issued within 120 days after initiation.[631]

The ITC will accept comments on the appropriateness of conducting an expedited review within 75 days of institution.[632] The ITC will then make its determination whether or not to conduct an expedited review and issue a staff report to the Commission and the parties, accept written comments on the merits, and issue a final determination within 150 days after institution.[633] The ITC will decide whether or not to expedite a review based on the vote of a majority of Commissioners.[634]

b. *Full Reviews*

Upon receipt of adequate substantive responses to the notice of initiation from both domestic and respondent interested parties, the DOC will conduct a full review.[635] Like an administrative review, the DOC will issue separate preliminary and final determinations.[636] The DOC will not nor-

---

[629]19 U.S.C. §1675(e).

[630]*Interim Regulations, supra* note 516, §§351.218(d)(4), 351.309(e)(ii).

[631]19 U.S.C. §1675(c)(3)(B); *Interim Regulations, supra* note 516, §351.218(e)(1).

[632]*Final Regulations, supra* note 516, at 30,611, §207.62.

[633]*See id.*; 19 U.S.C. §1675(c)(3)(B).

[634]*Id.* at 30,604.

[635]*Interim Regulations, supra* note 516, §351.218(e)(2)(i).

[636]*See id.* §351.218(f).

mally, however, automatically verify factual information unless it is submitted in the context of a full sunset review and only if the DOC makes a negative determination in its preliminary results and those results are not based on countervailing duty rates or dumping margins as determined in the investigation or subsequent reviews.[637] Interested parties will also be permitted to submit case and rebuttal briefs concerning the DOC's preliminary results and participate in a hearing in a full review.[638]

According to the ITC's regulations, the ITC expects to circulate a draft questionnaire to interested parties for comment.[639] Questionnaires will be issued within 225 days from the notice of institution. Interested parties will have at least 30 days to respond. [640] The ITC will receive the DOC's final determination within 240 days, unless the time limit is extended until 330 days after initiation.[641] If the DOC's final determination is negative, the DOC will revoke the order or terminate the suspended investigation.[642] If the DOC's final determination is affirmative, the ITC will proceed with its review.

Upon receipt of the questionnaires by day 255, the ITC staff will begin to prepare their prehearing report which will be forwarded to the ITC by day 285.[643] Just as if a sunset review were an investigation, the ITC will conduct a hearing and accept prehearing and posthearing briefs.[644] A final staff

---

[637]*Id.* §351.218(f)(2); *see* 19 U.S.C. §1677m(i)(2). Although the ITC has conducted verification of questionnaire responses filed in original investigations, it is not the ITC's practice to conduct verification of the questionnaire responses submitted by foreign producers. In comments on its final regulations, however, the ITC indicated that it would "consider verification of domestic interested party and respondent interested party information in appropriate circumstances and as staffing resources permit." *Final Regulations, supra* note 516, at 30,606. In addition, the ITC will also consider using the DOC's verification reports as appropriate. *Id.*

[638]*See* 19 C.F.R. §§351.309(c)(1)(i), 351.309(d)(1), 351.310(d)(1) (1997).

[639]*Final Regulations, supra* note 516, §207.63.

[640]*Id.* at 30,611.

[641]*Id.*; *Interim Regulations, supra* note 516, §351.218(f)(3)(ii). Where orders or suspended investigations have been grouped, the ITC shall, subject to the requirements on extensions of time limits, make its final determination not later than 120 days after the date that the DOC publishes notice of its final determination with respect to the last order or agreement in the group. 19 U.S.C. §1675(c)(5)(D).

[642]*Interim Regulations, supra* note 516, §351.222(i)(1)(ii).

[643]*Final Regulations, supra* note 516, at 30,611 & §207.64.

[644]*Id.* §§207.65-67.

report will be prepared and final comments will be accepted.[645] The ITC's vote will be held by day 348 and the final determination and views will be issued by day 360.[646] Consistent with the Agreements, the URAA provides that sunset reviews will normally be completed within 12 months.[647] The DOC and the ITC can each extend the deadlines for completion of the sunset review by not more than 90 days (approximately 3 months) if the review is considered to be "extraordinarily complicated."[648] The DOC and/or the ITC can extend the deadline for sunset reviews of transition orders because they are, by definition, "extraordinarily complicated."[649] The statute further requires that the first round of all sunset reviews of transition orders be completed by June 30, 2001.[650] Both the DOC and ITC will issue final determinations with reasons consistent with the Agreements.[651]

3. No Early Revocation or Termination of Transition Orders

According to the sunset provisions of the Agreements, "[t]he duty may remain in force pending the outcome of such a review."[652] Article 18.3 of

---

[645]*Id.* §§207.64(b), 207.68.

[646]*Id.* at 30,611. If the DOC makes a final affirmative determination, the ITC will issue a final determination within 360 days (approximately 12 months) after the date of initiation or, if a grouped review, within 120 days (approximately 4 months) after the date that the administering authority publishes notice of its final determination with respect to the last order or agreement in the group. 19 U.S.C. §§1675(c)(5)(A), (B), & (D).

[647]*Id.* §1675(c)(5); Antidumping Agreement, *supra* note 5, at art. 11.4; Subsidies Agreement, *supra* note 5, at art. 21.4.

[648]19 U.S.C. §§1675(c)(5)(B), (C); *Interim Regulations, supra* note 516, §351.218(f)(3)(ii). A sunset review is "extraordinarily complicated" if: (1) there is a large number of issues; (2) the issues to be considered are complex; (3) there is a large number of firms involved; (4) the orders or suspended investigations have been grouped; or (5) it is a review of a transition order. 19 U.S.C. §1675(c)(5)(C).

[649]*Id.*

[650]*Proposed Regulations, supra* note 516, at 55,185; *Policy Bulletin, supra* note 516, at 18,872.

[651]Antidumping Agreement, *supra* note 5, at art. 12.2.2; Subsidies Agreement, *supra* note 5, at art. 22.5; *Final Regulations, supra* note 516, §207.69; 19 C.F.R. §351.221(b)(5) (1997).

[652]Antidumping Agreement, *supra* note 5, at art. 11.3; Subsidies Agreement, *supra* note 5, at art. 21.3.

the Antidumping Agreement and Article 32.4 of the Subsidies Agreement provide that existing measures would be deemed to be imposed on a date not later than the date of entry into force for a Member of the WTO Agreement unless domestic legislation included a sunset provision.[653] Consistent with those provisions, the URAA provides that no transition order may be revoked before January 1, 2000.[654] Therefore, regardless of when a particular sunset review of a transition order is conducted or when the ITC issues its final determination, a measure will not be revoked or terminated earlier than January 1, 2000.[655] Likewise, the DOC's interim regulations suggested that a measure will not be revoked or terminated later than January 1, 2000, even if the determination is made subsequent to that date.[656]

It is unclear, however, whether the DOC will continue to collect duties on orders that have been revoked pursuant to a sunset determination before January 1, 2000. The URAA provides that a determination to revoke an order or terminate a suspended investigation "shall apply with respect to unliquidated entries of the subject merchandise which are entered, or withdrawn from warehouse, for consumption on or after the date determined by the administering authority."[657] To date, the DOC has not indicated the

---

[653]Antidumping Agreement, *supra* note 5, at art. 18.3; Subsidies Agreement, *supra* note 5, at art. 32.4.

[654]19 U.S.C. §1675(c)(6)(A)(iv). The statute clearly states that "[n]o transition order may be revoked under this subsection before the date that is 5 years after the date the WTO Agreement enters into force with respect to the United States." *Id.* Section 751(c)(3)(A) of the Tariff Act of 1930, as amended (19 U.S.C. §1675(c)(3)(A)), however, instructs the DOC to revoke an order within 90 days of initiation if no domestic interested party responds:

> If no interested party responds to the notice of initiation under this subsection, the administering authority shall issue a final determination, within 90 days after the initiation of a review, revoking the order or terminating the suspended investigation to which such notice relates. . . .

19 U.S.C. §1675(c)(3)(A). The DOC's interim regulations resolve this inconsistency by stating that the effective date for any revocation of a transition order will be January 1, 2000. *Interim Regulations, supra* note 516, §351.222(i)(2)(ii).

[655]*See id.* §351.222(i)(2).

[656]*Id.*

[657]19 U.S.C. §1675(d)(3). Potential interested parties have argued that the DOC should clarify whether revocation will force the DOC to terminate ongoing reviews of unliquidated entries. Japan Iron and Steel Exporters Association Comments at 7 (12/8/97); *see* Government du Quebec Comments at 3 (12/8/97). Others have argued

effectiveness date of a revocation determination for purposes of duty collection.

B. *THE LIKELIHOOD TEST IN THE URUGUAY ROUND AGREEMENTS ACT*

1. The DOC's Determination of Likelihood of Continuation or Recurrence of Dumping

The likelihood tests contained in pre- and post-URAA law are somewhat similar because they both require the DOC to ask and answer the same fundamental question: "Is it likely that they will they dump again?" Under pre-URAA law, the DOC was required to find that it *was not* likely that foreign producers or exporters would dump in the future in order to revoke or terminate.[658] Under the URAA, the DOC is required to determine that revocation *would be* likely to lead to continuation or recurrence of dumping to continue an order or suspension agreement.[659]

Unlike the discretionary revocation/termination test used in non-sunset revocations, Section 751(d)(2) of the Tariff Act of 1930, as amended (19 U.S.C. §1675(d)(2)), *requires* the DOC in sunset reviews to revoke an order or terminate a suspended investigation *unless* there is an affirmative finding that dumping (or a countervailable subsidy) is likely to continue or recur.[660]

Although the sunset provisions of the Agreements do not specifically dictate what factors should be considered in a likelihood analysis, the Agreements do provide general definitions for domestic industry, injury, dumping, and subsidization.[661] The URAA adopts those definitions in con-

---

that the DOC should issue an order suspending liquidation as of the fifth anniversary in cases or use other means to ensure that duties collected after the fifth anniversary month would be fully refunded with interest. International Advisory Services Group Ltd. Public Comments at 1-2 (12/8/97).

[658] *See supra* note 131 and accompanying text.

[659] 19 U.S.C. §1675(c)(1).

[660] 19 U.S.C. §1675(d)(2). In *Sanyo,* the Court of International Trade distinguished the bases for a negative finding that there is no likelihood of resumption of dumping from an affirmative finding that there is a likelihood of resumption of dumping. *Sanyo Electric Co., Ltd.,* 15 CIT at 611-12.

[661] Antidumping Agreement, *supra* note 5, at arts. 2-4; Subsidies Agreement, *supra* note 5, at arts. 1-2, 14-16.

structing its likelihood test for sunset reviews. Despite the predictive and speculative nature of the likelihood test,[662] the URAA directs the agency to rely on limited, readily-available, objective data to make its determination absent "good cause."[663] To determine the likelihood of continuation or recurrence of dumping, Section 752(c)(1) of the Tariff Act of 1930, as amended (19 U.S.C. §1675a(c)(1)), instructs the DOC to examine: (1) the weighted average dumping margins,[664] or the absence of margins, determined during the original investigation and subsequent reviews; and (2) the volume of imports of the subject merchandise, for the periods before and after the issuance of an order or the acceptance of a suspension agreement. If good cause is shown, the DOC is also required to consider such other price, cost, market, or economic factors as it deems relevant.[665]

The Statement of Administrative Action indicates that the DOC will consider the interplay between dumping margins and import volumes.[666] For example, the DOC should consider declining import volumes accompanied by the continued existence of dumping margins after the issuance of an order to be a strong indication that dumping would be likely to continue after revocation, because the evidence would indicate that the exporter needs to dump to sell at pre-order volumes. In contrast, the DOC should consider declining or lack of dumping margins combined with steady or

---

[662]SAA, *supra* note 516, at 883.

[663]The establishment of some objective basis for the likelihood test is in sharp contrast to the non-sunset revocation/termination standard found at 19 U.S.C. §1675(d)(1) (1997) and 19 C.F.R. §353.25(a)(1997). *See Toshiba Corp.*, 15 CIT at 600 (Court notes that the regulation presents no objective criterion for determining whether there is no likelihood of resumption of LTFV sales).

[664]The term "weighted average dumping margin" is defined in 19 U.S.C. §1677(35)(B) as "the percentage determined by dividing the aggregate dumping margins determined for a specific exporter or producer by the aggregate export prices and constructed export prices of such exporter or producer."

[665]19 U.S.C. §1675a(c)(1)-(2). The DOC will make its likelihood determination on an order-wide basis. *Policy Bulletin, supra* note 516, at 18,872.

[666]According to the Policy Bulletin, the DOC will consider the companies' relative market share to determine whether import volumes remained steady or increased. The parties will be responsible for supplying this information to the DOC. *Policy Bulletin, supra* note 516, at 18,872. Yet, if there are a number of producers that continue to dump but have not been reviewed under an antidumping duty order, the company-specific trends observed pursuant to that order would be inconclusive. Further, the trends observed by companies with declining margins would not reflect the experience of companies subject to a relatively high "all others" rate.

increasing imports to indicate that foreign companies do not have to dump to maintain market share in the United States and that dumping is less likely to continue or recur if the order were revoked.[667] According to the legislative history and the DOC's policy bulletin, declining margins alone will not normally be sufficient to show that dumping is less likely to continue or recur because continued margins *at any level above "de minimis" will lead to a finding of likelihood.*[668]

The Statement of Administrative Action further provides that the existence of dumping margins after the order, or the cessation of imports after the order, will be highly probative of the likelihood of continuation or recurrence of dumping. Like non-sunset revocation reviews, the existence of zero or *de minimis* margins at any time while the order was in effect will not, by itself, require the DOC to determine that there is no likelihood of continuation or recurrence of dumping.[669] Thus, under the formula established in the legislative history, the DOC is likely to make the following determinations absent countervailing considerations:[670]

Dumping is Likely to Recur	
Imports	*Margins*
• no post-order import volumes	
• sharply decreasing import volumes margins	• low or *de minimis* dumping
Dumping is Likely to Continue	
	• post-order dumping margins
• declining import volumes	• post-order dumping margins
Dumping is Less Likely to Continue or Recur	
• steady or increasing import volumes	• declining or no dumping margins

[667]SAA, *supra* note 516, at 889-90; S. Rep. No. 103-412, at 52 (1994); H.R. Rep. No. 103-826(I), at 63-64 (1994).

[668]*Policy Bulletin, supra* note 516, at 18,872.

[669]SAA, *supra* note 516, at 890. The DOC will treat as *de minimis* any weighted-average dumping margin that is less than 0.5 percent *ad valorem* or the equivalent specific rate. 19 U.S.C. §1675a(c)(4)(B); 19 C.F.R. §351.106(c)(1) (1997); *Policy Bulletin, supra* note 516, at 18,873.

[670]*See Policy Bulletin, supra* note 516, at 18,872.

Interested parties have the opportunity to dispute the DOC's conclusions based solely on the volume/margin data using positive evidence of "other factors."[671] According to the Statement of Administrative Action, the other factors the DOC could consider for "good cause" include the market share of foreign producers subject to the antidumping proceeding; changes in exchange rates, inventory levels, production capacity, and capacity utilization; any history of sales below cost of production; changes in manufacturing technology of the industry; and prevailing prices in relevant markets.[672] These factors are similar to those factors the DOC considered in making pre-URAA likelihood determinations.[673] According to its regulations, the DOC will only consider "other factors" in the context of a full sunset review.[674] The burden will be on the interested party to provide information or evidence justifying resort to "other factors."[675]

Whether or not an interested party has submitted sufficient information or evidence to establish "good cause" to consider other factors will be determined on a case-by-case basis. "Good cause" could be found in cases where the agency has reason to doubt the reliability of a determination based solely on volume and margin data. For example, "good cause" to consider other factors may exist where the agency's pre-sunset review administrative record is seriously outdated due to lack of frequent administrative reviews.[676] Likewise, "good cause" could exist where significant post-review information undermines the reliability of available volume and margin data. Finally, the DOC's Policy Bulletin recognizes that the import volume and margin data in a sunset review of a suspended investigation may not be conclusive with respect to the issue of likelihood. Therefore, the DOC anticipates that it will be more likely to entertain "good cause" arguments in a sunset review of a suspended investigation.[677] If "good cause" exists in a

---

[671]SAA, *supra* note 516, at 890 ("In practice, this will permit interested parties to provide information indicating that observed patterns regarding dumping margins and import volumes are not necessarily indicative of the likelihood of dumping. The list of factors is illustrative, and the Administration intends that Commerce will analyze such information on a case-by-case basis.").

[672]SAA, *supra* note 516, at 890.

[673]*See supra* Chapter II, Section A.4.b.

[674]*Interim Regulations, supra* note 516, §351.218(e)(2)(iii).

[675]*Policy Bulletin, supra* note 516, at 18,874.

[676]*See Toshiba Corp.*, 15 CIT at 602-03 (ITA relies on market factor evidence when company-specific margin data is seven years old in non-sunset review).

[677]*Policy Bulletin, supra* note 516, at 18,872-73.

review of a suspended investigation, the DOC will normally conduct the review consistent with its practice of examining likelihood in an administrative review under Section 751(a) of the Tariff Act of 1930, as amended (19 U.S.C. §1675(a)).[678]

2. The DOC's Determination of Likelihood of Continuation or Recurrence of a Countervailable Subsidy

The URAA also establishes standards to be applied by the DOC in determining the likelihood of continuation or recurrence of countervailable subsidies. Under new section 752(b)(1), the DOC will consider: (1) the net countervailable subsidies determined in the investigation and subsequent reviews;[679] and (2) any change in the program, such as whether the program has been continued, modified, or eliminated, that is likely to affect the net countervailable subsidy.[680]

As with the legislative history for the antidumping provisions, the legislative history for the countervailing duty provisions gives some guidance as to what scenarios would trigger an affirmative or negative likelihood finding. On the one hand, the legislative history indicates that the continued existence, temporary suspension, or partial termination of a program will favor an affirmative finding of likelihood of continuation or recurrence of subsidization.[681] On the other hand, the elimination of a subsidy program will not be dispositive of the likelihood issue. In addition to the elimination, the DOC will consider the permanency of the legal method used to eliminate the program and likelihood of reinstatement.[682] According to the Policy Bulletin,

---

678 *Id.* at 18,874.

679 For a definition of "net countervailable subsidy," see 19 U.S.C. §1677(6).

680 19 U.S.C. §1675a(b)(1); SAA, *supra* note 516, at 888; H.R. REP. NO. 103-826(I), at 63 (1994); *Policy Bulletin, supra* note 516, at 18,874. The DOC will make its determination on an order-wide basis. *Policy Bulletin, supra* note 516, at 18,874.

681 SAA, *supra* note 516, at 888; S. REP. NO. 103-412, at 52 (1994); *see Policy Bulletin, supra* note 516, at 18,874.

682 *See* Asociacion Colombiana de Exportadores de Flores v. United States, 19 CIT 490, 495 (1995) (Court affirms DOC's interpretation of 19 C.F.R. §355.25(a)(1) requiring that the government take "clearly identifiable actions" exceeding a mere "policy" to abolish a program); *Policy Bulletin, supra* note 516, at 18,875. According to the Policy

the DOC will normally conclude that a subsidy continues to exist when the benefit stream of an allocated subsidy will continue beyond the end of the sunset review without regard to whether the program continues to exist.[683]

Nor will company- or industry-specific renunciations of countervailable subsidies be dispositive: the DOC will require additional evidence that continuation or recurrence of subsidization is unlikely.[684] Where a company has a long track-record of non-use, the mere availability of the program, however, will not be sufficient to support an affirmative finding.[685]

The DOC has had occasion to consider program changes under pre-URAA law. For example, the DOC's long-standing practice was to adjust the estimated countervailing duty cash deposit rate to take into account a program-wide change occurring subsequent to a review period but before a preliminary determination.[686] According to the DOC's proposed regulations of 1989 and 1997, a program-wide change is a change that is (1) not limited to an individual firm or firms, and (2) effectuated by an official act, such as the enactment of a statute, regulation, or decree, or contained in the schedule of an existing statute, regulation, or decree. The DOC's consideration of a program-wide change in the context of an investigation will only affect the cash deposit rate and will not turn an affirmative determination into a negative determination. The DOC will not adjust the cash deposit

---

Bulletin, the DOC will normally find that programs eliminated through administrative action are more likely to be reinstated than those eliminated through legislative action.

[683] *Policy Bulletin, supra* note 516, at 18,875.

[684] SAA, *supra* note 516, at 888; *Policy Bulletin, supra* note 516, at 18,874; *see* S. REP. NO. 103-412, at 52 (1994).

[685] *Policy Bulletin, supra* note 516, at 18,874.

[686] Countervailing Duties, 54 Fed. Reg. 23,366, 23,385 (Dep't Comm. 1989) (proposed rules). Section 355.50 of the proposed regulations provided:

> (a) *In general.* Where
>
> (1) The Secretary determines that subsequent to a review period, but before a preliminary determination described in §355.15 or a preliminary results of review described in §355.22, a program-wide change has occurred, and
>
> (2) The Secretary is able to measure the change in the amount of countervailable subsidies provided under the program in question,
>
> the Secretary may take such program-wide change into account in establishing the estimated countervailing duty cash deposit rate.

Section 351.525 of the DOC's proposed regulations is almost identical to §355.50. *See* Countervailing Duties, 62 Fed. Reg. 8818, 8847 (Dep't Comm. 1997) (Comments).

rate for termination of a program if (1) residual benefits may continue to be bestowed under the terminated program, or (2) a substitute program has been introduced and the DOC has not been able to measure the amount of countervailable subsidies under the substitute program.

Likewise, the DOC may consider program changes that are not already reflected in the net subsidy rates calculated in the investigation or reviews in a sunset review. Based on its history of identifying program-wide changes, the DOC is likely to account for a program change in its sunset determination if the change would have an effect on the amount of countervailable subsidies, would not be limited in scope, and was effectuated by an official act.

If "good cause" is shown, the DOC shall also consider: (1) existing countervailable programs that could potentially be used by the producers/exporters subject to review and did not exist at the time of the measure; or (2) new programs that are found to be countervailable with respect to the producers/exporters subject to review:

> (A) programs determined to provide countervailable subsidies in other investigations or reviews under this subtitle, but only to the extent that such programs —
> (i) can potentially be used by the exporters or producers subject to the review under section 1675(c) of this title, and
> (ii) did not exist at the time that the countervailing duty order was issued or the suspension agreement was accepted, and
> (B) programs newly alleged to provide countervailable subsidies but only to the extent that the administering authority makes an affirmative countervailing duty determination with respect to such programs and with respect to the exporters or producers subject to the review.[687]

[687] 19 U.S.C. §1675a(b)(2); *cf.* 19 U.S.C. §1677d ("If, in the course of a proceeding under this subtitle, the administering authority discovers a practice which appears to be a countervailable subsidy, but was not included in the matters alleged in the countervailing duty petition, or if the administering authority receives notice from the Trade Representative that a subsidy or subsidy program is in violation of Article 8 of the Subsidies Agreement, then the administering authority — (1) shall include the practice, subsidy, or subsidy program in the proceeding if the practice, subsidy, or subsidy program appears to be a countervailable subsidy with respect to the merchandise which is the subject of the proceeding. . . ."); 19 C.F.R. §351.311(b) (the DOC will examine new subsidy if it concludes that sufficient time remains before scheduled date for final determination or final results of review).

The burden will be on interested parties to provide information or evidence justifying consideration of the subsidy program determined to provide countervailable subsidies in other investigations or reviews.[688]

Although neither the statute nor the legislative history defines "good cause" for raising a new subsidy allegation during a sunset review, the Statement of Administrative Action indicates that "good cause" could be found where the DOC did not have the opportunity to consider the applicability of "new" programs due to the lack of recent administrative reviews of the countervailing duty order or suspension agreement or where the program came into effect after the most recent review.[689] In order to conserve administrative resources, the DOC intends to refrain from pursuing new subsidy allegations in the context of a sunset review when the issue could have been addressed during previously conducted administrative reviews.[690] If "good cause" exists in a review of a suspended investigation, the DOC will normally conduct the review consistent with its practice of examining likelihood in an administrative review under Section 751(a) of the Tariff Act of 1930, as amended.[691]

3. The Role of Margins and *De Minimis* Rates

In making its determination as to whether revocation or termination is likely to lead to continuation or recurrence of dumping or subsidization, the DOC is directed to consider previously-determined margins or rates.[692] The Antidumping and Subsidies Agreements provide that a finding in "the most recent assessment proceeding . . . that no duty is to be levied shall not by itself require the authorities to terminate the definitive duty."[693] The URAA implements this precaution by stating that a dumping margin or net

[688] *Policy Bulletin, supra* note 516, at 18,876.

[689] SAA, *supra* note 516, at 889; *Policy Bulletin, supra* note 516, at 18,877.

[690] SAA, *supra* note 516, at 889.

[691] *Policy Bulletin, supra* note 516, at 18,877.

[692] 19 U.S.C. §§ 1675a(b)(1)(A), 1675a(c)(1)(A).

[693] Antidumping Agreement, *supra* note 5, at art. 11.3 n.22; Subsidies Agreement, *supra* note 5, at art. 21.3 n.52.

subsidy that is zero or *de minimis* shall *not*, by itself, require the DOC to make a negative determination.[694]

The legislative history notes that lack of dumping margins under an antidumping duty order or suspension agreement may simply be due to the existence of the order or agreement. With respect to a countervailing duty order, however, the legislative history states that "if the combined benefits of all programs considered by Commerce for purposes of its likelihood determination have never been above *de minimis* at any time the order was in effect, and if there is no likelihood that the combined benefits of such programs would be above *de minimis* in the event of revocation or termination, Commerce should determine that there is no likelihood of continuation or recurrence of countervailable subsidies."[695]

In addition to making a finding with respect to whether dumping or subsidization is likely to continue or recur, the DOC will provide to the ITC "the magnitude of the margin of dumping" and the "net countervailable subsidy" that is likely to prevail if the order is revoked or the suspended investigation is terminated.[696] The statute requires the DOC "normally" to choose a previously-determined margin from the final results of the original investigation, an administrative review, or a changed circumstance review. The legislative history explains that the DOC will "normally" select the rate from the original investigation to communicate to the ITC because "that is the only calculated rate that reflects the behavior of exporters and foreign governments without the discipline of an order or suspension agreement in place."[697] The DOC will calculate a net countervailable subsidy or a dumping margin in the context of a sunset review only in the most extraordinary circumstances.[698] Therefore, the DOC's regulations make it

---

[694]19 U.S.C. §§1675a(b)(4)(A), 1675a(c)(4)(A); SAA, *supra* note 516, at 817. The URAA instructs the DOC to apply the *de minimis* standards of reviews under 19 U.S.C. §1675(a) and (b)(1). The DOC regulations provide that the DOC will treat as *de minimis* any weighted-average dumping margin or countervailable subsidy rate that is less than 0.5 percent *ad valorem* or the equivalent of a specific rate. 19 C.F.R. §351.106.

[695]SAA, *supra* note 516, at 889.

[696]19 U.S.C. §§1675a(b)(3), 1675a(c)(3), 1677(35)(C).

[697]SAA, *supra* note 516, at 890.

[698]*Id.* at 891; H.R. REP. NO. 103-826(I), at 64 (1994). The Statement of Administrative Action also clarifies that the DOC was not intended to calculate "future" margins "because such an exercise would involve undue speculation regarding future selling

clear that the agency will not calculate margins for new shippers in the context of a sunset review.[699]

For antidumping duty orders, the DOC will normally provide company-specific margins and the "all others" rate[700] from the final determination in the original antidumping investigation.[701] The DOC may use the margins from the preliminary determination in "certain situations" such as where a final determination was not issued due to a suspended investigation. In cases where no company-specific margins or "all others" rates were included in a dumping finding[702] issued by the Treasury Department, the DOC will use the company-specific margin from the first final results of administrative review or, if unavailable, the first "new shippers" rate established for a particular company. In addition, the DOC will normally provide the ITC with a list of companies excluded or revoked from the order.[703]

Likewise, for countervailing duty orders, the DOC will normally provide to the ITC the company-specific countervailing duty rates from the final determination in the original investigation, regardless of whether the rate was based on "best information available" or "facts otherwise available."[704] If a company-specific rate is not available for a particular company, the DOC will normally provide the country-wide rate or "all others" rate determined in the original investigation.[705] The DOC may use the subsidy

---

prices, costs of production, selling expenses, exchange rates, and sales and production volumes." SAA, *supra* note 516, at 891.

[699] *Interim Regulations, supra* note 516, at §351.218(e)(2)(i).

[700] The "all others" rate has been calculated as an average rate for those companies that have not been individually investigated and new shippers. *See* Floral Trade Council v. United States, 822 F. Supp. 766, 768-71 (CIT 1993).

[701] *Policy Bulletin, supra* note 516, at 18,873.

[702] The Treasury Department issued antidumping "findings" prior to 1980 as opposed to "orders" issued by the Commerce Department after 1980.

[703] *Policy Bulletin, supra* note 516, at 18,873.

[704] *Id.* at 18,875-76.

[705] *Id.* at 18,876. Prior to the Uruguay Round, the DOC calculated a "country-wide" rate in countervailing duty cases and company-specific rates only if they were "significantly different" than the country-wide rate. 19 C.F.R. §355.20(d)(1995). The Uruguay Round Agreements Act, however, requires the DOC to calculate individual countervailing duty rates on a company-specific basis when possible. 19 U.S.C. §1677f-1(e).

from the preliminary determination in "certain situations" such as where a final determination was not issued due to a suspended investigation. In the case of an order where the original investigation was conducted by the Treasury Department, the DOC will normally rely on the final results of the first administrative review where the net countervailable subsidy was first calculated on an *ad valorem* basis. Finally, the DOC will provide the ITC with a list of companies excluded or revoked from the order.

The DOC, however, will have the discretion to choose a more recently calculated rate if it would be more "appropriate."[706] The legislative history describes a case where dumping margins have declined over the life of an order and imports have remained steady or increased as a case where the DOC could find the more recently calculated rates more illuminating.[707] According to the DOC's Policy Bulletin, unless the DOC makes a negative likelihood determination, the DOC may consider arguments in favor of providing a more recently calculated rate on a company-specific basis where, for example, that company's import volumes remained steady or increased and its dumping margins declined or were eliminated after an order.[708] Likewise, unless the DOC makes a negative likelihood determination, the DOC may consider arguments in favor of providing a more recently calculated rate for a company whose margins increased after the order, even if the increase is based on "best information available" or "facts available."[709]

---

[706]*Policy Bulletin, supra* note 516, at 18,873. At the same time, the DOC will be forced to initiate and proceed with administrative reviews while sunset reviews are pending for the same order or suspended investigation. *See* Matsushita Electric Industrial Co. v. United States, 688 F. Supp. 617 (CIT 1988), *aff'd,* 861 F. 2d 257 (Fed. Cir. 1988). Indeed, interested parties have an interest in requesting administrative reviews in an attempt to obtain favorable margins or lack thereof. Nothing in the statute or the legislative history prohibits the agencies from considering post-sunset review data. *See* UST, Inc. v. United States, 831 F.2d 1028, 1032-33 (Fed. Cir. 1987); Matsushita Electric Industrial Co. v. United States, 861 F. 2d 257 (Fed. Cir. 1988).

[707]SAA, *supra* note 516, at 890-91; H.R. REP. NO. 103-826(I), at 64 (1994).

[708]*Policy Bulletin, supra* note 516, at 18,873. In analyzing import volumes, the DOC will normally consider the company's relative market share which should be provided to the agency by the parties.

[709]*Id.* The DOC resorted to "best information available" before the Uruguay Round Agreements Act and "facts otherwise available" after the Uruguay Round Agreements Act when the requested information is not supplied. 19 U.S.C. §1677(e) (1994 & 1995).

According to the Policy Bulletin, the DOC may find the net countervailable subsidy rate from the original investigation is not the most appropriate rate if, for example, (1) the rate was derived (in whole or in part) from subsidy programs which were found in subsequent reviews to be terminated, (2) there has been a program-wide change, or (3) the rate ignores a program found to be countervailable in a subsequent administrative review.[710] Therefore, the DOC may make adjustments to the net countervailable subsidy in certain cases, including the following: (1) where a program has been terminated with no residual benefits and no likelihood of reinstatement; (2) where the DOC found a new countervailable program in an administrative review or found a program previously not used but subsequently found countervailable that was included in the new subsidy rate for the administrative review; (3) where the DOC has determined to increase the net countervailable subsidy rate for any reason including application of "best information available" or "facts otherwise available" in an administrative review; (4) where the DOC finds in an administrative review that a program is not countervailable because it is a qualifying research subsidy, a subsidy to disadvantaged regions, an environmental subsidy, or an agricultural subsidy within the meaning of Section 771(5B) (B), (C), (D) and (F) of the Tariff Act of 1930, as amended (19 U.S.C. §1677(5B) (B), (C), (D), & (F)); and (5) where the DOC finds that the program has been notified in accordance with Article 8.3 of the Subsidies Agreement unless the U.S. Trade Representative has notified the DOC that the program does not satisfy the conditions of the Subsidies Agreement.[711] The DOC will normally *not* adjust the net countervailable subsidy rate if it has not conducted an administrative review or for programs that still exist but were subsequently modified to eliminate exports to the United States (or subject merchandise).[712]

If the DOC makes an affirmative determination, the DOC will provide the ITC with the "magnitude of the margin" which the ITC will consider in

[710]*Policy Bulletin, supra* note 516, at 18,876.

[711]*Id.* According to Article 8.3 of the Subsidies Agreement, member states are required to notify the Committee on Subsidies and Countervailing Measures of any subsidy program which the member state claims is non-actionable under Article 8.2 (*i.e.*, qualifying research programs, assistance to disadvantaged regions, and environmental programs). Subsidies Agreement, *supra* note 5, at arts. 8.2-.3.

[712]*Policy Bulletin, supra* note 516, at 18,876.

the context of deciding whether revocation or termination is likely to lead to the continuation or recurrence of material injury.[713] In a countervailing duty case, the DOC will also transmit information concerning the nature of the subsidy and whether the subsidy is a subsidy described in Articles 3 or 6.1 of the Subsidies Agreement.[714] Consistent with the ITC's lack of authority to determine dumping or subsidy margins, under no circumstances will the ITC calculate its own margins to address the issue of potential injury in a sunset review.[715]

4. The ITC's Determination of Likelihood of Continuation or Recurrence of Material Injury

a. The URAA's Likelihood Test of Material Injury

i. Injury Factors

Pursuant to Section 752(a)(1) of the Tariff Act, as amended (19 U.S.C. §1675a(a)(1)), the ITC must decide in a sunset review whether revocation of an order or termination of a suspended investigation would be likely to lead to continuation or recurrence of injury within a reasonably foreseeable time.[716] The URAA directs the ITC to consider three factors as required by the Agreements: (1) the likely volume of imports of the subject merchandise; (2) the likely price effects of imports of the subject merchandise; and (3) the likely impact of imports of the subject merchandise on the industry.[717]

With respect to import volume, the ITC will consider whether the likely

---

[713]19 U.S.C. §1675a(a)(6).

[714]*Policy Bulletin, supra* note 516, at 18,876; 19 U.S.C. §1675a(a)(6). Note that Section 1675a(a)(6) requires the ITC to consider information regarding the nature of the subsidy involved and whether the subsidy is a subsidy described in Article 3 (prohibited subsidies) or 6.1 (subsidies causing serious prejudice to the interests of another member state) of the Subsidies Agreement.

[715]SAA, *supra* note 516, at 887.

[716]19 U.S.C. §1675a(a)(1). According to the House Report, no one factor is dispositive and the ITC "need not determine that both the volume and price effects of imports are likely to be significant to determine that material injury is likely within a reasonably foreseeable time." H.R. REP. NO. 103-826(I), at 61 (1994).

[717]19 U.S.C. §§1675a(a)(1), (2), (3), & (4).

volume of imports would be "significant" if the order were revoked or the suspended investigation were terminated.[718] In doing so, the ITC must consider "all relevant economic factors" including production capacity, inventories, import barriers in other countries, and the potential for product-shifting.[719]

Likewise, with respect to price effects, the ITC will consider whether there is likely to be "significant" price underselling by imports and whether imports are likely to enter the United States at prices that would otherwise have a "significant" depressing or suppressing effect on the price of domestic like products.[720] According to the legislative history, the ITC may rely on circumstantial, as well as direct, evidence of the adverse effects of unfairly traded imports on domestic prices.[721]

With respect to the likely impact of imports on the domestic industry in the event of a revocation or termination, the ITC is required to consider all relevant economic factors which are likely to have a bearing on the state of the industry, including but not limited to likely declines or negative effects on output, sales, market share, profits, productivity, return on investments, utilization of capacity, cash flow, inventories, employment, wages,

---

[718]19 U.S.C. §1675a(a)(2).

[719]Section 752(a)(2) of the Tariff Act of 1930, as amended, provides that the ITC should consider the following factors:

> (A) any likely increase in production capacity or existing unused production capacity in the exporting country,
> (B) existing inventories of the subject merchandise, or likely increases in inventories,
> (C) the existence of barriers to the importation of such merchandise into countries other than the United States, and
> (D) the potential for product-shifting if production facilities in the foreign country, which can be used to produce the subject merchandise, are currently being used to produce other products.

19 U.S.C. §1675a(a)(2).

[720]Section 752a(a)(3) of the Tariff Act of 1930, as amended, requires the ITC to consider whether:

> (A) there is likely to be significant price underselling by imports of the subject merchandise as compared to domestic like products, and
> (B) imports of the subject merchandise are likely to enter the United States at prices that otherwise would have a significant depressing or suppressing effect on the price of domestic like products.

19 U.S.C. §1675a(a)(3).

[721]SAA, *supra* note 516, at 886.

growth, ability to raise capital, investment, and existing development and production efforts of the industry, including efforts to develop a derivative or more advanced version of the domestic like product.[722] The statute requires the ITC to consider all relevant economic factors within the context of the business cycle and the conditions of competition that are distinctive to the domestic industry. Although the ITC must consider all the statutory factors, no one factor is necessarily dispositive.[723] For example, the ITC is not required to find that both the likely volumes and price effects would be "significant."[724]

ii. A "Reasonably Foreseeable Time"

Despite the similarity to the material injury or threat thereof standards used in original investigations, the likelihood standard differs in that it requires the ITC to determine whether revocation or termination would be likely to lead to continuation or recurrence of material injury within a "reasonably foreseeable time."[725] The analysis is prospective in nature and does not require a determination of current material injury.[726] Injury must be likely to "continue" or "recur." On the one hand, the legislative history explains that "an improvement in the state of the industry related to an order . . . may suggest that the state of the industry is likely to deteriorate if the order is revoked. . . ."[727] On the other hand, a domestic industry that

[722]19 U.S.C. §1675a(a)(4).

[723]19 U.S.C. §1675a(5); SAA, *supra* note 516, at 886.

[724]SAA, *supra* note 516, at 886.

[725]Although the additional "reasonably foreseeable time" requirement is not mandated by the Agreements, it comports with the Agreements' phrase "likely to lead to." *See* Antidumping Agreement, *supra* note 5, at art. 11.3; Subsidies Agreement, *supra* note 5, at art. 21.3.

[726]SAA, *supra* note 516, at 884; *see* S. Rep. No. 103-412, at 48 (1994) ("the ITC must decide the likely impact, in the reasonably foreseeable future, of an important change in the status quo — the revocation of an antidumping or countervailing duty order or the termination of a suspended investigation"); H.R. Rep. No. 103-826(I), at 60 (1994) ("Nonetheless, the Commission may consider relevant factors such as current and likely continued depressed shipment levels and current and likely continued prices for the domestic like product in the U.S. market in making its determination of the likelihood of continuation or recurrence of material injury if the order is revoked.").

[727]SAA, *supra* note 516, at 884.

continues to experience material injury is not required to show a further decline in its condition to satisfy the likelihood of continuation standard.[728]

Unlike the threat of injury standard that requires the ITC to consider whether further dumped or subsidized imports are "imminent," the likelihood standard requires the ITC to recognize that "the effects of revocation or termination may not be imminent, but may manifest themselves only over a longer period of time."[729] According to the legislative history, a "reasonably foreseeable time" will vary from case-to-case but will normally exceed the "imminent" timeframe utilized under the threat standard in original investigations.[730]

One of the issues that will presumably be addressed in individual cases is the question of how far into the future the DOC and the ITC should look to assess the likelihood of a continuation or recurrence of dumping. Given that an order or suspended investigation will have a useful life of an additional five years if the sunset review is affirmative, a five-year period could be the benchmark for a "reasonably foreseeable time" for most industries.[731] The DOC has also used a five-year period to confirm non-use of

---

[728]*Id.*

[729]19 U.S.C. §1675a(a)(5), 1677(7)(F)(ii).

[730]SAA, *supra* note 516, at 887; *see* S. REP. NO. 103-412, at 51 (1994); H.R. REP. NO. 103-826(I), at 61 (1994); 19 U.S.C. §§1675a(a)(5), 1677(7)(F)(ii). In an investigation, the ITC will not find a threat of material injury imminent based on a "mere possibility that injury might occur at some remote future time." Alberta Gas Chemicals, Inc. v. United States, 515 F. Supp. 780, 791 (CIT 1981). The ITC has distinguished the standard for pre-URAA Section 751(b) changed circumstance reviews which had a "substantially different conceptual basis." Television Receiving Sets from Japan, Inv. No. 751-TA-2, USITC Pub. 1153, at 5 n.4 (June 1981).

[731]*See* Frozen Concentrated Orange Juice from Brazil, Inv. No. 751-TA-10, USITC Pub. 1623, at 12, 23 (Dec. 1984) the ITC has found that a series of freezes left the domestic frozen concentrated orange juice industry in a vulnerable state and found that revocation would threaten the industry with material injury. The ITC noted that "[s]uch injury would not manifest itself immediately upon revocation of the suspension, but would begin to be apparent in subsequent crop years as the opportunity for recovery slips by, and the industry is unable fully to recover." In the case of oranges, production normally does not recover fully to prefreeze levels until three to five years after a freeze. *See also* Conditions of Competition Between U.S. and Mexican Fabricated Automotive Glass in the U.S. Market, Inv. No. 332-286, USITC Pub. 2299, at 89 (July 1990); Potassium Chloride from Canada, Inv. No. 751-TA-3, USITC Pub. 1137, at 16-17 (April 1981)

countervailable subsidies by producers/exporters requesting revocation of a countervailing duty order, and to revoke or terminate an order or suspended investigation for lack of interest. The ITC has also considered a three to five year period when determining whether to revoke orders in a Section 751(b) review.[732] As noted above, other countries have looked several years in the future in administering their likelihood test.[733]

iii. Other Factors

To determine whether material injury will continue or recur within a reasonably foreseeable time, the legislative history indicates that the ITC will consider "the fungibility or differentiation within the product in question, the level of substitutability between the imported and domestic products, the channels of distribution used, the methods of contracting (such as spot sales or long-term contracts), and lead times for delivery of goods, as well as other factors that may only manifest themselves in the longer term, such as planned investment and the shifting of production facilities."[734]

These "other factors" are similar to considerations typically made in original investigations. For example, in an original investigation, the ITC will consider the product characteristics and other market phenomena to define the "conditions of competition."[735] For example, the ITC will consider the degree to which the imported and domestic products are substitutable to determine whether import volumes and price effects are so significant that they cause or threaten to cause material injury to the domestic industry.[736]

(ITC considers as many as 8 years in the future to determine likely condition of U.S. industry); Certain Scissors and Shears from Brazil, Inv. No. 104-TA-19, USITC Pub. 1456, at 10 n.27 (Dec. 1983) (ITC considers future based on period of five years).

[732] *See* Television Receiving Sets from Japan, Inv. No. 751-TA-2, USITC Pub. 1153, at 16 (June 1981).

[733] *See, e.g.*, Stainless Steel Bars and Stainless Steel Wire in Cut Lengths, Originating In or Exported From Brazil, the Federal Republic of Germany, France, Japan, the Republic of Korea, and Spain, Review No.: RR-89-009, at 9 (July 20, 1990). As explained above, the CIT will focus on circumstances within the next year or two placing less weight on the events later in the five-year period during which a finding could be continued.

[734] SAA, *supra* note 516, at 887.

[735] Vector Supercomputers from Japan, Inv. No. 731-TA-750 (Final), USITC Pub. 3062, at 13 (Oct. 1997).

[736] *See* Fresh Cut Roses from Colombia and Ecuador, Inv. Nos. 731-TA-684 and 685 (Final), USITC Pub. 2862, at I-21 (March 1995) ("The more substitutable products are,

The ITC has also considered whether the market segments prevent imports from competing directly with domestic production.[737]

Finally, the ability of foreign producers or exporters to shift production towards producing the subject merchandise after revocation or termination is likely to weigh in favor of an affirmative determination. For example, in the ITC's threat determinations in an original investigation, the statute requires consideration of the potential for foreign product shifting "if production facilities in the foreign country, which can be used to produce the subject merchandise, are currently being used to produce other products."[738] Thus, in a sunset review, it would appear that the ITC would consider not only the ready availability of production facilities for the subject merchandise but also evidence of any planned investment in those facilities to support an affirmative determination.

iv. Condition of the Domestic Industry

The URAA and its legislative history provide some guidance with respect to the ITC's consideration of the condition of the domestic industry

---

the more likely that potential purchasers will make their relative purchasing decisions based upon price differences between the products. Conversely, where there is a high degree of product differentiation, products are less substitutable, and price is less likely to be a determining factor in purchasing decisions."); Fresh Kiwifruit from New Zealand, Inv. No. 731-TA-516 (Final), USITC Pub. 2510, at 14 (May 1992); *but see* Large Newspaper Printing Presses and Components Thereof, Whether Assembled or Unassembled, from Germany and Japan, Inv. Nos. 731-TA-736, 737 (Final), USITC Pub. 2988, at 29 (Aug. 1996) (ITC made unanimous affirmative determination even though "pricing analysis . . . is complicated by . . . the fact . . . every LNPP or addition sold is customized to the specifications of the individual customer"). The ITC, however, has not been required to follow its prior determinations regarding substitutability from prior determinations involving the same product. U.S. Steel Group v. United States, 873 F. Supp. 673, 697 (CIT 1994), *aff'd*, 96 F.3d 1352 (Fed. Cir. 1996).

[737] *See* Fresh Cut Roses from Colombia and Ecuador, Inv. Nos. 731-TA-684 and 685 (Final), USITC Pub. 2862, at I-18 (March 1995); Nippon Steel Corp. v. United States, 19 CIT 450, 471 (1995).

[738] 19 U.S.C. §1677(7)(F). The ITC has also relied on the product-shifting capability of Japanese television exporters to support its 751(b) finding that the domestic industry would be threatened with material injury if the antidumping duty order were to be modified or revoked. Television Receiving Sets from Japan, Inv. No. 751-TA-2, USITC Pub. 1153, at 18 (June 1981).

in making its likelihood determination. In addition to the volume, price, and impact considerations, Section 752(a)(1) of the Tariff Act of 1930, as amended (19 U.S.C. §1675a(a)(1)), requires the ITC to consider prior injury determinations, the effect of imports on the subject merchandise prior to the order or agreement, any industry improvement attributable to the order or agreement, the vulnerability of the industry, and any DOC duty absorption findings.[739] The URAA requires the ITC to consider the pre-order or agreement condition of the industry which shows the impact of imports on the industry without the remedial effects of an order or agreement.[740] The ITC is also required to consider any post-order or agreement improvement in the condition of the domestic industry which could deteriorate absent the order or suspension agreement.[741]

(A) vulnerability of the domestic industry

According to the legislative history, the "vulnerability" of the domestic industry relates to whether the industry would be susceptible to material injury by reason of dumped or subsidized imports.[742] According to the statute, the term "material injury" is harm that is "not inconsequential, immaterial, or unimportant."[743] "Material injury" means an amount of injury

---

[739]Section 752(a)(1) of the Tariff Act of 1930, as amended requires the ITC to consider:

> (A) its prior injury determinations, including the volume, price effect, and impact of imports of the subject merchandise on the industry before the order was issued or the suspension agreement was accepted,
>
> (B) whether any improvement in the state of the industry is related to the order or the suspension agreement,
>
> (C) whether the industry is vulnerable to material injury if the order is revoked or the suspension agreement is terminated, and
>
> (D) in an antidumping proceeding under section 1675(c) of this title, the findings of the administering authority regarding duty absorption under section 1675(a)(4) of this title.

19 U.S.C. §1675a(a)(1).

[7440]SAA, *supra* note 516, at 884; S. Rep. No. 103-412, at 48 (1994).

[741]SAA, *supra* note 516, at 884; S. Rep. No. 103-412, at 49 (1994); H.R. Rep. 103-826(I), at 60 (1994).

[742]SAA, *supra* note 516, at 885.

[743]19 U.S.C. §1677(7)(A).

that is greater than *de minimis*. The term "by reason of" is a causation standard that has been interpreted to require a finding that dumped or subsidized imports have contributed even minimally to the injury.[744] Thus, the ITC must consider whether the domestic industry is susceptible to greater than *de minimis* harm by reason of dumped or subsidized imports that contribute even minimally to that harm if the order or suspension agreement is revoked or terminated.

The ITC may find that injury is likely to continue or recur based on a finding that the industry is "vulnerable" to injury from the subject imports due to "other" causes of current injury. For example, the ITC found that an industry would be materially injured by reason of imports of drycleaning machinery covered by an antidumping duty order if the order were modified or revoked under Section 751(b) in view of the vulnerable condition of the domestic industry.[745] In that case, the ITC noted that, although it does not weigh causes, the domestic industry was made even more vulnerable to the impact of imports due to severe competition from imports from a country not covered by the antidumping duty order. In another Section 751(b) case, the ITC found that revocation of a suspension agreement on frozen concentrated orange juice would not have a significant effect on foreign producers, exporters, or importers but that revocation would threaten the extremely vulnerable domestic industry with material injury.[746] In that case, the domestic industry's condition had declined in large part due to the effects of an unprecedented number and severity of freezes.[747]

---

[744]Hyundai Electronics Industries Co. v. United States, Slip Op. 97-53, at 11-12 (CIT 1997); *but see* Gerald Metals, Inc. v. United States, 132 F.3d 716, 722 (Fed. Cir. 1997).

[745]Drycleaning Machinery from the Federal Republic of Germany, Inv. No. 751-TA-9, USITC Pub. 1617, at 3, 13 (Dec. 1984), *aff'd,* American Permac, Inc. v. United States, 656 F. Supp. 1228 (CIT 1986), *aff'd,* 831 F.2d 269 (Fed. Cir. 1987), *cert. dismissed,* 485 U.S. 901 (1988).

[746]Frozen Concentrated Orange Juice from Brazil, Inv. No. 751-TA-10, USITC Pub. 1623, at 5 (Dec. 1984).

[747]*See id.* at 12. According to the ITC:

> The nature of an agricultural industry such as that under consideration here renders it vulnerable to the vagaries of weather and other growing conditions. Freezes are an accepted fact in the domestic FCOJ industry, as is the expectation that the industry will recover from the freeze. However, if imports act to hinder or prevent the industry's recovery, we conclude that this would be injury to the industry. Such injury

According to the legislative history, the ITC must also consider whether the industry will deteriorate further upon revocation or termination and whether the vulnerable state of the domestic industry is due to the ineffectiveness of the order or suspension agreement or its circumvention.[748] Neither the statute nor the legislative history explains, however, how the ITC should interpret data indicating that the domestic industry's vulnerability is due to the ineffectiveness of the order or suspension agreement or its circumvention. The ITC could consider the following findings as evidence of the industry's vulnerability due to the ineffectiveness of the order: (1) scope rulings that include a particular product within the scope of an order; (2) Customs' findings regarding importers' failure to properly classify subject merchandise; and (3) Customs' findings regarding improper country of origin markings.[749]

While a formal finding of circumvention pursuant to 19 U.S.C. §1677j could satisfy the circumvention criterion, a formal finding of circumvention may not be necessary for the ITC's sunset analysis. For example, the CITT has considered evidence of "circumvention" in deciding whether dumping was likely to resume.[750] In the case of *Whole Potatoes from the State of Washington*, the CITT found that evidence of U.S. producers circumventing the antidumping order by shipping non-subject grades of potatoes at times when the U.S. price for those potatoes was below established normal values supported a finding of the likelihood of resumed dumping. Likewise, *in Carbon Steel Welded Pipe from the Republic of Korea*, the CITT relied on evidence that Korean exporters had attempted to cir-

---

> would not manifest itself immediately upon revocation of the suspension, but would begin to be apparent in subsequent crop years as the opportunity for recovery slips by, and the industry is unable fully to recover.

Id. at 23.

[748]SAA, *supra* note 516, at 885; S. Rep. No. 103-412, at 49 (1994).

[749]As explained *infra*, ineffectiveness of the order could also be due to duty absorption when the affiliated importer chooses to pay the duties rather than raising the U.S. resale price. *See* SAA, *supra* note 516, at 885; Stewart and Stewart Rebuttal Comments at 27 (1/21/98).

[750]*See* Whole Potatoes With Netted or Russeted Skin, Excluding Seed Potatoes, in Non-Size A, Also Commonly Known as Strippers, Originating In or Exported From the State of Washington, United States of America, For Use or Consumption In the Province of British Columbia, Review No.: RR-89-010, at 10-11 (Sept. 14, 1990).

cumvent the antidumping order by describing the subject goods as non-subject goods at the time of entry into Canada.[751]

At the same time, the legislative history also indicates that the ITC can, in "appropriate circumstances," make an affirmative determination of likelihood notwithstanding the lack of any likely further deterioration of the current condition of the domestic industry upon revocation or termination.[752] No guidance is provided as to what Congress or the Administration would accept to be "appropriate circumstances." Because this portion of the legislative history does not refer again to cases in which the order was ineffective or circumvented, the ITC could find "appropriate circumstances" to include those cases in which the domestic industry is in difficulty. In such cases, the status quo after revocation would be continued injury.

(B) consideration of duty absorption

In addition to the magnitude of the margin, the DOC will also communicate its finding with respect to duty absorption to the ITC.[753] Upon request, the DOC will investigate during any administrative review initiated 2 or 4 years after an order, if antidumping duties have been absorbed by a foreign producer or exporter on sales through an affiliated importer. The DOC will also take duty absorption findings into account in determining the magnitude of the margin if an order were revoked. Specifically, the legislative history states that "[d]uty absorption is a strong indicator that the current dumping margins calculated by [DOC] . . . in reviews may not be indicative of the margins that would exist in the absence of an order. Once an order is revoked, the importer could achieve the same pre-revocation return on its sales by lowering its prices in the U.S. in the amount of the duty that previously was being absorbed."[754] Although a duty absorption finding

[751]Carbon Steel Welded Pipe in the Nominal Size Range 12.7 mm to 406.4 mm (1/2 in. to 16 in.) Inclusive, In Various Forms and Finishes, Usually Supplied to Meet ASTM A53, ASTM A120, ASTM A252, ASTM A589 or AWWA C200-80 or Equivalent Specifications, Including Water Well Casing, Piling Pipe, Sprinkler Pipe and Fencing Pipe, But Excluding Oil and Gas Line Pipe Made to API Specifications Exclusively, Originating In or Exported From the Republic of Korea, Review No.: RR-94-004, at 9 (June 5, 1995).

[752]SAA, *supra* note 516, at 884; H.R. REP. NO. 103-826(I), at 60 (1994).

[753]19 U.S.C. §1675(a)(4).

[754]SAA, *supra* note 516, at 885.

will not affect the calculation of margins in reviews, the DOC's duty absorption finding in the second year is intended to have a deterrent effect on the continued absorption of duties by affiliated importers. If the DOC finds duty absorption in the fourth year, the legislative history indicates that the DOC will consider that information in making its likelihood determination in a sunset review.[755]

In addition, Section 751(a)(4) of the Tariff Act of 1930, as amended (19 U.S.C. §1675(a)(4)), directs the DOC to notify the ITC as to its findings regarding duty absorption for consideration in a sunset review. The Policy Bulletin states that the DOC will provide the ITC with company-specific duty absorption findings for all reviews in which a duty absorption analysis was conducted.[756] Specifically, if the DOC finds duty absorption in the fourth review, the DOC normally will (1) determine that a company's current dumping margin is not indicative of the margin likely to prevail if the order is revoked, and (2) provide to the ITC the higher of the margin that the DOC otherwise would have reported or the most recent margin for that company as adjusted to account for duty absorption findings.[757]

The ITC is to consider evidence of duty absorption in determining whether material injury is likely to continue or recur.[758] According to the legislative history, the ITC will consider evidence of duty absorption as increasing the likelihood of continuation or recurrence of material injury because the producer or exporter would be able to market more aggressively in the absence of an order or suspension agreement.[759]

(C) causation

Finally, the legislative history cautions the ITC not to weigh causes of likely injury. According to the legislative history, the ITC is expected to make an affirmative finding if there is a likelihood of continued or recurring material injury upon revocation or termination despite the possibility of other likely outcomes. There is no indication that the thresholds for in-

---

[755] *Id.* at 886.

[756] *Policy Bulletin, supra* note 516, at 18,874.

[757] *Id.* at 18,874. The DOC will adjust a company's most recent margin by increasing the margin by the amount of duty absorption on those sales for which the DOC found duty absorption. *Id.*

[758] SAA, *supra* note 516, at 886.

[759] *Id.*; S. Rep. No. 103-412, at 49-50 (1994); H.R. Rep. No. 103-826(I), at 61 (1994).

jury and causation in a sunset review differ from those in original investigations. Therefore, if the ITC can find that the revocation or termination is likely to be *a contributing cause* of material injury to the domestic industry, the ITC should make an affirmative determination. The legislative history of the sunset review provision acknowledges the difficulty of applying a "likelihood" test which requires an "inherently predictive and speculative" determination and suggests:

> There may be more than one likely outcome following revocation or termination. The possibility of other likely outcomes does not mean that a determination that revocation or termination is likely to lead to continuation or recurrence of dumping or countervailable subsidies, or injury, is erroneous, as long as the determination of likelihood of continuation or recurrence is reasonable in light of the facts of the case. In such situations, the order or suspended investigation *will be* continued.[760]

Thus, one way to interpret this suggestion is to find that the role of the DOC and the ITC is *not* to establish that the continuation or recurrence of dumping, subsidization, or injury is the only likely outcome upon revocation or termination. Rather, the agencies "will" make an affirmative determination if there is evidence that the continuation or recurrence of dumping, subsidization, or injury is *a* likely outcome upon revocation or termination.

b. Comparison of "Likelihood Tests" in Sunset, Section 751(b), and Section 104(b) Reviews

i. Section 751(b)

In a Section 751(b) changed circumstances review, the ITC would assess whether (1) there were changed circumstances sufficient to warrant review; and, if so, (2) whether the U.S. industry would be materially injured,

---

[760]SAA, *supra* note 516, at 883 (emphasis added); H.R. Rep. No. 103-826(I), at 59 (1994); *see* S. Rep. No. 103-412, at 47-48 (1994).

threatened with material injury, or whether establishment of an industry in the United States would be materially retarded by imports if the order were revoked or modified.[761] In the URAA, however, Congress amended the language of Section 751(b) and inserted language identical to the ITC's likelihood test required for sunset reviews. Accordingly, under Section 751(b), the ITC is now required to determine whether or not revocation or termination is "likely to lead to continuation or recurrence of material injury."[762] According to the Statement of Administrative Action, the change in language for Section 751(b) is consistent with prior practice.[763]

Based on these origins, there are numerous similarities between the likelihood test in sunset and prior Section 751(b) reviews. For example, the ITC's analysis under both tests is necessarily prospective (predictive) in nature. Both reviews require consideration of injury factors such as production capacity, ability for product shifting, and third country market outlets. The purpose of both reviews is not to determine whether or not an industry is experiencing current injury but to assess the condition of the industry in light of the likely impact of future imports. In both reviews, the vulnerability of the domestic industry can weigh in favor of an affirmative determination.

There are distinctions, however, between changed circumstances and sunset reviews. One distinction is that the ITC is required to presume that dumping or subsidization will resume or continue in a changed circumstances review. [764] In contrast, the ITC's sunset review will not proceed in the absence of an affirmative DOC determination. The ITC will also receive information concerning the magnitude of the margin likely to prevail upon revocation or termination and duty absorption findings in a sunset re-

---

[761] 19 U.S.C. §1675(b)(1994); 19 C.F.R. §207.45(a), (c); 19 U.S.C. §1671 (note).

[762] 19 U.S.C. §1675(b) (1995).

[763] SAA, *supra* note 516, at 878. Not only did the URAA extend the same likelihood test to both sunset and Section 751(b) reviews, but the ITC is also instructed to consider the same factors in Section 752 to determine likelihood in both reviews. *Id.* at 883.

[764] *See* Matsushita Electric Industrial Co., Ltd. v. United States, 569 F. Supp. 853, 856-57 (CIT 1983), *rev'd on other grounds* 750 F.2d 927, 929 (Fed. Cir. 1984); American Permac, Inc. v. United States, 831 F.2d 269, 274 (Fed. Cir. 1987); Salmon Gill Fish Netting of Manmade Fibers from Japan, Inv. No. 751-TA-5, USITC Pub. 1234, at 8 (March 1982).

view.[765] In Section 751(b) reviews, however, the ITC has found that the "presence or absence of a dumping margin, or its magnitude within a limited range, is of no use in predicting how a company will set prices when no longer constrained by the order."[766]

In a Section 751(b) review, the ITC has also assumed that any dumping or subsidization is being offset by the existing order or suspension agreement, whereas in a sunset review the ITC will not necessarily assume the same.[767] Another distinction is that the focus of a sunset review is on ending the entire order or suspended investigation whereas the focus of a changed circumstances review can be on simply modifying the order or agreement.[768]

Finally, both Section 751(b) and sunset reviews do not begin from a "clean slate."[769] Unlike Section 751(b), however, the sunset review provisions do not allocate the burden of proof to any interested party.[770] Prior to

---

[765] 19 U.S.C. §1675a(c)(3).

[766] Television Receiving Sets from Japan, Inv. No. 751-TA-2, USITC Pub. 1153, at 8 (June 1981). The ITC's consideration of margin information may, however, change in post-URAA Section 751(b) reviews given published DOC determinations regarding duty absorption. *See* 19 U.S.C. §1675(a)(4).

[767] *See, e.g.,* Drycleaning Machinery from the Federal Republic of Germany, Inv. No. 751-TA-9, USITC Pub. 1617, at 5 (Dec. 1984). It is unclear whether the ITC will continue to assume that dumping or subsidization is being offset by the existing order or agreement in light of Congressional concern regarding duty absorption.

[768] SAA, *supra* note 516, at 879 ("Commerce and the Commission will make their sunset determinations on an order-wide, rather than a company-specific, basis."); *see* Television Receiving Sets from Japan, Inv. No. 751-TA-2, USITC Pub. 1153, at 19 (June 1981), *citing* 19 C.F.R. §207.45(a) (1981) and S. Rep. 93-1298, 93d Cong., 2d Sess. 181 (1974); Synthetic L-Methionine from Japan, Inv. No. 751-TA-4, USITC Pub. 1167, at 1 (July 1981).

[769] Matsushita Elec. Indus. Co., Ltd. v. United States, 750 F.2d 927, 932 (Fed. Cir. 1984) (ITC changed circumstance review); Zenith Electronics Corp. v. United States, 872 F. Supp. 992, 996 (CIT 1994) (DOC administrative review).

[770] According to the U.S. Court of Appeals for the Federal Circuit, the "burden of proof" is the "ultimate burden of persuasion in convincing a fact finder." Creswell Trading Co., Inc. v. United States, 15 F.3d 1054, 1059 (Fed. Cir. 1994). In contrast, the "burden of production" is the burden of going forward with the evidence. *Id.* The burden then shifts to the opposing party who has the burden of producing enough evidence to

the URAA, U.S. law placed the burden of demonstrating changed circumstances or the existence of fair trading on the foreign producers/exporters, the parties found to have been dumping or receiving countervailable subsidies.[771] In contrast, the URAA's sunset provisions do not specifically allocate the burden to interested parties. The statutory language makes it clear that the agencies are charged with the burden of conducting a review and, thus, have the ultimate burden of proof or "burden of persuasion" on the merits.[772] Indeed, in comments on its final regulations, the DOC stated that it found "no basis in either the statute or the agreement for placing the burden of proof on the domestic industry."[773]

---

raise a question of material fact. *See* U.S. Steel Group v. United States, 873 F. Supp. 673, 691(CIT 1994), *aff'd,* 96 F.3d 1352, 1359 n.9 (Fed. Cir. 1996), *citing* Environmental Defense Fund, Inc. v. EPA, 548 F.2d 998, 1004 (D.C. Cir. 1976), *cert. denied,* 431 U.S. 925 (1977) (noting that §556(d) of the Administrative Procedure Act allocates the burden to the proponent of a rule or order.); *see also* Zenith Electronics Corp. v. United States, 872 F. Supp. 992, 996 (CIT 1994).

[771] 19 U.S.C. §1675(b)(1994). Section 751(b) of the Tariff Act of 1930, as amended (19 U.S.C. §1675(b)(1994)) stated that "[d]uring an investigation by the Commission, the party seeking revocation of an antidumping or countervailing duty order shall have the burden of persuasion with respect to whether there are changed circumstances sufficient to warrant revocation of the antidumping or countervailing duty order." The U.S. Congress specifically allocated the burden to the requesting party pursuant to the requirements of Articles 9.2 and 4.9 of the Tokyo Round's Antidumping and Subsidies Agreements, respectively. *See* Appendix I.

[772] *See* Creswell Trading Co., Inc. v. United States, 15 F.3d 1054, 1059 (Fed. Cir. 1994); *see also Conference Report to Accompany H.R. 3398,* H.R. Rep. No. 98-1156, at 182 (1984).

> In section 751 review investigations, as in all Commission antidumping and countervailing duty investigations, neither petitioner nor respondent has a burden of proof. The Commission conducts its own fact-finding in antidumping and countervailing duty investigations. The duty of the parties is to cooperate with the Commission's requests for information. The Commission, for its part, has a duty to conduct a thorough investigation within the context of the strict time constraints of the dumping and countervailing duty law and to seek the information necessary for a reasoned determination.

Conference Report to Accompany H.R. 3398, H.R. Rep. No. 98-1156, at 182 (1984), *citing* Budd Company Railway Division v. United States, 507 F. Supp. 997, 1003 (CIT 1980).

[773] Antidumping Duties; Countervailing Duties, 62 Fed. Reg. 27,296, 27,325 (Dep't Comm. 1997) (Final Rule); *see* Michael Stein, *The Uruguay Round and the Trade Laws: Antidumping, Countervailing Duties, Common Provisions, in* 1 The Commerce Depart-

iii. Section 104(b)

The ITC at one time found the inquiry under Section 751(b) to be more challenging than the inquiry required under Section 104(b). The ITC reasoned that Section 104(b) determinations required predictions of the benefit to a foreign producer of its government's subsidy policy, often based on relatively stable legislation, which was less demanding than that based on the reaction of individual companies to the lifting of restraints on their pricing.[774]

Although many of the injury factors considered in a Section 104(b) review are identical to those considered in a Section 751(b) review, there are a few different considerations in Section 104(b) reviews. For example, in a Section 104(b) case, the ITC made no previous finding of injury to the domestic industry. Yet, according to at least one Commissioner, the ITC assumed in a Section 104(b) case that "as a threshold matter, . . . any subsidy-related injury to the U.S. industry has been remedied during the period in which the duties have been imposed."[775] In contrast, in a sunset review, the outstanding order or suspension agreement will likely be based on a prior injury determination, and the ITC will not necessarily assume that import-related injury to the U.S. industry has been remedied.[776]

In addition, the ITC will not usually consider the most recent subsidy rate information to determine the likelihood of revocation in a sunset re-

---

MENT SPEAKS ON INTERNATIONAL TRADE AND INVESTMENT 877, 890 (PLI 1994) (the sunset provision creates a presumption that the order will expire and shifts the burden of showing that the duty should not terminate to the administering authority).

[774]Television Receiving Sets from Japan, Inv. No. 751-TA-2, USITC Pub. 1153, at 9 n.8 (June 1981).

[775]Certain Nonrubber Footwear from Brazil, India, and Spain, Inv. Nos. 104-TAA-16, 17, and 18, USITC Pub. 1388, at 14 (May 1983) (views of Commissioner Stern); *see* Certain Tomato Products from Greece, Inv. No. 104-TAA-23, USITC Pub. 1594, at 3-4 (Oct. 1984) ("Instead of an evaluation of whether a domestic industry is materially injured or threatened with material injury, section 104(b) evaluations assume that any subsidy is being offset by the existing CVD order and require us to forecast what will happen if the CVD order is revoked."); Sugar Content of Certain Articles from Australia, Inv. No. 104-TAA-26, USITC Pub. 1748, at 3-4 (Sept. 1985).

[776]*See supra* Section A.1.e. In sunset reviews, the statutory language specifically requires the ITC to consider whether revocation or termination would be likely to lead to the continuation or recurrence of material injury. The statute also recognizes that remedial antidumping duties may not have accomplished their intended purpose by requiring consideration of duty absorption. 19 U.S.C. §1675(a)(4).

view or Section 751(b) review as was done in the Section 104(b) reviews.[777] Although a consideration in Section 104(b) reviews requested by a foreign government, there is no indication that the ITC will consider the level of the domestic industry's participation in a sunset review after the industry has responded adequately to requests for information. Finally, despite consideration of foreign producers/exporters' intent in Section 751(b) and 104(b) reviews, there is a noticeable absence of any statutory requirement to consider statements of intent in a sunset review.

c. *Regional Industry Sunset Reviews*

Consistent with the Agreements, the URAA gives the ITC the option to base its likelihood determination on (1) the regional industry as defined in the original determination, (2) a newly defined regional industry according to 19 U.S.C. §1677(7)(4)(C), or (3) the domestic industry as a whole in the United States.[778] According to the legislative history, the URAA provides the ITC with flexibility to redefine the domestic industry given that the existence of an order or suspension agreement may have affected the marketing and distribution patterns of the product.[779] Therefore, the ITC's analysis of a regional industry takes into account whether the market isolation and import concentration criteria[780] are likely to be satisfied in the event of revo-

---

[777]SAA, *supra* note 516, at 890.

[778]19 U.S.C. §1675a(a)(8). Pursuant to Section 771(4)(C) of the Tariff Act of 1930, as amended (19 U.S.C. §1677(4)(C)), a "regional industry" is defined as the "domestic producers within a region who are treated as a separate industry. . . ." Under post-Uruguay Round law, the CITT also reconsiders its regional industry finding in sunset reviews. *See, e.g.,* Whole Potatoes With Netted or Russeted Skin, Excluding Seed Potatoes, in Non-Size A, Also Commonly Known as Strippers, Originating in or Exported from the State of Washington, United States of America, For Use or Consumption in the Province of British Columbia; and Whole Potatoes, Originating in or Exported from the United States of America, For Use or Consumption in the Province of British Columbia, Excluding Seed Potatoes, and Excluding Whole Potatoes With Netted or Russeted Skin in Non-Size A, Originating in or Exported from the State of Washington, Review No.: RR-94-007, at 14 (Sept. 14, 1995).

[779]SAA, *supra* note 516, at 888; S. Rep. No. 103-412, at 51 (1994).

[780]SAA, *supra* note 516, at 888. Section 771(4)(C) provides as follows:

> In appropriate circumstances, the United States, for a particular product market, may be divided into 2 or more markets and the producers within each market may be treated as if they were a separate industry if—

cation or termination.[781] The ITC is also instructed to take into account any prior regional industry definition, whether the product at issue has characteristics that naturally lead to the formation of regional markets, and whether any changes to the isolation of the region or in import concentration are related to the imposition of the order or the acceptance of a suspension agreement.[782]

C. *SUBSEQUENT SUNSET REVIEWS*

When an order or suspension agreement survives the scrutiny of the first fifth year sunset review, the sunset provisions in the Agreement and the

---

(i) the producers within such market sell all or almost all of their production of the domestic like product in question in that market, and

(ii) the demand in that market is not supplied, to any substantial degree, by producers of the product in question located elsewhere in the United States.

> In such appropriate circumstances, material injury, the threat of material injury, or material retardation of the establishment of an industry may be found to exist with respect to an industry even if the domestic industry as a whole, or those producers whose collective output of a domestic like product constitutes a major proportion of the total domestic production of that product, is not injured, if there is a concentration of dumped imports or imports of merchandise benefiting from a countervailable subsidy into such an isolated market and if the producers of all, or almost all, of the production within that market are being materially injured or threatened by material injury, or if the establishment of an industry is being materially retarded, by reason of the dumped imports or imports of merchandise benefiting from a countervailable subsidy. . . .

19 U.S.C. §1677(4)(C).

[781]SAA, *supra* note 516, at 888; H.R. REP. NO. 103-826(I), at 62 (1994).

[782]SAA, *supra* note 516, at 888; H.R. REP. NO. 103-826(I), at 63 (1994). According to the Statement of Administrative Action, "import concentration" will be found to exist if the ratio of the subject imports to consumption is clearly higher in the regional market than in the rest of the U.S. market and if such imports into the region account for a substantial proportion of total subject imports entering the United States. Neither the statute nor its legislative history, however, provides a benchmark ratio. SAA, *supra* note 516, at 860. This statement was intended to overrule the ITC's prior practice of requiring specific benchmark ratios. *See* Crushed Limestone from Mexico, Inv. No. 731-TA-562 (Prelim.), USITC Pub. 2533, at 13-14, 22-24 (July 1992).

URAA specifically establish a subsequent five-year sunset deadline.[783] For subsequent sunset reviews of transition orders, the statute states that the time limits for conducting transition reviews extend to all subsequent sunset reviews.[784] Presumably, the agencies will initiate sunset reviews for continued transition orders in a manner similar to the first round with staggered starting dates although all will arguably be much closer to the five years from the first decision. Thus, within three and a half years after the date of the previous continuation determinations, a sunset review will be initiated not later than the fifth anniversary of the continuation determinations. The review will be completed not later than 18 months after initiation, and a review of *all* transition orders will be completed not later than 18 months after the fifth anniversary of the last continuation determination.[785] According to the Statement of Administrative Action, the statute provides for extended initiation and completion dates for subsequent sunset reviews of transition orders "because the five-year anniversary of such orders will always occur at the same time, thereby creating an extraordinary burden on the agencies' resources." A review of the Antidumping and Subsidies Agreements and the statute and its legislative history also reveals that there is no directive to retire older orders or suspension agreements merely because of their age.[786]

D. *APPEALS OF SUNSET REVIEW DETERMINATIONS*

Article 13 of the Antidumping Agreement and Article 23 of the Subsidies Agreement require member states to provide judicial, arbitral or administrative tribunals or procedures for the purpose of providing prompt review of administrative actions relating to final determinations or reviews of determinations, including sunset reviews.[787] According to the Statement of

---

[783] 19 U.S.C. §1675(c)(1)(C).

[784] 19 U.S.C. §1675(c)(6)(A)(iii).

[785] 19 U.S.C. §1675(c)(6)(A)(ii).

[786] SAA, *supra* note 516, at 882 ("subsequent five-year reviews of transition orders will follow the same time frame as initial five-year reviews — reviews will begin eighteen months prior to, and will be completed within eighteen months after, the fifth anniversary of the date of a determination to continue the transition order"); *see* 62 Fed. Reg. at 27, 324.

[787] Antidumping Agreement, *supra* note 5, at art. 13; Subsidies Agreement, *supra* note 5, at art. 23.

Administrative Action, the current U.S. system of judicial and binational panel review of final determinations satisfies these WTO requirements.[788]

Final determinations of sunset reviews are subject to judicial review pursuant to Section 516A of the Tariff Act of 1930, as amended (19 U.S.C. §1516a).[789] Section 516A provides two separate standards of review for sunset determinations: one standard of review for final determinations for expedited sunset reviews, and one standard for final determinations for full determinations.[790] With respect to final determinations for expedited reviews, the court shall hold unlawful any determination found to be arbitrary, capricious, an abuse of discretion, or otherwise not in accordance with law. With respect to final determinations for full reviews, the court shall hold unlawful any determination found to be unsupported by substantial evidence on the record, or otherwise not in accordance with law.[791] According to the legislative history, Congress assigned the arbitrary and capricious standard of review to final determinations in expedited sunset reviews because those determinations would be based on the limited record from limited responses to the notice of initiation.[792]

---

[788]SAA, *supra* note 516, at 817-18. The Court of International Trade has exclusive jurisdiction of any civil action commenced under section 516A of the Tariff Act of 1930. 28 U.S.C. §1581(c). Court of International Trade decisions can be appealed to the Court of Appeals for the Federal Circuit and then to the U.S. Supreme Court. 28 U.S.C. §§1254, 1292(d)(1), 1295(a)(5), 2645(c). For a discussion of WTO dispute settlement procedures applied to antidumping and countervailing duty disputes, see James R. Cannon, Jr., *Dispute Settlement in Antidumping and Countervailing Duty Cases, in* THE WORLD TRADE ORGANIZATION: MULTILATERAL TRADE FRAMEWORK FOR THE 21ST CENTURY AND U.S. IMPLEMENTING LEGISLATION 359 (Terence P. Stewart ed., ABA 1996).

[789]Alternatively, if the case involves an order or suspension agreement involving Canada or Mexico, interested parties can seek review from the North American Free Trade Agreement's Chapter 19 binational panel. 19 U.S.C. §1516a(g)(8). Finally, if foreign interested parties are dissatisfied with the final determination in a sunset review, their government, as a WTO member, can resort to dispute settlement measures as provided in the WTO Understanding on Rules and Procedures Governing the Settlement of Disputes, including a request for a WTO panel. Antidumping Agreement, *supra* note 5, at art. 17; Subsidies Agreement, *supra* note 5, at art. 30; Understanding on the Rules and Procedures Governing the Settlement of Disputes at art. 6, *in* Final Act, supra note 4, at 1659.

[790]19 U.S.C. §§1516a(a)(1)(D) & 1516a(b)(1)(B)(ii).

[791]19 U.S.C. §§1516a(a)(2)(A)(i)(I), 1516a(a)(2)(B)(i), & 1516a(b)(1)(B)(iii).

[792]SAA, *supra* note 516, at 880. According to the Statement of Administrative Action, the application of two standards of review is consistent with the legislative history of the 1979 Act. *Id., citing* H.R. Rep. 317, 96th Cong., 1st Sess. 180 (1979).

Judicial review of the ITC's determinations not to initiate a changed circumstance review under Section 751(b) of the Tariff Act of 1930, as amended (19 U.S.C. §1675(b)), likewise proceeded under the "arbitrary and capricious" standard of review. According to the Supreme Court, substantial deference must be afforded to the agency's determinations under the arbitrary and capricious standard so long as they possess a rational basis in fact.[793]

In contrast, the agencies' non-sunset revocation/termination decisions have been reviewed under the substantial evidence standard. Under that standard, the Court of International Trade has concluded that "a decision whether to revoke an antidumping-duty order does not depend on the weight of the evidence on the record, rather on the agency's expert analysis of that evidence." [794]

Finally, interested parties have other alternatives if judicial review is not pursued or is unsuccessful. Foreign interested parties will be able to establish entitlement to revocation or termination under the DOC's regulations within three years.[795] The statute allows the domestic industry to file a petition within the first 24 months after sunset covering the same merchandise and benefit from expedited consideration, to the "maximum extent practicable."[796] Therefore, if it becomes clear that the agencies' projections were incorrect and injurious dumped or subsidized imports enter the market, the domestic industry can refile its petition.

---

[793] *See* Avesta AB v. United States, 914 F.2d 233, 237 (Fed. Cir. 1990) *cert. denied* 499 U.S. 920 (1991), *citing* Consolo v. Federal Maritime ITC, 383 U.S. 607, 620-21 (1966); Zenith Radio Corp. v. United States, 437 U.S. 443, 450-51 (1978).

[794] PPG Industries, Inc. v. United States, 780 F. Supp. 1389, 1394 (CIT 1991), *vacated,* 979 F.2d 215 (Fed. Cir. 1992), *citing Sanyo Electric Co., Ltd.*, 15 CIT at 612; *Toshiba Corp.*, 15 CIT at 600.

[795] 19 C.F.R. §351.222(e). The DOC repealed its regulations allowing for automatic revocations or terminations on the basis of lack of administrative review requests because the procedures resulted in "considerable administrative burden" which is unnecessary with sunset reviews. *Final Rule,* 62 Fed. Reg. at 27,326 (Comments on 19 C.F.R. §351.222). The statute, however, allows the DOC to revoke an order or terminate an investigation if producers accounting for substantially all of the production of that domestic like product have expressed a lack of interest in the order or suspended investigation. 19 U.S.C. §1677m(h); 19 C.F.R. §351.222(g)(1)(i).

[796] 19 U.S.C. §§1671a(c)(1)(C) & 1673a(c)(1)(C). The statute further allows the agency in possession of proprietary information submitted in conjunction with a sunset review resulting in revocation or termination to use that information in a subsequent investigation covering the same merchandise filed within two years. 19 U.S.C. §1677f(b)(3); SAA, *supra* note 516, at 891.

CHAPTER VII

Conclusion

Of the four major historic users of antidumping and countervailing duty laws, only the United States was forced to undertake major legislative changes to adopt the Uruguay Round's sunset requirement. As the United States approaches its first sunset review in July 1998, a review of its implementing legislation, legislative history, and regulations as compared to the legislation and practice of the European Union, Canada, and Australia reveals a large number of similarities in "sunset" (or expiry/continuation) review provisions:

Summary of Sunset Review Provisions				
Issue	***EU***	***Canada***	***Australia***	***U.S.***
The government can self-initiate a sunset review	Yes	Yes	No	Yes
Interested parties can file a request for a sunset review.	Yes	Yes	Yes	No
The government requires factual information to be submitted within 30 days of the notice of initiation.	No (37-40)	No (35)	No (60)	Yes (30+50)
The government conducts verification in a sunset review.	Yes	Yes	Yes	Yes
The government can conduct an expedited sunset review.	Yes	No	Yes	Yes
The government can group reviews.	Yes	Yes	Yes	Yes

Summary of Sunset Review Provisions (Continued)				
Issue	***EU***	***Canada***	***Australia***	***U.S.***
The government can cumulate imports.	Yes	Yes	Yes	Yes
The government calculates a current margin in a sunset review.	Yes	No	Yes	No
The government considers historic margins over the course of a measure in a sunset review.	No	Yes	Yes	Yes
The government considers duty absorption in a sunset review.	Yes	No	No	Yes
The government considers evidence of measures against foreign producers/exporters in third countries to weigh in favor of an affirmative determination in a sunset review.	Yes	Yes	Yes	Unclear
The government considers foreign capacity data in a sunset review.	Yes	Yes	Yes	Yes
The government considers evidence of circumvention of existing measures in a sunset review.	Yes	Yes	No	Yes
The government reconsiders or describes the domestic industry and/or like product definitions in a sunset review.	Yes	Yes	Yes	Yes
The government considers the current condition of the domestic industry in a sunset review.	Yes	Yes	Yes	Yes
The government considers the domestic industry's vulnerability in a sunset review.	Yes	Yes	Unclear	Yes
The government considers the domestic industry's investment in production in a sunset review.	Yes	Yes	Unclear	Yes
The government considers evidence of likely price depression or suppression in a sunset review.	Yes	Yes	Yes	Yes
The government applies a "foreseeable" future test.	Yes	Yes	No	Yes
Usual deadline for completion of sunset review.	1 year	1 year	less than 1 year	1 year

Unlike the procedures in the three other countries, the U.S. sunset review provisions require the government to self-initiate a review and base the length and thoroughness of that review on interested parties' desire and ability to supply necessary information. In contrast, the three other countries primarily rely on interested parties to file a substantiated request for a sunset review. Once initiated, however, the three countries do not appear to limit their review based on the participation of interested parties as in the U.S. "expedited" review.

Procedurally, all four sunset systems provide an opportunity for interested parties to participate in the process with written and oral submissions. The four governments conduct some form of verification of submitted information to ensure accuracy. Unlike other countries, however, the EU conducts what is tantamount to a new investigation. As a result, the EU calculates current margins whereas Canada and Australia rely on previously calculated margins or duties collected during the five year period.

Substantively, the four governments will consider many of the same factors identified above in determining whether dumping or subsidies are likely to continue or recur after revocation or termination. For example, a review of the decisions in the three countries with pre-Uruguay Round sunset provisions reveals repeated reliance on evidence of continued margins, excess foreign capacity, the existence of measures in third countries, and/or the vulnerability of the domestic industry to support an affirmative finding. Given the U.S. reliance on similar evidence in its revocation decisions in prior years, it is likely that the ITC will consider similar evidence in its sunset reviews.

Based on a review of prior pre- and post-Uruguay Round decisions, however, the emphasis on factors that would support an affirmative finding differ in the EU, Canada, and Australia. For example, the EU and Australia tend to rely more on evidence of price undercutting and market shares of imports to support an affirmative determination than Canada. Both the EU and Canada have expressed concern over the domestic industry's investments in future production in making affirmative determinations. Of the three countries with pre-Uruguay sunset reviews, the Canadian decisions favor evidence showing the attractiveness of the Canadian market for future imports in support of an affirmative determination.

The Agreements require a wide range of factors to be considered in making injury determinations and, therefore, sunset review determinations. These requirements are reflected in the four countries' statutes, regulations, or practice.[797] Thus, on the eve of the first round of U.S. sunset reviews, it can be anticipated that the U.S. agencies' decisions are likely to reflect the same factors that have proven to be important in prior cases in other jurisdictions. What is certain is that the sunset case law across the countries will be in an important phase during the next few years.

[797]See Appendix III for a comparison of the legislative provisions governing sunset reviews in the EU, Canada, Australia, and the United States.

APPENDIX I

Sunset Provision in Antidumping Agreement

Tokyo	*Carlisle I*	*Carlisle II*	*NZ I*	*NZ 2*	*NZ 3*	*Dunkel*	*Final*
9.1 An anti-dumping duty shall remain in force only as long as, and to the extent necessary to counteract dumping which is causing injury.	11.1 An anti-dumping duty shall remain in force only as long as and to the extent necessary to counteract dumping which is causing injury.	11.1 An anti-dumping duty shall remain in force only as long as and to the extent necessary to counteract dumping which is causing injury.	11.1 An anti-dumping duty shall remain in force only as long as and to the extent necessary to counteract dumping which is causing injury.	11.1 An anti-dumping duty shall remain in force only as long as and to the extent necessary to counteract dumping which is causing injury.	11.1 An anti-dumping duty shall remain in force only as long as and to the extent necessary to counteract dumping which is causing injury.	11.1 An anti-dumping duty shall remain in force only as long as and to the extent necessary to counteract dumping which is causing injury.	11.1 An anti-dumping duty shall remain in force only as long as and to the extent necessary to counteract dumping which is causing injury.
9.2 The investigating authorities shall review the need for the continued imposition of the duty, where warranted, on their own initiative or if any interested party so requests and submits positive information substantiating the need for review.	11.2 The authorities shall review the need for the continued imposition of the duty, where warranted, on their own initiative or if any interested party so requests and submits positive information substantiating the need for a review. In such a review, the authorities shall in particular examine whether	11.2 The authorities shall review the need for the continued imposition of the duty, where warranted, on their own initiative or if any interested party so requests and submits positive information substantiating the need for a review,* provided that a reasonable period of time has elapsed since	11.2 The authorities shall review the need for the continued imposition of the duty, where warranted, on their own initiative or, provided that a reasonable period of time has elapsed since the imposition of the definitive anti-dumping duty, upon request by any interested party which sub-	11.2 The authorities shall review the need for the continued imposition of the duty, where warranted, on their own initiative or, upon request by any interested party which submits positive information substantiating the need for a review.* Interested parties shall have the right to request the au-	11.2 The authorities shall review the need for the continued imposition of the duty, where warranted, on their own initiative or, provided that a reasonable period of time has elapsed since the imposition of the definitive anti-dumping duty, upon request by any interested party which sub-	11.2 The authorities shall review the need for the continued imposition of the duty, where warranted, on their own initiative or, provided that a reasonable period of time has elapsed since the imposition of the definitive antidumping duty, upon request by any interested party which sub-	11.2 The authorities shall review the need for the continued imposition of the duty, where warranted, on their own initiative or, provided that a reasonable period of time has elapsed since the imposition of the definitive anti-dumping duty, upon request by any interested party which sub-

Sunset Provision in Antidumping Agreement

Tokyo	Carlisle I	Carlisle II	NZ I	NZ 2	NZ 3	Dunkel	Final
	the continued imposition of the duty is necessary to offset injurious dumping. If subsequent to a review under this paragraph the evidence discloses that the anti-dumping duty is no longer warranted, it shall be terminated immediately.	the imposition of the definitive anti-dumping duty. Reviews should be carried out as quickly as possible and should normally not exceed twelve months. In the review, the authorities shall in particular examine whether the continued imposition of the duty is necessary to offset dumping and to prevent injury from recurring. If subsequent to a review under this paragraph, the authorities determine that the anti-dumping duty is no longer	mits positive information substantiating the need for a review.* Interested parties shall have the right to request the authorities to examine whether the continued imposition of the duty is necessary to offset dumping, whether recurrence of the injury would occur if the duty were removed or varied, or both. If as a result of the review under this paragraph, the authorities determine that the anti-dumping duty is not longer warranted, it shall	thorities to examine whether the continued imposition of the duty is necessary to offset dumping, whether recurrence of the injury would occur if the duty were removed or varied, or both. If, as a result of the review under this paragraph, the authorities determine that the anti-dumping duty is no longer warranted, it shall be terminated immediately. ____ *The term "review" as used in this Article does not include a determination of	mits positive information substantiating the need for a review.* Interested parties shall have the right to request the authorities to examine whether the continued imposition of the duty is necessary to offset dumping, whether recurrence of the injury would occur if the duty were removed or varied, or both. If, as a result of the review under this paragraph, the authorities determine that the anti-dumping duty is no longer warranted, it shall	mits positive information substantiating the need for a review.* Interested parties shall have the right to request the authorities to examine whether the continued imposition of the duty is necessary to offset dumping, whether recurrence of the injury would occur if the duty were removed or varied, or both. If, as a result of the review under this paragraph, the authorities determine that the anti-dumping duty is no longer warranted, it shall	mits positive information substantiating the need for a review.* Interested parties shall have the right to request the authorities to examine whether the continued imposition of the duty is necessary to offset dumping, whether the injury would be likely to continue or recur if the duty were removed or varied, or both. If, as a result of the review under this paragraph, the authorities determine that the anti-dumping duty is no longer

Sunset Provision in Antidumping Agreement

Tokyo	Carlisle I	Carlisle II	NZ I	NZ 2	NZ 3	Dunkel	Final
		warranted, it shall be terminated immediately. ——— * For the purposes of this Code, the term "review" shall mean a formal proceeding, to be conducted by the authorities, at which the matter or matters under review shall be subject to a full examination and during which all parties referred to in Article 6.10 and 6.11 shall have a full opportunity to present information.	be terminated immediately. ——— * The term "review" as used in this Article does not include a determination of final liability for payment of anti-dumping duties as provided for in Article 9.3.1.	final liability for payment of anti-dumping duties as provided for in Article 9.3.	be terminated immediately. ——— * The term "review" as used in this Article does not include a determination of final liability for payment of anti-dumping duties as provided for in Article 9.3.	be terminated immediately. ——— * A determination of final liability for payment of anti-dumping duties as provided for in Article 9.3 does not by itself constitute a review within the meaning of this Article.	warranted, it shall be terminated immediately. ——— * A determination of final liability for payment of anti-dumping duties, as provided for in paragraph 3 of Article 9, does not by itself constitute a review within the meaning of this Article.

Sunset Provision in Antidumping Agreement

Tokyo	Carlisle I	Carlisle II	NZ I	NZ 2	NZ 3	Dunkel	Final
	11.3 Notwithstanding the provisions of paragraphs 1 and 2, any definitive antidumping duty shall be terminated within 5 years of its imposition, unless the authorities determine on the basis of a review carried out before the date of termination that there is good cause for the continuation of the anti-dumping duty, after all parties referred to in Article 6:10 and 11 have had a full opportunity to present information.	11.3 Notwithstanding the provisions of paragraphs 1 and 2, any definitive anti-dumping duty shall [be terminated within [3][5] years of its imposition, unless the authorities determine on the basis of a review carried out before the date of termination that the continued imposition of the duty is necessary to offset dumping and to prevent injury from recurring.] [continue to apply unless it is demonstrated, in a review to be conducted within [3][5] years of the	11.3 Notwithstanding the provisions of paragraphs 1 and 2, any definitive antidumping duty shall be terminated not later than five years from the date of its imposition (or from the date of its most recent review under paragraph 2 if that review has covered both dumping and injury), unless the authorities determine, on the basis of a review initiated before that date upon a duly substantiated request made by or on behalf of the domestic industry	11.3 Notwithstanding the provisions of paragraphs 1 and 2, any definitive anti-dumping duty shall be terminated not later than five years from the date of its imposition (or from the date of its most recent review under paragraph 2 if that review has covered both dumping and injury), unless the authorities determine, on the basis of a review initiated before that date upon a duly substantiated request made by or on behalf of the domestic industry	11.3 Notwithstanding the provisions of paragraphs 1 and 2, any definitive anti-dumping duty shall be terminated not later than five years from the date of its imposition (or from the date of its most recent review under paragraph 2 if that review has covered both dumping and injury, or under this paragraph), unless the authorities determine, on the basis of a review initiated before that date on their own initiative or upon a duly substantiated request made	11.3 Notwithstanding the provisions of paragraphs 1 and 2, any definitive anti-dumping duty shall be terminated on a date not later than five years from its imposition (or from the date of the most recent review under paragraph 2 if that review has covered both dumping and injury, or under this paragraph), unless the authorities determine, in a review initiated before that date on their own initiative or upon a duly substantiated request made by or on behalf of the domestic industry	11.3 Notwithstanding the provisions of paragraphs 1 and 2, any definitive anti-dumping duty shall be terminated on a date not later than five years from its imposition (or from the date of the most recent review under paragraph 2 if that review has covered both dumping and injury, or under this paragraph), unless the authorities determine, in a review initiated before that date on their own initiative or upon a duly substantiated request made by or on

Sunset Provision in Antidumping Agreement

Tokyo	Carlisle I	Carlisle II	NZ I	NZ 2	NZ 3	Dunkel	Final
		imposition of the duty, that a revocation of the duty would not result in a resumption of dumping which would cause injury.]	within a reasonable period of time prior to that date, that the continued imposition of the duty to offset dumping and prevent injury from recurring. The duty may remain in force pending the outcome of such a review.	within a reasonable period of time prior to that date, that the continued imposition of the duty is necessary to offset dumping and prevent injury from recurring. The duty may remain in force pending the outcome of such a review.	by or on behalf of the domestic industry within a reasonable period of time prior to that date, that the continued imposition of the duty is necessary to offset dumping and prevent the continuation or recurrence of the injury. The duty may remain in force pending the outcome of such a review.	within a reasonable period of time prior to that date, that the continued imposition of the duty is necessary to prevent the continuation or recurrence of injury by dumped imports.* The duty may remain in force pending the outcome of such a review. ——— *When the amount of the anti-dumping duty is assessed on a retrospective basis, a finding in the most recent assessment proceeding under Article 9.3.1 that no duty is to be levied shall not by itself	behalf of the domestic industry within a reasonable period of time prior to that date, that the expiry of the duty would be likely to lead to continuation or recurrence of dumping and injury.* The duty may remain in force pending the outcome of such a review. ——— * When the amount of the anti-dumping duty is assessed on a retrospective basis, a finding in the most recent assessment proceeding under subparagraph 3.1 of Article 9 that

Sunset Provision in Antidumping Agreement

Tokyo	*Carlisle I*	*Carlisle II*	*NZ I*	*NZ 2*	*NZ 3*	*Dunkel*	*Final*
						require the authorities to determine under this paragraph that the continued imposition of the antidumping duty is not necessary.	no duty is to be levied shall not by itself require the authorities to terminate the definitive duty.

Sunset Provision in Subsidies Agreement

Tokyo	*Carlisle I*	*Carlisle II*	*Carlisle III*	*Carlisle IV*	*Dunkel*	*Final*
4.9 A countervailing duty shall remain in force only as long as, and to the extent necessary to counteract the subsidization which is causing injury. The investigating authorities shall review the need for continued imposition of the duty, where warranted, on their own initiative or if any interested party so requests and submits positive information substantiating the need for review.	20.1 A countervailing duty shall remain in force only as long as, and to the extent necessary to counteract the subsidization which is causing injury. The investigating authorities shall review the need for continued imposition of the duty, where warranted, on their own initiative or if any interested party so requests and submits positive information substantiating the need for review.	20.1 A countervailing duty shall remain in force only as long as, and to the extent necessary to counteract the subsidization which is causing injury. The investigating authorities shall review the need for continued imposition of the duty, where warranted, on their own initiative or if any interested party so requests and submits positive information substantiating the need for review.	20.1 A countervailing duty shall remain in force only as long as, and to the extent necessary to counteract the subsidization which is causing injury. The investigating authorities shall review the need for continued imposition of the duty, where warranted, on their own initiative or if any interested party so requests and submits positive information substantiating the need for review.	20.1 A countervailing duty shall remain in force only as long as, and to the extent necessary to counteract the subsidization which is causing injury. The investigating authorities shall review the need for continued imposition of the duty, where warranted, on their own initiative or if any interested party so requests and submits positive information substantiating the need for review.	20.1 A countervailing duty shall remain in force only as long as, and to the extent necessary to counteract the subsidization which is causing injury. The investigating authorities shall review the need for continued imposition of the duty, where warranted, on their own initiative or if any interested party so requests and submits positive information substantiating the need for review.	21.1 A countervailing duty shall remain in force only as long as and to the extent necessary to counteract subsidization which is causing injury.
	20.2 Notwithstanding the provisions of paragraph 1, every countervail	20.2 Notwithstanding the provisions of paragraph 20.1, every countervail	20.2 Notwithstanding the provisions of paragraph 1 above, every coun	20.2 Notwithstanding the provisions of paragraph 1 above, every coun	20.2 Notwithstanding the provisions of paragraph 1 above, every coun	21.2 The authorities shall review the need for the continued imposition

Sunset Provision in Subsidies Agreement

Tokyo	Carlisle I	Carlisle II	Carlisle III	Carlisle IV	Dunkel	Final
	ing duty shall be terminated within 5 years of its imposition unless the investigating authorities determine on the basis of a review that there is "good cause" for the continuation of the duty, after all interested parties have had a full opportunity to present their views.	ing duty shall be terminated within 5 years of its imposition unless the investigating authorities determine on the basis of a review that there is "good cause" for the continuation of the duty, after all interested parties have had a full opportunity to present their views.	tervailing duty shall be terminated within 5 years of its imposition unless the investigating authorities determine on the basis of a review that there is "good cause" for the continuation of the duty, after all interested parties have had a full opportunity to present their views.	tervailing duty shall be terminated within 5 years of its imposition unless the investigating authorities determine on the basis of a review that there is "good cause" for the continuation of the duty, after all interested parties have had a full opportunity to present their views.	tervailing duty shall be terminated within 5 years of its imposition unless the investigating authorities determine on the basis of a review that there is "good cause" for the continuation of the duty, after all interested parties have had a full opportunity to present their views.	of the duty, where warranted, on their own initiative or, provided that a reasonable period of time has elapsed since the imposition of the definitive countervailing duty, upon request by any interested party which submits positive information substantiating the need for a review. Interested parties shall have the right to request the authorities to examine whether the continued imposition of the duty is necessary to offset subsidization, whether the injury would be likely to continue or

Sunset Provision in Subsidies Agreement

Tokyo	*Carlisle I*	*Carlisle II*	*Carlisle III*	*Carlisle IV*	*Dunkel*	*Final*
						recur if the duty were removed or varied, or both. If, as a result of the review under this paragraph, the authorities determine that the countervailing duty is no longer warranted, it shall be terminated immediately.
						21.3 Notwithstanding the provisions of paragraphs 1 and 2, any definitive countervailing duty shall be terminated on a date not later than five years from its imposition (or from the date of the most recent review under paragraph 2 if that review has covered both subsidization and injury, or under this paragraph), unless the authorities determine, in a review initiated before that date on

Tokyo	*Carlisle I*	*Carlisle II*	*Carlisle III*	*Carlisle IV*	*Dunkel*	*Final*
						their own initiative or upon a duty substantiated request made by or on behalf of the domestic industry within a reasonable period of time prior to that date, that the expiry of the duty would be likely to lead to continuation or recurrence of subsidization and injury.* The duty may remain in force pending the outcome of such a review. * When the amount of the countervailing duty is assessed on a retrospective basis, a finding in the most recent assessment proceeding that no duty is to be levied shall not by itself require the authorities to terminate the definitive duty.

APPENDIX II

The Initiation Phase	
DOC Schedule*	**ITC Schedule****
Notice of Initiation and Request for Information *19 U.S.C. §1675(c)(2) *19 C.F.R. §§351.218(c), 351.221(c)(5)(i)	Notice of Institution and Request for Information *19 C.F.R. §207.60(d)
15 Days after Initiation: Notice of Intent to Participate Filed by Domestic Interested Parties *19 C.F.R. §351.218(d)(1)(i)	
20 Days after Initiation: DOC Notification to the ITC That No Domestic Interested Party has Responded to Notice of Initiation *19 C.F.R. §351.218(d)(1)(iii)(B)(2)	
	21 Days After Institution: Entries of Appearance/APO Application *19 C.F.R. §201.11(b)
30 Days After Initiation: Substantive Responses to Notice of Initiation; Statement of Waiver *19 C.F.R. §351.218(d)(2) & (3)	
35 Days After Initiation: Filing of Rebuttal Comments to Substantive Responses *19 C.F.R. §351.218(d)(4)	
40 Days After Initiation: Notification to ITC that No Domestic Interested Party Has Responded (Based on Inadequate Responses) *19 C.F.R. §351.218(e)(1)	
50 Days After Initiation: Notification to the ITC That Respondent Interested Parties Have Provided Inadequate Responses *19 C.F.R. §351.218(e)(1)	50 Days After Institution: Responses to Notice of Institution *19 C.F.R. §207.61

70 Days After Initiation: Comments on Adequacy of Responses and Appropriateness of Expedited Review *19 C.F.R. §351.309(e)(ii)	
	75 Days After Institution: Comments on Appropriateness of Expedited Review *19 C.F.R. §207.62
90 Days After Initiation: Final DOC Determination If No Domestic Interested Party Responds *19 U.S.C. §1675(c)(3)(A) *19 C.F.R. §351.218(d)(1)(iii) *19 C.F.R. §351.222(i)(1)(i)	
	95 Days After Institution: Notice of Expedited or Full Review *19 C.F.R. §§207.62(c), (d)
An Expedited Review	
120 Days After Initiation: Final Determination Based on Facts Available *19 U.S.C. §1675(c)(3)(B) *19 C.F.R. §351.218(e)(1)	
	122 Days After Institution: Staff Report/Data Compilation to ITC and Parties *19 C.F.R. §207.62(d)
	127 Days After Institution: Written Submission on Merits Due *19 C.F.R. §207.62(d)
	140 Days After Institution: Commission Vote
	150 Days After Institution: Final Determination Based on Facts Available and Views to the DOC *19 U.S.C. §1675(c)(3)(B)

The Full Review	
DOC Schedule	**ITC Schedule**
	Notice of Scheduling *19 C.F.R. §207.62(c)
110 After Initiation: Preliminary Results of Full Review *19 C.F.R. §351.218(f)(1)	
120 After Initiation: Verification in a Full Sunset Review *19 C.F.R. §351.218(f)(2)(ii)	
160 Days After Initiation: Case Briefs Due *19 C.F.R. §351.309(c)(1)(i)	
165 Days After Initiation: Rebuttal Briefs Due *19 C.F.R. §351.309(d)(1)	
167 Days After Initiation: Hearing in Full Sunset Review *19 C.F.R. §351.310(d)(1)	
	180 Days After Institution: New Entries of Appearance/APO Applications *19 C.F.R. §201.11(b)(5)
	190 Days After Institution: Draft Questionnaire to Parties for Comments *19 C.F.R. §207.63
	205 Days After Institution: Written Comments on Draft Questionnaire *19 C.F.R. §207.63
	225 Days After Institution: Questionnaire Mail Date *63 Fed. Reg. at 30,611

240 Days After Initiation: DOC Final Dumping/Subsidy Determination, Unless Extension of Time *19 U.S.C. §1675(c)(5)(A) *19 C.F.R. §351.218(f)(3)(i)	
	255 Days After Institution: Questionnaire Return Date *63 Fed. Reg. at 30,611
	285 Days After Institution: Prehearing Staff Report *19 C.F.R. §207.64
	295 Days After Institution: Prehearing Briefs Due *19 C.F.R. §207.65
	305 Days After Institution: Hearing *19 C.F.R. §207.66
	315 Days After Institution: Posthearing Briefs Due *19 C.F.R. §207.67
330 Days After Initiation: Final Results of Sunset Review With Full Extension of Time *19 C.F.R. §351.218(f)(3)(ii)	330 Days After Institution: Final Staff Report *19 C.F.R. §207.64(b)
	340 Days After Institution: Final Comments Due *19 C.F.R. §207.68
	348 Days After Institution: Commission Vote *63 Fed. Reg. at 30,611
	360 Days After Institution: Final Determination and Views to DOC *19 C.F.R. §207.69

* *Interim Regulations, supra* note 516, at 13,524-25.
** *Final Regulations, supra* note 516, at 30,611.

APPENDIX III

Primary Sunset Review Provisions in Domestic Legislation

European Union*	Canada**	Australia***	United States****
Council Regulation 384/96 **Article 11** **Duration, reviews and refunds** 1. An anti-dumping measure shall remain in force only as long as, and to the extent that, it is necessary to counteract the dumping which is causing injury. 2. A definitive anti-dumping measure shall expire five years from its imposition or five years from the date of the conclusion of the most recent review which has covered both dumping and injury, unless it is determined in a review that the expiry would be likely to lead to a continuation or recurrence of dumping and injury. Such an expiry review shall be initiated on the initiative of	Special Import Measures Act **Finality and Review of Orders and Findings** **Application for judicial review** 76.(1) Subject to 61(3) and Part I.1 or II, an application for judicial review of an order or finding of the Tribunal under this Act may be made to the Federal Court of Appeal on any of the grounds set out in Subsection 18.1(4) of the Federal Court Act. **Review of orders by Tribunal and re-hearing** (2) At any time after the making of an order or finding described in any of Sections 3 to 6, the Tribunal may, on its own initiative or at the request of the Deputy Min-	Customs Act of 1901, as amended **Section 269TM Period During Which Certain Notices and Undertakings To Remain in Force** **269TM(1) [After publication of notice]** Where a notice is published after section 17 of the *Customs Legislation (Tariff Concessions and Anti-Dumping) Amendment Act of 1992* commences under a relevant notification provision in respect of goods of a particular kind, that notice expires 5 years after the day on which it is published unless it is revoked before the end of that period. **269TM(2) [Where undertaking entered into]** Where an undertaking is entered into after section 17 of the *Customs Legislation*	Tariff Act of 1930, as amended **§1675. Administrative review of determinations** *** **(c) Five-year review** **(1) In general** Notwithstanding subsection (b) of this section and except in the case of a transition order defined in paragraph (6), 5 years after the date of publication of — (A) a countervailing duty order (other than a countervailing duty order to which subparagraph (B) applies or which was issued without an affirmative determination of injury by the Commission under section 1303 of this title), an antidumping

Primary Sunset Review Provisions in Domestic Legislation

European Union*	Canada**	Australia***	United States****
the Commission, or upon request made by or on behalf of Community producers, and the measure shall remain in force pending the outcome of such review. An expiry review shall be initiated where the request contains sufficient evidence that the expiry of the measures would be likely to result in a continuation or recurrence of dumping and injury. Such a likelihood may, for example, be indicated by evidence of continued dumping and injury or evidence that the removal of injury is partly or solely due to the existence of measures or evidence that the circumstances of the exporters, or market conditions, are such that they would indicate the likelihood of further injurious dumping. In carrying out investigations under this paragraph, the ex-	ister or any other person or of any government, review the order or finding and, in the making of the review, may re-hear any matter before deciding it. **Idem** (2.1) Where the Tribunal receives notice of action taken pursuant to paragraph 41.1(1)(a) or (2)(a) [action on final determination or decision referred back by Court or panel] in respect of goods to which an order or finding of the Tribunal, other than an order or finding described in any of Section 3 to 6, applies, the Tribunal may, on its own initiative or at the request of the Deputy Minister or any other person or of any government, review the order or finding and, in making such a review, may re-hear any matter before deciding it.	*(Tariff Concessions and Anti-Dumping) Amendment Act 1992* commences under a relevant undertaking provision in respect of goods of a particular kind, that undertaking expires 5 years after the day on which it was entered into unless provision is made for its earlier expiration. **269TM(3) [Notices previously in force]** If: (a) a notice was or is published before section 17 of the *Customs Legislation (Tariff Concessions and Anti-Dumping) Amendment Act 1992* commences; and (b) the notice is in force immediately before the commencement of that section; the notice expires 5 years after the day on which it was published unless it is sooner revoked.	duty order, or a notice of suspension of an investigation, described in subsection (a)(1) of this section, (B) a notice of injury determination under section 1675b of this title with respect to a countervailing duty order, or (C) a determination under this section to continue an order or suspension agreement, the administering authority and the Commission shall conduct a review to determine, in accordance with section 1675a of this title, whether revocation of the countervailing or antidumping duty order or termination of the investigation suspended under section 1671c or 1673c of this title would be likely to lead to continuation or recurrence of dumping or a countervailable subsidy (as the case may be) and of material injury.

Primary Sunset Review Provisions in Domestic Legislation

European Union*	Canada**	Australia***	United States****
porters, importers, the representatives of the exporting country and the Community producers shall be provided with the opportunity to amplify, rebut or comment on the matters set out in the review request, and conclusions shall be reached with due account taken of all relevant and duly documented evidence presented in relation to the question as to whether the expiry of measures would be likely, or unlikely, to lead to the continuation or recurrence of dumping and injury. A notice of impending expiry shall be published in the *Official Journal of the European Communities* at an appropriate time in the final year of the period of application of the measures as defined in this paragraph. Thereafter, the Community producers shall, no later than three	**Idem** (2.2) Where an order or finding of the Tribunal is referred back to the Tribunal under Subsection 77.015(3) or (4) or 77.019(5) [panel review], or under Subsection 77.15(3) or (4) or 77.19(4) [panel review], the Tribunal shall review the order or finding and, in making such a review, may rehear any matter before deciding it. **Refusal** (3) The Tribunal shall not initiate any review pursuant to Subsection (2) or (2.1) at the request of any person or government unless the person or government satisfies the Tribunal that a review is warranted. **Order of refusal** (3.1) Where the Tribunal decides not to initiate a review pursuant	**269TM(3A)** [**Undertakings previously in force**] If: (a) an undertaking was or is entered into force before section 17 of the *Customs Legislation (Tariff Concessions and Anti-Dumping) Amendment Act 1992* commence; and (b) the undertaking is in force immediately before that section commences; the Minister must, by notice in writing, give the person who gave the undertaking the opportunity, before the undertaking expires, to extend the undertaking so that it expires 5 years after the day on which it was entered into unless provision is made for its earlier expiration. **269TM(3B)** [**Expiry of undertaking**] If a person who gave an undertaking of the kind referred to	(2) **Notice of initiation of review** Not later than 30 days before the fifth anniversary of the date described in paragraph (1), the administering authority shall publish in the Federal Register a notice of initiation of a review under this subsection and request that interested parties submit — (A) a statement expressing their willingness to participate in the review by providing information requested by the administering authority and the Commission, (B) a statement regarding the likely effects of revocation of the order or termination of the suspended investigation, and (C) such other information or industry data as the administering

European Union*	Canada**	Australia***	United States****
months before the end of the five-year period, be entitled to lodge a review request in accordance with the second sub-paragraph. A notice announcing the actual expiry of measures pursuant to this paragraph shall also be published. *** 5. The relevant provisions of this Regulation with regard to procedures and the conduct of investigations, excluding those relating to time limits, shall apply to any review carried out pursuant to paragraphs 2, 3 and 4. Any such review shall be carried out expeditiously and shall normally be concluded within 12 months of the date of initiation of the review. 6. Reviews pursuant to this Article shall be initiated by the Commis-	to Subsection (2) at the request of a person or government, the Tribunal shall make an order to that effect and give reasons therefor, and the Secretary shall forward a copy of the order and the reasons by registered mail to that person or government and cause notice of the order to be published in the Canada Gazette. **Completion of review** (4) On completion of a review pursuant to Subsection (2) of an order or finding, the Tribunal shall make an order rescinding the order or finding or continuing it with or without amendment, as the circumstances require, and give reasons for the decision. **Idem** (4.1) On completion of a review pursuant to Subsection (2.1) or	in subsection (3A) refuses or fails to extend its operation in the manner referred to in subsection (3A) before the undertaking expires, the Minister may, in substitution for the extension of the undertaking, publish a dumping duty notice or a countervailing duty notice that commences on the day after the undertaking expired and ends 2 years after that day unless it is sooner revoked. *** Antidumping Authority Act of 1988 **Section 8A Authority May Make Recommendations of Continuation of Dumping Duty Notices Etc.** **8A(1) [Publication of notice]** Not later than 8 months before an anti-dumping measure expires,	authority or the Commission may specify. **(3) Responses to notice of initiation** **(A) No response** If no interested party responds to the notice of initiation under this subsection, the administering authority shall issue a final determination, within 90 days after the initiation of a review, revoking the order or terminating the suspended investigation to which such notice relates. For purposes of this paragraph, an interested party means a party described in section 1677(9)(C), (D), (E), (F), or (G) of this title. **(B) Inadequate response** If interested parties provide inadequate responses to a notice of initi-

European Union*	Canada**	Australia***	United States****
sion after consultation of the Advisory Committee. Where warranted by reviews, measures shall be repealed or maintained pursuant to paragraph 2, or repealed, maintained or amended pursuant to paragraphs 3 and 4, by the Community institution responsible for their introduction. Where measures are repealed for individual exporters, but not for the country as a whole, such exporters shall remain subject to the proceeding and may, automatically, be reinvestigated in any subsequent review carried out for that country pursuant to this Article. 7. Where a review of measures pursuant to paragraph 3 [interim reviews] is in progress at the end of the period of application of measures as defined in paragraph 2, such review shall also cover the	(2.2) of an order or finding, the Tribunal shall confirm the order or finding or rescind it and make such other order or finding with respect to the goods to which the order or finding under review applies as the nature of the matter may require, shall give reasons for the decision and, where it makes another order or finding, shall declare to what goods, including, where applicable, from what supplier and from what country of export, the order or finding applies. **Separate order or finding** (4.11) Where a review pursuant to subsection (2.1) involves goods of: (a) more than one NAFTA country, or	the Authority must publish in the *Gazette* and in a newspaper circulating in each State, in the Australian Capital Territory and in the Northern Territory, a notice: (a) informing that the dumping duty notice, countervailing duty notice or undertaking is due to expire on a specific day (the "**specified expiry day**"); and (b) inviting interested parties to apply to the Authority in accordance with this section, within 60 days, for the continuation of the anti-dumping measure. **8A(1A) [Time of issue]** If the Minister makes a declaration under paragraph 269ZG(3)(b) of the *Customs Act 1901*, the original dumping duty notice or countervailing duty notice and that notice as modified because of that	ation, the administering authority, within 120 days after the initiation of the review, or the Commission, within 150 days after such initiation, may issue, without further investigation, a final determination based on the facts available, in accordance with section 1677e of this title. **(4) Waiver of participation by certain interested parties** **(A) In general** An interested party described in section 1677(9)(A) or (B) of this title may elect not to participate in a review conducted by the administering authority under this subsection and to participate only in the review conducted by the Commission under this subsection. **(B) Effect of waiver** In a review in which an interested party waives its participation pur-

Primary Sunset Review Provisions in Domestic Legislation

European Union*	Canada**	Australia***	United States****
circumstances set out in paragraph 2. *** 9. In all review or refund investigations carried out pursuant to this Article, the Commission shall, provided that circumstances have not changed, apply the same methodology as in the investigation which led to the duty, with due account being taken of Article 2 [determination of dumping], and in particular paragraphs 11 and 12 thereof, and of Article 17 [sampling]. 10. In any investigation carried out pursuant to this Article, the Commission shall examine the reliability of export prices in accordance with Article 2 [determination of dumping]. However, where it is decided to	(b) one or more NAFTA countries and goods of one or more other countries and the Tribunal makes another order or finding pursuant to Subsection (4.1), the Tribunal shall make a separate order or finding under that Subsection with respect to the goods of each NAFTA country. **Suspension of S.(4.2)** (4.12) The operation of Subsection (4.2) is suspended during the period in which Subsection (4.11) is in force. **Separate order or finding** (4.2) Where a review pursuant to Subsection (2.1) involves goods of the United States as well as goods of other countries and the Tri-	declaration are both to be treated, for the purpose of this section as if they had been issued at the time of the issue of the original notice. **8A(2) [Expiry of notice or undertaking]** If no application is received by the Authority within the period specified in the notice then, on the specified expiry day: (a) the dumping duty notice expires; or (b) the countervailing duty notice expires; or (c) the person who gave the undertaking is taken to be released from the undertaking; as the case requires.	suant to this paragraph, the administering authority shall conclude that revocation of the order or termination of the investigation would be likely to lead to continuation or recurrence of dumping or a countervailable subsidy (as the case may be) with respect to that interested party. **(5) Conduct of review** **(A) Time limits for completion of review** Unless the review has been completed pursuant to paragraph (3) or paragraph (4) applies, the administering authority shall make its final determination pursuant to section 1675a(b) or (c) of this title within 240 days after the date on which a review is initiated under this subsection. If the administering authority makes a final affirmative

European Union*	Canada**	Australia***	United States****
construct the export price in accordance with Article 2(9), it shall calculate it with no deduction for the amount of anti-dumping duties paid when conclusive evidence is provided that the duty is duly reflected in resale prices and the subsequent selling prices in the Community.	bunal makes another order or finding pursuant to Subsection (4.1), the Tribunal shall make a separate order or finding under that Subsection with respect to goods of the United States. **Notice** (4.3) On completion of a review pursuant to Subsection (2), (2.1) or (2.2), the Secretary shall (a) forward by registered mail to the Deputy Minister, such other persons and such governments as may be specified by the rules of the Tribunal and, in the case of a review under Subsection (2.2), the Canadian Secretary: (i) forthwith after the review is completed, a copy of the order or finding made under Subsection (4) or (4.1), as the case may be, and	**8A(3) [Form of application]** An application must: (a) be in writing; and (b) be in an approved form; and (c) contain such information as the form requires; and (d) be signed in the manner indicated in the form. **8A(4) [Report by the Authority]** If: (a) an application is received for the continuation of an anti-dumping measure; and (b) the Authority is satisfied that the application complies with the requirements of this section; the Authority must, within 120 days or such other period as is	determination, the Commission shall make its final determination pursuant to section 1675a(a) of this title within 360 days after the date on which a review is initiated under this subsection. **(B) Extension of time limit** The administering authority or the Commission (as the case may be) may extend the period of time for making their respective determinations under this subsection by not more than 90 days, if the administering authority or the Commission (as the case may be) determines that the review is extraordinarily complicated. In a review in which the administering authority extends the time for making a final determination, but the Commission does not extend the time for making a determination, the Commission's determination shall be made not later than 120 days

European Union*	Canada**	Australia***	United States****
	(ii) not later than 15 days after the completion of the review, a copy of the reasons for the decision; and (b) cause notice of the order or finding to be published in the Canada Gazette. **Order or finding deemed to be rescinded** (5) Where the Tribunal has not initiated a review pursuant to Subsection (2) with respect to an order or finding before the expiration of five years after: (a) if no order continuing the order or finding has been made pursuant to Subsection (4), the day on which the order or finding was made, or (b) if one or more orders continuing the order or finding have been	prescribed after the receipt of the application, give the Minister a report recommending whether the measure should be continued. **8A(5)** [**Inquiry**] For the purpose of giving the Minister a report in respect of a matter, the Authority must hold an inquiry into the matter. **8A(6)** (Omitted by No. 150 of 1994) **8A(7)** [**Late submissions**] If an inquiry is held under subsection (5), the Authority must have regard to all submissions it receives within the period specified in the notice of inquiry under section 23 but may disregard any submission received after the end of that period. **8A(7A)** [**Expiration of notice**] The Authority must not recommend the continuation of an	after the date on which the final determination of the administering authority is published. **(C) Extraordinarily complicated** For purposes of this subsection, the administering authority or the Commission (as the case may be) may treat a review as extraordinarily complicated if — (i) there is a large number of issues, (ii) the issues to be considered are complex, (iii) there is a large number of firms involved, (iv) the orders or suspended investigations have been grouped as described in subparagraph (D), or (v) it is a review of a transition order.

Primary Sunset Review Provisions in Domestic Legislation

European Union*	Canada**	Australia***	United States****
	made pursuant to Subsection (4), the day on which the last such order was made, the order or finding shall be deemed to have been rescinded as of the expiration of the five years.	anti-dumping measure unless it is satisfied that the expiration of the notice would lead, or would be likely to lead, to a continuation of, or recurrence of the material injury that the anti-dumping measure is intended to prevent. **8A(8)** [**Continuation of anti-dumping measures**] The Minister may, after having regard to the report in relation to the continuation of an anti-dumping measure and before the specified expiry day, take steps to secure the continuation of the measure. **8A(9)** [**Expiry of anti-dumping measures**] If the Minister does not take steps to secure the continuation of an anti-dumping measure before the specified expiry day, the measure expires in accordance with section 269TM of the *Customs Act 1901*.	**(D) Grouped reviews** The Commission, in consultation with the administering authority, may group orders or suspended investigations for review if it considers that such grouping is appropriate and will promote administrative efficiency. Where orders or suspended investigations have been grouped, the Commission shall, subject to subparagraph (B), make its final determination under this subsection not later than 120 days after the date that the administering authority publishes notice of its final determination with respect to the last order or agreement in the group. **(6) Special transition rules** **(A) Schedule for reviews of transition orders**

Primary Sunset Review Provisions in Domestic Legislation

European Union*	Canada**	Australia***	United States****
		8A(10) [**Minister's decision**] If the Minister decides to secure the continuation of an anti-dumping measure, the continuation of that measure is so secured: (a) if the measure is a dumping duty notice or countervailing duty notice — by the Minister determining, in writing, that the notice continues in force after the specified expiry day; and (b) if the measure is an undertaking — by the person who gave that undertaking agreeing to extend the undertaking beyond the specified expiry day or, if the person will not so agree, by the Minister publishing a dumping duty notice or a countervailing duty notice to take effect from the day after the specified expiry day in substitution for that undertaking.	**(i) Initiation** The administering authority shall begin its review of transition orders in the 42d calendar month after the date such orders are issued. A review of all transition orders shall be initiated not later than the 5th anniversary after the date such orders are issued. **(ii) Completion** A review of a transition order shall be completed not later than 18 months after the date such review is initiated. Reviews of all transition orders shall be completed not later than 18 months after the 5th anniversary of the date such orders are issued. **(iii) Subsequent reviews** The time limits set forth in clauses (i) and (ii) shall be applied to all

European Union*	Canada**	Australia***	United States****
		8A(11) [In force for 5 years] If the Minister secures continuation of an anti-dumping measure in accordance with this section, the measure continues in force for a period of 5 years after the specified expiry day unless: (a) in the case of a dumping duty notice or countervailing duty notice — it is revoked before the end of that period; or (b) in the case of an undertaking — provision is made for its earlier expiration. **8A(12) [Meaning of anti-dumping measure]** In this section: **"antidumping measure"** means: (a) a dumping duty notice or a countervailing duty notice; or	subsequent 5-year reviews of transition orders by substituting "date of the determination to continue such orders" for "date such orders are issued". **(iv) Revocation and termination** No transition order may be revoked under this subsection before the date that is 5 years after the date the WTO Agreement enters into force with respect to the United States. **(B) Sequence of transition reviews** The administering authority, in consultation with the Commission, shall determine such sequence of review of transition orders as it deems appropriate to promote administrative efficiency. To the extent practicable, older orders shall be reviewed first.

Primary Sunset Review Provisions in Domestic Legislation

European Union*	Canada**	Australia***	United States****
		(b) an undertaking given under subsection 269TG(4) or 269TJ(3) of the *Customs Act 1901*; that is in force when this section commences or that comes into force after this section commences.	**(C) Definition of transition order** For purposes of this section, the term "transition order" means — (i) a countervailing duty order under this subtitle or under section 1303 of this title, (ii) an antidumping duty order under this subtitle or a finding under the Antidumping Act, 1921, or (iii) a suspension of an investigation under section 1671c or 1673c of this title, which is in effect on the date the WTO Agreement enters into force with respect to the United States. **(D) Issue date for transition orders** For purposes of this subsection, a transition order shall be treated as issued on the date the WTO

Primary Sunset Review Provisions in Domestic Legislation

European Union*	Canada**	Australia***	United States****
			Agreement enters into force with respect to the United States, if such order is based on an investigation conducted by both the administering authority and the Commission. **(d) Revocation of order or finding; termination of suspended investigation** **(1) In general** The administering authority may revoke, in whole or in part, a countervailing duty order or an antidumping duty order or finding, or terminate a suspended investigation, after review under subsection (a) or (b) of this section. The administering authority shall not revoke, in whole or in part, a countervailing duty order or terminate a suspended investigation on the basis of any export taxes, duties, or other charges levied on the ex-

Primary Sunset Review Provisions in Domestic Legislation

European Union*	Canada**	Australia***	United States****
			port of the subject merchandise to the United States which are specifically intended to offset the countervailable subsidy received. **(2) Five-year reviews** In the case of a review conducted under subsection (c) of this section, the administering authority shall revoke a countervailing duty order or an antidumping duty order or finding, or terminate a suspended investigation, unless — (A) the administering authority makes a determination that dumping or a countervailable subsidy, as the case may be, would be likely to continue or recur, and (B) the Commission makes a determination that material injury would be likely to continue or

Primary Sunset Review Provisions in Domestic Legislation

European Union*	Canada**	Australia***	United States****
			recur as described in section 1675a(a) of this title. (3) Application of revocation or termination A determination under this section to revoke an order or finding or terminate a suspended investigation shall apply with respect to unliquidated entries of the subject merchandise which are entered, or withdrawn from warehouse, for consumption on or after the date determined by the administering authority. **(e) Hearings** Whenever the administering authority or the Commission conducts a review under this section, it shall, upon the request of an interested party, hold a hearing in accordance with section 1677c(b) of

European Union*	Canada**	Australia***	United States****
			this title in connection with that review. *** **§1675a. Special rules for section 1675(b) and 1675(c) reviews** **(a) Determination of likelihood of continuation or recurrence of material injury** (1) **In general** In a review conducted under section 1675(b) or (c) of this title, the Commission shall determine whether revocation of an order, or termination of a suspended investigation, would be likely to lead to continuation or recurrence of material injury within a reasonably foreseeable time. The Commission shall consider the likely volume, price effect, and impact of imports

Primary Sunset Review Provisions in Domestic Legislation

European Union*	Canada**	Australia***	United States****
			of the subject merchandise on the industry if the order is revoked or the suspended investigation is terminated. The Commission shall take into account — (A) its prior injury determinations, including the volume, price effect, and impact of imports of the subject merchandise on the industry before the order was issued or the suspension agreement was accepted, (B) whether any improvement in the state of the industry is related to the order or the suspension agreement, (C) whether the industry is vulnerable to material injury if the order is revoked or the suspension agreement is terminated, and (D) in an antidumping proceeding under section 1675(c) of this title,

European Union*	Canada**	Australia***	United States****
			the findings of the administering authority regarding duty absorption under section 1675(a)(4) of this title. **(2) Volume** In evaluating the likely volume of imports of the subject merchandise if the order is revoked or the suspended investigation is terminated, the Commission shall consider whether the likely volume of imports of the subject merchandise would be significant if the order is revoked or the suspended investigation is terminated, either in absolute terms or relative to production or consumption in the United States. In so doing, the Commission shall consider all relevant economic factors, including — (A) any likely increase in production capacity or existing unused

Primary Sunset Review Provisions in Domestic Legislation

European Union*	Canada**	Australia***	United States****
			production capacity in the exporting country, (B) existing inventories of the subject merchandise, or likely increases in inventories, (C) the existence of barriers to the importation of such merchandise into countries other than the United States, and (D) the potential for product-shifting if production facilities in the foreign country, which can be used to produce the subject merchandise, are currently being used to produce other products. **(3) Price** In evaluating the likely price effects of imports of the subject merchandise if the order is revoked or the suspended investigation is termi-

European Union*	Canada**	Australia***	United States****
			nated, the Commission shall consider whether — (A) there is likely to be significant price underselling by imports of the subject merchandise as compared to domestic like products, and (B) imports of the subject merchandise are likely to enter the United States at prices that otherwise would have a significant depressing or suppressing effect on the price of domestic like products. **(4) Impact on the industry** In evaluating the likely impact of imports of the subject merchandise on the industry if the order is revoked or the suspended investigation is terminated, the Commission shall consider all relevant economic factors which are likely to have a bearing on the state of the industry

Primary Sunset Review Provisions in Domestic Legislation

European Union*	Canada**	Australia***	United States****
			in the United States, including, but not limited to — (A) likely declines in output, sales, market share, profits, productivity, return on investments, and utilization of capacity, (B) likely negative effects on cash flow, inventories, employment, wages, growth, ability to raise capital, and investment, and (C) likely negative effects on the existing development and production efforts of the industry, including efforts to develop a derivative or more advanced version of the domestic like product. The Commission shall evaluate all relevant economic factors described in this paragraph within the context of the business cycle and the conditions of competition that are distinctive to the affected industry.

European Union*	Canada**	Australia***	United States****
			(5) Basis for determination The presence or absence of any factor which the Commission is required to consider under this subsection shall not necessarily give decisive guidance with respect to the Commission's determination of whether material injury is likely to continue or recur within a reasonably foreseeable time if the order is revoked or the suspended investigation is terminated. In making that determination, the Commission shall consider that the effects of revocation or termination may not be imminent, but may manifest themselves only over a longer period of time. **(6) Magnitude of margin of dumping and net countervailable subsidy; nature of countervailable subsidy** In making a determination under section 1675(b) or (c) of this title,

European Union*	Canada**	Australia***	United States****
			the Commission may consider the magnitude of the margin of dumping or the magnitude of the net countervailable subsidy. If a countervailable subsidy is involved the Commission shall consider information regarding the nature of the countervailable subsidy and whether the subsidy is a subsidy described in Article 3 or 6.1 of the Subsidies Agreement. (7) **Cumulation** For purposes of this subsection, the Commission may cumulatively assess the volume and effect of imports of the subject merchandise from all countries with respect to which reviews under section 1675(b) or (c) of this title were initiated on the same day, if such imports would be likely to compete with each other and with domestic like products in the

European Union*	Canada**	Australia***	United States****
			United States market. The Commission shall not cumulatively assess the volume and effects of imports of the subject merchandise in a case in which it determines that such imports are likely to have no discernible adverse impact on the domestic industry. **(8) Special rule for regional industries** In a review under section 1675(b) or (c) of this title involving a regional industry, the Commission may base its determination on the regional industry defined in the original investigation under this subtitle, another region that satisfies the criteria established in section 1677(4)(C) of this title, or the United States as a whole. In determining if a regional industry analysis is appropriate for the determination in the review, the Commission shall consider

European Union*	Canada**	Australia***	United States****
			whether the criteria established in section 1677(4)(C) of this title are likely to be satisfied if the order is revoked or the suspended investigation is terminated. **(b) Determination of likelihood of continuation or recurrence of a countervailable subsidy** **(1) In general** In a review conducted under section 1675(c) of this title, the administering authority shall determine whether revocation of a countervailing duty order or termination of a suspended investigation under section 1671c of this title would be likely to lead to continuation or recurrence of a countervailable subsidy. The administering authority shall consider — (A) the net countervailable subsidy determined in the investigation and subsequent reviews, and

European Union*	Canada**	Australia***	United States****
			(B) whether any change in the program which gave rise to the net countervailable subsidy described in subparagraph (A) has occurred that is likely to affect that net countervailable subsidy. **(2) Consideration of other factors** If good cause is shown, the administering authority shall also consider — (A) programs determined to provide countervailable subsidies in other investigations or reviews under this subtitle, but only to the extent that such programs — (i) can potentially be used by the exporters or producers subject to the review under section 1675(c) of this title, and (ii) did not exist at the time that the countervailing duty order was

European Union*	Canada**	Australia***	United States****
			issued or the suspension agreement was accepted, and (B) programs newly alleged to provide countervailable subsidies but only to the extent that the administering authority makes an affirmative countervailing duty determination with respect to such programs and with respect to the exporters or producers subject to the review. **(3) Net countervailable subsidy** The administering authority shall provide to the Commission the net countervailable subsidy that is likely to prevail if the order is revoked or the suspended investigation is terminated. The administering authority shall normally choose a net countervailable subsidy that was determined under section 1671d of this title or sub-

European Union*	Canada**	Australia***	United States****
			section (a) or (b)(1) of section 1675 of this title. **(4) Special rule** **(A) Treatment of zero and de minimis rates** A net countervailable subsidy described in paragraph (1)(A) that is zero or de minimis shall not by itself require the administering authority to determine that revocation of a countervailing duty order or termination of a suspended investigation would not be likely to lead to continuation or recurrence of a countervailable subsidy. **(B) Application of de minimis standards** For purposes of this paragraph, the administering authority shall apply

European Union*	Canada**	Australia***	United States****
			the de minimis standards applicable to reviews conducted under subsections (a) and (b)(1) of section 1675 of this title. **(c) Determination of likelihood of continuation or recurrence of dumping** **(1) In general** In a review conducted under section 1675(c) of this title, the administering authority shall determine whether revocation of an antidumping duty order or termination of a suspended investigation under section 1673c of this title would be likely to lead to continuation or recurrence of sales of the subject merchandise at less than fair value. The administering authority shall consider — (A) the weighted average dumping margins determined in the investigation and subsequent reviews, and

Primary Sunset Review Provisions in Domestic Legislation

European Union*	Canada**	Australia***	United States****
			(B) the volume of imports of the subject merchandise for the period before and the period after the issuance of the antidumping duty order or acceptance of the suspension agreement. (2) **Consideration of other factors** If good cause is shown, the administering authority shall also consider such other price, cost, market, or economic factors as it deems relevant. (3) **Magnitude of the margin of dumping** The administering authority shall provide to the Commission the magnitude of the margin of dumping that is likely to prevail if the order is revoked or the suspended investigation is terminated. The administering authority shall normally choose a margin that was

European Union*	Canada**	Australia***	United States****
			determined under section 1673d of this title or under subsection (a) or (b)(1) of section 1675 of this title. **(4) Special rule** **(A) Treatment of zero or de minimis margins** A dumping margin described in paragraph (1)(A) that is zero or de minimis shall not by itself require the administering authority to determine that revocation of an antidumping duty order or termination of a suspended investigation would not be likely to lead to continuation or recurrence of sales at less than fair value. **(B) Application of de minimis standards** For purposes of this paragraph, the administering authority shall apply the de minimis standards applica-

European Union*	Canada**	Australia***	United States****
			ble to reviews conducted under subsections (a) and (b) of section 1675 of this title. **§1675b. Special rules for injury investigations for certain section 1303 countervailing duty orders and investigations** *** **(e) Request for simultaneous expedited review under section 1675(c)** **(1) General rule** **(A) Requests for reviews** Notwithstanding section 1675(c)(6)(A) of this title and except as provided in subparagraph (B), an interested party may request a review of an order under section 1675(c) of this title at the same time the party requests an investigation under subsection (a) of

European Union*	Canada**	Australia***	United States****
			this section, if the order involves the same or comparable subject merchandise. Upon receipt of such request, the administering authority, after consulting with the Commission, shall initiate a review of the order under section 1675(c) of this title. The Commission shall combine such review with the investigation under this section. **(B) Exception** If the administering authority determines that the interested party who requested an investigation under this section is a related party or an importer within the meaning of section 1677(4)(B) of this title, the administering authority may decline a request by such party to initiate a review of an order under section 1675(c) of this title which involves the same or comparable subject merchandise.

European Union*	Canada**	Australia***	United States****
			(2) Cumulation If a review under section 1675(c) of this title is initiated under paragraph (1), such review shall be treated as having been initiated on the same day as the investigation under this section, and the Commission may, in accordance with section 1677(7)(G) of this title, cumulatively assess the volume and effect of imports of the subject merchandise from all countries with respect to which such investigations are treated as initiated on the same day. **(3) Time and procedure for Commission determination** The Commission shall render its determination in the investigation conducted under this section at the same time as the Commission's determination is made in the review

Primary Sunset Review Provisions in Domestic Legislation

European Union*	Canada**	Australia***	United States****
			under section 1675(c) of this title that is initiated pursuant to this subsection. The Commission shall in all other respects apply the procedures and standards set forth in section 1675(c) of this title to such section 1675(c) of this title reviews.

* Council Regulation 384/96, 1995 O.J. (L 56) 1996 (antidumping regulation).

** Special Import Measures Act, ch. 25, §76, 1996 S.C.(Can.).

*** Customs Act 1901, as amended, §269TM, *reprinted in* Australian Customs Law and Practice (CCH) ¶74,701-02; Anti-Dumping Authority Act 1988, as amended, §8A, *reprinted in* Australian Customs Law and Practice (CCH) ¶91,873-74.

**** 19 U.S.C. §§1675(c), 1675a, 1675b(e) (1980 & 1998 Supp.)

BIBLIOGRAPHY

Books and Articles:

Alan F. Holmer, Gary N. Horlick, & Terence P. Stewart, *Enacted and Rejected Amendments to the Antidumping Law: In Implementation or Contravention of the Antidumping Agreement?*, 29 INT'L LAW. 483 (Summer 1995).

AUSTRALIAN CUSTOMS LAW AND PRACTICE (CCH).

Barbara R. Stafford & Linda S. Chang, *The Sunset Provisions: Mortality and the Uruguay Round, in* 1 THE COMMERCE DEPARTMENT SPEAKS ON INTERNATIONAL TRADE AND INVESTMENT 721 (PLI, 1994).

Bernard Carreau, *Revocation of Antidumping and Countervailing Duty Orders: New Procedures and Recent Trends in Commerce Practice*, 669 THE COMMERCE DEPARTMENT SPEAKS 43 (PLI, 1990).

CITT RESEARCH BRANCH, CANADA'S USE OF THE GATT ANTI-DUMPING CODE (June 1991).

Clive Stanbrook & Philip Bentley, DUMPING AND SUBSIDIES: THE LAW AND PROCEDURES GOVERNING THE IMPOSITION OF ANTI-DUMPING AND COUNTERVAILING DUTIES IN THE EUROPEAN COMMUNITY (1996).

Debra P. Steger, *Canadian Implementation of the Agreement Establishing the World Trade Organization, in* IMPLEMENTING THE URUGUAY ROUND 243 (John H. Jackson & Alan Sykes eds., 1997).

Edwin A. Vermulst, ANTIDUMPING LAW AND PRACTICE IN THE UNITED STATES AND THE EUROPEAN COMMUNITIES: A COMPARATIVE ANALYSIS 251 (North-Holland, 1987).

Edwin A. Vermulst, *The Anti-Dumping Systems of Australia, Canada, the EEC and the United States of America: Have Anti-Dumping Laws Become a Problem in International Trade?*, 10 MICH. J. INT'L L 765 (Summer 1989).

Frank Montag & Andre Fiebig, *The European Union, in* ANTI-DUMPING UNDER THE WTO: A COMPARATIVE REVIEW 97 (Keith Steele ed., 1996).

Gerd Hollander & Fred Gruen, *Australia's Antidumping Policies and Practices* (Oct. 3, 1997), presented at the Brookings Trade Policy Forum on "Private Practices and Trade Policy: The Future of International Rules on Antidumping and Competition" (Nov. 13-14, 1997).

Greyson Bryan & Dominique Guy Boursereau, *Antidumping Law in the European Communities and the United States: A Comparative Analysis*, 18 GEO. WASH. J. INT'L L. & ECON. 631 (1985).

H. Keith C. Steele, *The Australian Antidumping System, in* ANTIDUMPING LAW AND PRACTICE: A COMPARATIVE STUDY 223 (John H. Jackson & Edwin A. Vermulst eds., 1989).

Hon. John Moore MP & Hon. Warren Truss MP, JOINT PRESS RELEASE (036/98) (Feb. 24, 1998).

Ivo Van Bael & Jean-Francois Bellis, ANTI-DUMPING AND OTHER TRADE PROTECTION LAWS OF THE EEC 209 (CCH 2nd ed., 1990).

James R. Cannon, Jr., *Dispute Settlement in Antidumping and Countervailing Duty Cases, in* THE WORLD TRADE ORGANIZATION: MULTILATERAL TRADE FRAMEWORK FOR THE 21ST CENTURY AND U.S. IMPLEMENTING LEGISLATION 359 (Terence P. Stewart ed., ABA 1996).

Jean-Francois Bellis, *The EEC Antidumping System, in* ANTIDUMPING LAW AND PRACTICE: A COMPARATIVE STUDY 41 (John H. Jackson & Edwin A. Vermulst eds., 1989).

Launching the Uruguay Round, GATT FOCUS NEWSLETTER (Oct. 1986).

Lawrie Willet AO, *Review of Australia's Anti-Dumping and Countervailing Administration* (Sept. 1996).

Leonard M. Shambon, *Revocation Under the Antidumping and Countervailing Duty Laws?: You Should Live So Long!*, 2 THE COMMERCE DEPARTMENT SPEAKS 241 (PLI, 1987).

Michael Stein, *The Uruguay Round and the Trade Laws: Antidumping, Countervailing Duties, Common Provisions, in* 1 THE COMMERCE DEPARTMENT SPEAKS ON INTERNATIONAL TRADE AND INVESTMENT 877 (PLI 1994).

Patrick J. McDonough, *Subsidies and Countervailing Measures, in* 1 THE

GATT URUGUAY ROUND: A NEGOTIATING HISTORY (1986-1992) 803 (Terence P. Stewart ed., 1993).

Peter A. Magnus, *The Canadian Antidumping System, in* ANTIUMPING LAW AND PRACTICE: A COMPARATIVE STUDY 167 (John H. Jackson & Edwin A. Vermulst eds., 1989).

Peter L.H. Van den Bossche, *The European Community and the Uruguay Round Agreements, in* IMPLEMENTING THE URUGUAY ROUND 23 (John H. Jackson & Alan O. Sykes eds., 1997).

Philippe De Smedt, *Survey of the Revised Basic EC Anti-Dumping Regulation*, 17 INT'L BUS. LAW. 13 (1989).

Po-Yee Lee, *Canadian & International Use of Anti-Dumping and Countervailing Measures* 29 (Research Branch, CITT May 1997).

Robert A. Weaver, *Functioning of the GATT System, in* 2 THE GATT URUGUAY ROUND: A NEGOTIATING HISTORY (1986-1992) 1891 (Terence P. Stewart ed., 1993).

Ronald C. Cheng, *Canada*, ANTI-DUMPING UNDER THE WTO: A COMPARATIVE REVIEW 73 (Keith Steele ed., 1996).

Shane B. Brown, Richard S. Gottlieb & Darrel H. Pearson, 5 INTERNATIONAL TRADE LAWS OF CANADA: SPECIAL IMPORT MEASURES 34 (R.S. Gottlieb & D.H. Peason eds., 1992).

Terence P. Stewart, *Administration of the Antidumping Law: A Different Perspective, in* DOWN IN THE DUMPS: ADMINISTRATION OF THE UNFAIR TRADE LAWS 288 (Richard Boltuck & Robert E. Litan eds., 1991).

Terence P. Stewart, *Antidumping Practice of the United States and the European Union*, Vol. 1, Before the Russian Chamber of Commerce and Industry Conference on GATT/WTO (Oct. 1995).

Terence P. Stewart, *Antidumping, Subsidies and Countervailing Measures: The Negotiations Are Still a Long Way From Completion in* URUGUAY ROUND TRADE NEGOTIATIONS: WHERE DO WE GO FROM HERE? (ABA, March 21-22, 1991).

Terence P. Stewart, *Overview of the Uruguay Round of Trade Negotiations*, GATT/WTO Seminar in Conjunction With the Chamber of Commerce and Industry of the Russian Federation (Oct. 16-17, 1995).

Terence P. Stewart, *The Important Function of Antidumping Laws*, IV.6 INT'L ECON. 46 (Insights, Inst. for Int'l Econ., Nov.-Dec. 1993).

Terence P. Stewart, Susan G. Markel & Michael T. Kerwin, *Antidumping, in* 2 THE GATT URUGUAY ROUND: A NEGOTIATING HISTORY (1986-1992) 1383 (Terence P. Stewart ed., 1993).

U.S. Antidumping Proposals: Special Report, INSIDE U.S. TRADE (Dec. 3, 1993).

U.S. Tables Proposal For 11 Changes To GATT Antidumping Text: Special Report, INSIDE U.S. TRADE (12/3/93).

Reports:

AUSTRALIAN ANTI-DUMPING AUTHORITY, ANNUAL REPORT 1988-89.

AUSTRALIAN ANTI-DUMPING AUTHORITY, ANNUAL REPORT 1990-91.

AUSTRALIAN ANTI-DUMPING AUTHORITY, ANNUAL REPORT 1991-92.

AUSTRALIAN ANTI-DUMPING AUTHORITY, ANNUAL REPORT 1994-95.

CITT, ANNUAL REPORT FOR FISCAL YEAR ENDING MARCH 31, 1989.

CITT, ANNUAL REPORT 1995-96.

CITT, *Guideline: Changes in the Tribunal's Practice in Proceedings Related to the Expiry of Orders and Findings and to Reviews Under Section 76 of the "Special Import Measures Act"* (Nov. 20, 1996).

CITT, *Information on Dumping and Subsidizing Inquiries and Reviews.*

CITT, *Introductory Guide on the Canadian International Trade Tribunal.*

Conference Report to Accompany H.R. 3398, H.R. REP. NO. 98-1156 (1984).

Fourteenth Annual Report from the Commission to the European Parliament on the Community's Anti-Dumping and Anti-Subsidy Activities: 1995, COM(96) 428 final (Brussels, Sept. 16, 1997).

GATT, ANTI-DUMPING AND COUNTERVAILING MEASURES LEGISLATION (June 1987).

H.R. Doc. No. 103-316, vol. 1 (1994).

H.R. REP. NO. 103-826(I) (1994), *reprinted in* 1994 U.S.C.C.A.N. 3773.

Ninth Annual Report of the Commission on the Community's Anti-Dumping and Anti-Subsidy Activities: 1990, SEC(91) 974 final (Brussels, May 31, 1991).

S. REP. NO. 103-412 (1994).

USITC, THE YEAR IN TRADE 1993: OPERATION OF THE TRADE AGREEMENTS PROGRAM, 45th REPORT, USITC Pub. 2971 (June 1991).

GATT and WTO Documents:

Anti-dumping and Countervailing Duties, GATT Sales No. GATT/1958-2 (July 1958).

Anti-dumping and Countervailing Duties, Report adopted on 13 May 1959, GATT Doc. No. L/978, *reprinted in* GATT BISD (8th Supp.).

Anti-dumping and Countervailing Duties, Report of Group of Experts, GATT Sales No. GATT/1961-2 (1961).

Anti-dumping Checklist, Comments by Australia, GATT Doc. No. TN.64/NTB/W/10/Add. 8 (May 20, 1966).

Anti-dumping Checklist, Comments by Denmark, GATT Doc. No. TN.64/NTB/W/10/Add. 6 (May 5, 1966).

Anti-dumping Checklist, Comments by the European Economic Community, GATT Doc. No. TN.64/NTB/W/10/Add.1 (April 21, 1966).

Anti-dumping Checklist, Comments of Finland, GATT Doc. No. TN.64/NTB/W/10/Add. 10 (June 30, 1966).

Antidumping Checklist, Comments by the Government of Canada, GATT Doc. No. TN.64/NTB/W/10/Add. 5 (May 5, 1966).

Anti-dumping Checklist, Comments by Japan, GATT Doc. No. TN.64/NTB/W/10/Add.2 (April 22, 1966).

Anti-dumping Checklist, Comments by Norway, GATT Doc. No. TN.64/NTB/W/10/Add.4 (April 29, 1966).

Anti-dumping Checklist, Comments by Sweden, GATT Doc. No. TN.64/NTB/W/10/Add. 7 (May 6, 1966).

Anti-dumping Checklist, Comments by the United Kingdom, GATT Doc. No. TN.64/NTB/W/10 (April 19, 1966).

Anti-dumping Checklist, Comments by the United States, GATT Doc. No. TN.64/NTB/W/10/Add.3 (April 28, 1966).

Australian Dumping and Countervailing Administrative Guidelines (Division A5, Section 6), reprinted in Inventory of Review and Sunset Clause Provisions in the Legislation and Administrative Procedures of Parties to the Code, GATT Doc. No. ADP/W/106 (Jan. 16, 1986).

Communication from Japan, GATT Doc. No. MTN.GNG/NG8/W/30 (June 20, 1988).

Communication from the European Communities to the GATT Uruguay Round — Anti-dumping, GATT Doc. No. MTN.GNG/NG8/W/74 (March 21, 1990).

Communication from the International Chamber of Commerce, GATT Doc. No. TN.64/NTB/42 (June 20, 1966).

Communication from the Republic of Korea, GATT Doc. No. MTN.GNG/NG8/W/40 (Nov. 22, 1988).

Drafting Proposals of the Nordic Countries Regarding Amendments of the Anti-dumping Code, GATT Doc. No. MTN.GNG/NG8/W/76 (April 11, 1990).

Draft Int'l Code on Anti-dumping Procedure and Practice: Note by the United Kingdom Delegation, GATT Doc. No. Spec(65) 86 (Oct. 7, 1965).

Elements on the Framework for Negotiations, Submission by Japan, GATT Doc. No. MTN.GNG/NG10/W/27 (Oct. 6, 1989).

Elements of the Framework for Negotiations, Submission by India, GATT Doc. No. MTN.GNG/NG10/W/33 (Nov. 30, 1989).

Elements of the Framework for Negotiations, Submission by the Nordic Countries, GATT Doc. No. MTN.GNG/NG10/W/30 (Nov. 27, 1989).

Explanations by the Republic of Korea on the Occasion of Submitting Concrete Negotiating Text on the Anti-dumping Code, GATT Doc. No. MTN.GNG/NG8/W/40/Add.1 (Nov. 23, 1989).

Framework for Negotiations, Communication from Canada, GATT Doc. No. MTN.GNG/NG10/W/25 (June 28, 1989).

Meeting of 30 April - 1 May 1990, Note by Secretariat, GATT Doc. No. MTN/GNG/NG10/18 (May 28, 1990).

Meeting of October 19-20, 1989, Note by the Secretariat, GATT Doc. No. MTN.GNG/NG10/14 (Nov. 15, 1989).

Meeting of October 29, 1987, Note by the Secretariat, GATT Doc. No. MTN.GNG/NG10/4 (Nov. 10, 1987), at 1-2.

Memorandum by the Government of Canada, GATT Doc. No. TN.64/NTB/W/15 (Feb. 21, 1967).

Ministerial Declaration of 20 September 1986 (Punta del Este Declaration), GATT Doc. No. MIN(86)/6 (Sept. 20, 1986).

Minutes of the Meeting Held on 21 and 24 October 1985, GATT Doc. No. ADP/M/16 (Jan. 9, 1986).

Note by the Secretariat, GATT Doc. No. MTN.GNG/NG8/5 (Dec. 15, 1987).

Notes on Meeting on 20-21 October 1965, GATT Doc. No. TN.64/NTB/W/2 (Nov. 23, 1965).

Proposed Elements for a Framework for Negotiations: Principles and Objec-

tives for Anti-dumping Rules, Communication from the Delegation of Singapore, GATT Doc. No. MTN.GNG/NG8/W/55 (Oct. 13, 1989).

Submission by Australia, GATT Doc. No. MTN.GNG/NG8/W/66 (Dec. 22, 1989).

Submission by Canada, GATT Doc. No. MTN.GNG/NG8/W/65 (Dec. 22, 1989).

Submission of Japan on the Amendments to the Anti-Dumping Code, GATT Doc. No. MTN.GNG/NG8/W/48 (Aug. 3, 1989).

Submission from the Nordic Countries, GATT Doc. No. MTN.GNG/NG8/W/15 (Nov. 16, 1987).

WTO Committee on Anti-Dumping Practices & Committee on Subsidies and Countervailing Measures, *Notification of Laws and Regulations Under Articles 18.5 and 32.6 of the Agreements: Canada*, G/ADP/N/1/CAN/1, G/SCM/N/1/CAN/1 (March 24, 1995).

INDEX

adequacy, 72–73, 92, 135, 144–145, 147, 149–150, 152–154, 213
Advisory Committee, 72, 222
affiliation*****
Antidumping Agreement, 2–3, 58–59, 64, 66–67, 128, 134–135, 149, 157, 160–162, 169, 176, 192–193, 199–205
antidumping duty, 9, 11, 27–31, 36–38, 45–46, 51–53, 88, 128, 132, 143, 163, 170–171, 179, 181, 200, 203, 219, 229–231, 246–248
appeal, 105–106, 218
appearance, 40, 49, 212, 214
application, 10, 19, 22, 26, 47–48, 55, 64, 105, 112–114, 121, 149, 173, 193, 212, 218, 220, 222–225, 232, 245, 248
Australia, 2–3, 5, 8, 11–12, 19–20, 22–25, 49–51, 53–55, 57, 63, 111–112, 114–117, 121–124, 189, 195–198, 218–252
Australian Anti–Dumping Authority or ADA, 19–20, 22, 25, 54, 111–113
Brazil, 12, 36, 40–45, 49–52, 79, 81, 91, 96–99, 101, 104, 115–116, 118, 177–178, 181, 189
burden, 32, 39, 45–46, 52, 60–62, 65, 103–104, 134, 136, 150, 156, 165, 169, 187–189, 192, 194

Canada, 2–3, 5–6, 9, 11–12, 16–18, 34, 36, 41–42, 49–50, 53–55, 57–58, 63, 89–90, 92–93, 96–100, 102, 106, 108–109, 116, 177, 183, 193, 195–198, 218–252
Canadian Import Tribunal or CIT, 16–18, 30, 32–34, 36, 38–39, 45, 47, 131, 151, 162–163, 165–166, 171–172, 177–179, 181, 186–188, 194
Canadian International Trade Tribunal or CITT, 12, 16–18, 54–55, 89–110, 182, 190
capacity, 41–42, 44, 50–52, 79–80, 83, 93, 97, 99, 101, 103–105, 109, 115–116, 118–119, 122–123, 165, 175, 186, 196–197, 235–236, 238
capital, 24, 176, 222, 238
Cartland, 58, 60–61, 63

Carlisle, 58–61, 63, 200–209
cause or causation, 2, 7, 16, 20, 26–27, 37, 42, 47, 60–62, 97, 102, 105, 108–110, 118, 121, 124, 133, 136, 141, 163, 165, 168–169, 178, 181, 184–185, 203–204, 207, 221, 225, 243, 247
changed circumstances, 14–15, 26–30, 35–39, 45–46, 53–54, 61, 96, 137, 140, 185–188
circumvent or circumvention, 43, 83, 100, 105, 137, 140, 182, 196
comment, 7, 38, 69, 113, 133, 142, 159, 220
competition, 22, 38, 49, 61, 74, 82, 93, 102, 104, 143, 176–178, 181, 238
confidential, 22, 67, 69, 91, 95, 157
consumer, 67, 83, 124, 140, 157
consumption, 2, 21, 28–29, 50, 79, 82, 87, 95, 97, 100–101, 110, 161, 182, 190–191, 232, 235
continuation, 3, 11, 24–25, 39, 60–63, 65–66, 69, 72, 76, 78, 80, 83–86, 91–92, 97, 101–102, 104, 107, 110–115, 117–122, 124–125, 134, 136, 149, 156, 162–164, 166–167, 169–170, 174, 176–177, 184–186, 189, 192, 195, 203–204, 207, 209, 218–228, 233, 242, 245–246, 248
continuation inquiry, 24–25, 111–114, 117, 120–122
continuation or recurrence, 3, 11, 24–25, 39, 60–63, 65–66, 69, 72, 76, 78, 80, 82, 83–87, 91–92, 97, 101–102, 104, 107, 110–115, 117–125, 134, 136, 149, 156, 162–164, 166–167, 169–170, 174, 176–177, 184–186, 189, 192, 195, 201, 203–204, 207, 209, 218–228, 233, 242, 245–246, 248
continue, 3, 7, 17–18, 42, 61–62, 74, 84, 96–97, 107, 110, 114–115, 117–121, 128, 132, 155–156, 161–164, 167–168, 170, 176, 178, 181, 184, 186–187, 192, 197, 201, 203, 207, 219, 228, 231, 239
corporate planning, 41
countervailing duty, 1–3, 5, 10–13, 17, 19–31, 34, 37–41, 45, 47–49, 51–52, 54–57, 63, 66, 71–72, 89, 96, 112, 118, 120, 124, 127–129, 136–140, 143, 149, 151, 154, 157, 159, 166–171, 174, 176, 178, 188, 193, 195, 206–209, 218–219, 221–223, 227–231, 242–245, 249
Court of First Instance, 84
cumulate or cumulation, 73–75, 90, 129–133, 154–155, 196, 240, 251
currency, 32–34
Customs Service, 19, 25, 27, 30, 56

demand, 40–42, 81, 92, 104–105, 108, 143, 191
de minimis, 31, 34, 74, 164, 169–170, 181, 245–246, 248
Denmark, 8, 114–115
Department of Commerce or DOC, 1, 3, 6–9, 21, 25, 27–38, 41–42, 46, 55–58, 63–64, 73, 127–142, 145–152, 155–174, 177, 180, 183–188, 194, 212–215
depression, 65, 69, 118, 122, 196
disclosure, 69, 157
domestic industry, 2–3, 6–7, 11–12, 15–16, 25, 36–40, 43–45, 47, 49–

51, 55, 60, 62, 65–66, 69, 79–81, 83, 92–93, 95, 101–105, 107, 110, 114, 118, 122, 131, 134–136, 143, 147–148, 150–151, 162, 175–176, 178–183, 185–186, 188–191, 194, 196–197, 203–204, 209, 241
dumped or dumping, 3, 6, 8–10, 13, 15–16, 18–19, 21–26, 28–34, 36, 41–42, 44–47, 53–54, 60–62, 65–66, 69, 71–72, 74–87, 90–93, 96–105, 108–112, 114–117, 119–124, 134, 136–138, 140, 149–150, 156, 159, 162–165, 169–172, 174, 177, 180–188, 191, 194, 197, 200–201, 203–204, 215, 218–223, 227–228, 231, 239–240, 246–248
Dunkel, 58–59, 61–62, 200–209
duration, 5, 7–10, 23, 56–57, 60, 63, 103, 218
duty absorption, 77–78, 83, 137, 180, 182–184, 186–187, 189, 235

economic indicator*****
employment, 44, 50, 79, 97, 175, 238
enforcement, 97–98
European Commission or Commission, 13–16, 18, 22, 25–26, 38, 48, 50, 52, 55, 71–88, 92, 95, 107, 128, 131, 133, 142, 145, 148, 158, 176, 187–188, 213, 215, 218–226, 228, 230–235, 237–241, 244, 247, 250–252
European Council, 13
European Court of Justice, 84
European Economic Community, 8, 12, 96
European Union or EU, 2–3, 11–15, 17–18, 25, 53–55, 57, 59, 63, 71–74, 76–77, 79, 81, 83, 85, 87, 95, 116, 195–198, 218–252
evidence, 6, 8–9, 13–14, 31–33, 36, 38–40, 42–43, 45, 50, 52, 65, 67, 69, 72, 74–75, 77, 80–83, 86, 97–104, 106–107, 115–117, 119, 122–123, 136, 141, 147, 163, 165, 167, 169, 175, 179, 182, 184–185, 187, 193–194, 196–197, 201, 219–220, 224
exchange rate*****
expedited review, 72, 91, 129–130, 146–148, 154–156, 158, 195, 197, 213, 249
expiry review, 18, 55, 71–77, 83–86, 90–91, 94–95, 99, 103–106, 108, 119, 195, 218–219
exporter, 19, 40–41, 43, 74, 102, 117, 122, 136, 142, 145–146, 156, 163, 183–184
exports, 27, 33, 43–44, 48–49, 51–52, 80–81, 87, 93, 121, 123–124, 138, 140, 144, 152–153, 173

facts available or facts otherwise available, 68–69, 73, 76, 129, 145, 148–149, 171–173, 213, 222
Federal Court of Appeal, 105, 218
finding, 3, 17–20, 26, 28–31, 33, 36, 38, 62, 66, 69, 77–78, 83, 90–92, 94–110, 115–116, 118–119, 128, 156, 162, 164, 166–167, 169–170, 178–179, 181–184, 189–190, 197, 204, 209, 218–226, 229–232
foreseeable or foreseeable future, 21, 80, 82, 98, 143, 174, 176–178, 196, 233, 239

full review, 91, 129–130, 135, 142, 144, 146–148, 150, 152–153, 157–159, 165, 213–214
fungibility, 131, 178

General Agreement on Tariffs and Trade or GATT, 1–2, 5–14, 16–19, 21, 47–49, 53, 55, 57–59, 61, 63, 107
good cause, 26–27, 60–62, 136, 141, 163, 165, 168–169, 203, 207, 243, 247
grouping, 3, 90, 112, 129–130, 132–134, 226
Gruen Report, 22, 56

health, 49, 101
hearing, 13, 16, 40, 49, 75, 85, 94, 158–159, 214–215, 232

idle, 101
imminent, 33, 80, 177, 239
importer, 8, 40–41, 53, 74, 86, 132, 136, 142, 145–146, 155–156, 182–183, 250
imports, 2, 7, 9, 11–13, 16–18, 25, 27–28, 30, 35, 38–44, 49–51, 61–62, 65, 74–77, 79–83, 85, 87–88, 92, 97, 99–100, 103, 105, 108, 112, 115, 117–119, 121–124, 129–131, 133, 135–136, 143–144, 153–155, 163–164, 172, 174–175, 177, 179–181, 186, 191, 194, 196–197, 204, 233–237, 240–241, 247, 251
inadequate, 91, 129–130, 144–148, 154, 156, 158, 212, 221
industry, 1–3, 6–7, 11–16, 19–22, 25, 36–40, 42–53, 55, 60, 62, 65–66, 69, 78–83, 85–88, 92–93, 95, 101–105, 107–108, 110, 114, 116, 118, 121–124, 131, 134–136, 142–143, 145, 147–148, 150–151, 154–155, 162, 165, 174–183, 185–186, 188–191, 194, 196–197, 203–204, 209, 220, 234, 237–238, 241
initiation, 15, 17–18, 36, 60, 67–69, 73, 75–77, 85, 91–92, 95–96, 129, 131–132, 134–142, 144–146, 148–152, 156–161, 192–193, 195, 212–215, 220–222, 227
injury, 2–3, 6–13, 15–17, 19, 21, 25–26, 30, 37–42, 44–49, 51–54, 61–62, 65–66, 69, 71–72, 74, 76, 78–88, 92–93, 97, 101–105, 108–112, 114, 117–121, 123–124, 128, 130–131, 133–134, 154–155, 162, 174, 176–181, 183–186, 189, 191, 197, 200–201, 203–204, 206–209, 218–220, 226, 231, 233–234, 239, 249
institution, 14, 38, 40, 129, 142, 147–148, 153, 158–159, 212–215, 222
intent or intention, 41–43, 52, 81, 135–136, 150, 190, 212
interim review, 14, 54, 73–74, 85, 87–88, 103
interrogatories, 94–95
inventory, 21, 57, 165
invest*****
investing or investment, 50, 82–83, 88, 103, 105, 110, 133, 176, 178–179, 189, 196, 238

116–120, 122, 124, 128, 130, 132, 134, 136, 138, 140, 142, 144, 146–148, 150, 152, 154, 156, 158, 160, 162, 164, 166–174, 176, 178, 180, 182, 184–192, 194, 196, 198, 206–209, 212, 214–215, 219, 223, 231, 239–240, 242–245
substitutability, 178–179
successor*****
sunset review, 2–3, 17, 21, 24, 55–56, 58, 63–64, 68, 96, 128–129, 132, 134–137, 139–141, 145–146, 148–150, 152, 154–156, 159–161, 165, 167–171, 174, 177, 179, 184–187, 189–197, 214–215, 218–252
supply, 69, 87–88, 92, 101, 103, 123, 135, 143, 197
suppression, 65, 69, 97, 118, 122, 196
Supreme Court of Canada, 106
suspension agreement, 3, 26–27, 32, 35, 37–38, 40, 42, 63, 128–129, 143, 147, 150, 153, 162–163, 168–170, 180–182, 184, 187, 189–191, 193, 219, 234, 244, 247
Sweden, 5, 8, 38, 40, 49–50, 52, 79–81, 96–97
switch, 82, 88

testimony, 40, 49, 102
third country, 2, 83, 85, 88, 104, 115–116, 119, 122, 186
threat, 3, 13, 15, 19, 21, 41–42, 45–46, 61, 65, 76, 78, 80, 82, 88, 90–91, 131, 176–177, 179, 191
threatened, 38, 40, 48, 51, 87, 121, 179, 186, 189, 191
Tokyo Round, 10, 12, 16, 21, 27, 47, 58, 103, 188
transition order, 128, 160–161, 192, 218, 225, 227–229

undercut or undercutting, 65, 69, 80, 83, 87, 118–119, 122, 197
undertaking, 19, 23–24, 111–112, 120, 218–223, 227–229
union, 2–3, 11–13, 19, 53, 55, 71, 73, 75, 77, 79, 81, 83, 85, 87, 94, 102, 142, 144, 153, 195, 218–252
United States or U.S., 2–3, 5, 8–9, 11–13, 15, 18, 25–43, 45–49, 52–57, 59, 61–62, 64, 68, 72–73, 80, 92–93, 95–97, 100–101, 103–104, 106–110, 115–116, 118, 127–198, 215, 218–252
Uruguay Round, 1–3, 5, 7, 9, 11–13, 15–17, 19, 21, 23, 25, 27, 29, 31, 33, 35, 37, 39, 41, 43, 45, 47, 49, 51, 53, 55, 57–61, 63, 65, 67, 69, 76, 89, 96, 111–112, 127–128, 133, 154, 162, 171–172, 188, 195
Uruguay Round Agreements Act or URAA, 3, 31, 127–129, 132, 135, 149, 151, 154–155, 157–158, 160–163, 166, 169–172, 174, 179–180, 186, 188, 190, 192
utilization, 41, 44, 50, 79, 97, 118, 165, 175, 238

value, 2, 26, 28, 33–34, 39, 53, 85, 114, 123, 138, 140, 144, 152, 246, 248
verify, , 13, 157, 159
verification or verified, 13, 29, 68–69, 115, 159, 195, 197, 214

volume, 6, 39, 41, 65, 69, 74, 80, 87, 97, 109, 118, 122–124, 131, 138, 140, 143, 152, 155, 163, 165, 174–175, 180, 233–235, 240–241, 247, 251
vulnerable or vulnerability, 43, 80–81, 83, 101–104, 177, 180–182, 186, 196–197, 234

waiver, 129, 155–156, 212, 222

warranted, 9–10, 14, 17, 21, 90–91, 93, 96, 102, 106, 200–202, 206–208, 220, 222
World Trade Organization or WTO, 1–2, 6, 8, 10–14, 16, 18, 20, 22, 24, 26, 28, 30, 32, 34, 36, 38, 40, 42, 44, 46, 48–50, 52–54, 56, 58, 60, 62, 64, 66, 68, 72, 74, 76, 78, 80, 82, 84, 86, 88–92, 94, 96, 98, 100, 102, 104, 106, 108–112, 114, 116, 118, 120, 122, 124, 128–130, 132, 134, 136, 138, 140, 142, 144, 146, 148, 150, 152, 154, 156, 158, 160–162, 164, 166, 168, 170, 172, 174, 176, 178, 180, 182, 184, 186, 188, 190, 192–194, 196, 198, 212, 214, 228–229
World Trade Organization Agreement Implementation Act, 89